MOTOR CYCLE
ADVENTURES

In The Central Appalachians

Virginia's Blue Ridge

•

Shenandoah Valley

•

West Virginia Highlands

By Hawk Hagebak

milestone press

Milestone Press, PO Box 158, Almond NC 28702

Book design by Ron Roman/Treehouse Communications
www.treehousecomm.com

Front cover and interior photos (pp. 5, 9, 13, 14, 23, 29, 31, 32, 134, 165-168, 173, 174, 176, 181, 183, 184, 189-192) by Mary Ellen Hammond; all other photos by the author.

Maps by Jim Parham

Printed in the United States on recycled paper

Acknowledgments

I'm the one who gets the byline on the cover of this book, but I certainly did not write it in a vacuum. During my research, I soaked up facts and opinions from hundreds of sources. While writing, I called upon countless friends, family, and riders I met on roadside overlooks to help me decide what should end up on the pages of this book. Regardless of what information I ultimately included, all of those influences flavored the final product.

My family didn't get to ride a single mile of these adventures with me. My wife Lisa remained at home while I went out like a modern-day Don Quixote (slaying the dragons of Virginia and West Virginia), and then she patiently proofread every word I wrote. She's currently looking for a support group for "moto-journalist widows"—women who lose their spouses to book research for months at a time. The wonder of my daughter Annabelle, even though she's too young to read, boosted my energy to ride. My older daughters Stacie, Savannah, and Shannon are all adventuresome young women who inspired me to discover what lay around the next bend. My sister-in-law Pepper brought a fresh perspective to the sport of motorcycling by buying a scooter. Pepper introduced me to the "Vespa Wave" you'll read about in the Code of the Road.

My friends, many of whom are pictured in this book, were gracious enough to ride all the way to Virginia and West Virginia with me. Friends I made along the way also helped considerably. Spanky Watkins, Bobby McGee, Randy Rogers (who learned first-hand the importance of having a tire repair kit), Paul Rushing (who did not crash), Mary Ellen Hammond (first time rider!), and Laird Knight made my travels more entertaining and eye opening. Motorcyclists I met at roadside overlooks shared their secrets and warned me away from long rides to nowhere. Many of them knew I was writing a book, but shared anyway. As a social group, motorcyclists are tops! I'm never disappointed when I meet a fellow biker. I always learn something new.

It takes time, energy, money, and rubber to write a motorcycle guidebook, and I'm grateful I had company along the way. I thank everyone I met, everyone who listened to my creative processes, and everyone who was willing to share their advice. I hear Lisa wants to reintroduce herself to my saddle and say good-bye to her support group, so, it's time to wear out some more tires—gotta ride.

Contents

APPENDIX

WEST VIRGINIA'S
SOUTHERN HIGHLANDS

WEST VIRGINIA'S
NORTHERN HIGHLANDS

Introduction

From early spring to late fall, the roads of Virginia and West Virginia are not only clear of ice and snow, they're also clear for great rides along lonely stretches of roadway. These long stretches will take you away from the monotonous rhythm of the interstate highways, snaking you through mountain passes, along pristine creeks and rivers, and into quaint towns. Whether you're on a sportbike, a luxoliner touring bike, or a highly customized cruiser, you're sure to find these adventures interesting and fun.

I wrote this book with my friends in mind. I considered, "How much fun would this mountain pass be for Eric?" and, "Would Mike want to know about the Cass Scenic Railroad State Park?" I have found my "friends litmus test" to be handy. While each of my cohorts is unique—all ride different machines, have different experience levels, and enjoy different kinds of motorcycles— they all share the desire to ride.

As you carve out these adventures on your bike, chances are you'll run into one or two new riding buddies of your own. You never know how new friends can help you until you're in need. Maybe you're looking for directions, advice, or just someone to bounce your road lie off of. A riding buddy or two is good to have along on an adventure. I know, because I usually drag one or two along with me, if not in body, then in spirit.

THE STATES

Virginia and West Virginia were once a single state. They were separated during the Civil War on June 19, 1863, when West Virginia was admitted to the Union after seceding from the Confederacy.

VIRGINIA IS FOR LOVERS

In Virginia, the above phrase takes on a wider meaning. You probably love motorcycles and love great roads. If so, you can add those two items to the end of the phrase. Virginia is for Lovers—of Motorcycles and Great Roads. Virginia offers so much, you can add nearly anything to the end of the phrase, and it's likely you'll find your own "love" in Virginia. This is particularly true if you love rich history, beautiful scenery, good food, and warm, friendly natives.

One of the original 13 colonies, Virginia once stretched from the Atlantic coast as far west as white men could reach. In 1792, the Kentucky line became Virginia's western border. Still, crossing from one side of Virginia to the other was a challenge. With fertile farmland in the east and rich mineral deposits in the west, Virginians had a hard time getting their products from one side to the other. In the 1830s, a plan to link the western and eastern parts of the state was conceived, but there was a problem—not a single U.S. company would take on such a daunting job. Finally, Napoleon's engineers, out of work at the time, came to America to build a road that wound like a wild snake over the Allegheny Mountains. That road's foundation is still in use today.

WILD, WONDERFUL WEST VIRGINIA

It has been said that a flattened West Virginia would cover an area larger than Texas. Let me be the first to vote against a plan to flatten those great mountains! The rugged terrain that makes West Virginia "Wild and Wonderful" also makes much of it remote and scenic. The awesome New River Gorge, carved by the ancient New River (second only to the Nile in age!), is also where the first West Virginia coal was found. Coal mining is still a major component of the local economy. More recently, tourism and technology have been added to the state's industries, bringing people from all across the globe to the remote reaches of West Virginia.

If you enjoy thinking you're better than West Virginians because of their ignorance and backward ways, consider this: West Virginia had electricity before most other states, hosts the National Radio Astronomy Observatory, and is home to the engineering marvel that is the New River Gorge Bridge. Those three facts alone dispel the bucktoothed hillbilly stereotype. And West Virginians might just be smarter than the rest of us— after all, *we* just visit; *they're* smart enough to build a life there.

ABOUT MOTORCYCLES

What kind of motorcycle you choose to ride for these adventures won't really matter. Most motorcycles are pretty much the same—two (sometimes three) wheels, engine in the middle, a twist-grip throttle, hand- and foot-actuated brakes, a saddle, and a lamp pointing forward so you can see your way in the dark. The basic motorcycle hasn't changed from that design since its wide introduction in the early 1900s. Sure,

there were a few motorcycles before 1900, but around 1900 was when owning a motorcycle became within easy reach of the general public.

So much of the technology in this country can be attributed to the bicycling industry. In their bicycle shop, the Wright brothers tinkered and tinkered, creating the first powered flying machine with a simple gasoline-burning engine. Similar engines were added to bicycle frames, creating an inexpensive means of transportation well within the means of the average household. These powered bicycles quickly replaced the horse as the preferred method of getting around. The new "Iron Horses" didn't need to be fed, brushed, or pastured. Riders just had to keep them fueled and replace the tires when they became too worn to grip the muddy roads of the day.

In the decades that followed, motorcycles morphed from their "powered bicycle" form to the vehicles we recognize as motorcycles today. As the motorcycle grew in power and ability, European and North American designers had very different ideas of what motorcycles should look like.

In Europe, horses had been trained for short, fast rides with little to carry. Riding horses were light and fast with trim saddles and bridles. European riders dressed in high boots, tight trousers, special helmets, and rode with their feet tucked tightly underneath them, their hands forward and close together. Geographically, most of what the riders needed was close by. So in Europe, "light and fast" became the watchword of motorcycle design.

In North America, horses were bred for long rides over varying terrain, having to carry all the rider would need for weeks at a time. The horse packed saddlebags, a bedroll, and other gear strapped on anywhere it might fit. The rider wore boots, gloves, chaps, a hat, and a scarf to keep the dust out of his nose. Astride, the American rider adopted a more relaxed posture than his European cousin. He rode with his feet directly below his knees or even a little further forward, hands apart, and body nearly erect. This posture was comfortable for long rides across the expansive countryside that is North America. So, "large and comfortable" became the mantra of North American motorcycle designers.

That trend continues to this day. When introduced, Japanese motorcycles followed European design—fast and light. The Japanese also added "inexpensive" to the list of attributes for good motorcycle design and construction. The Japanese brands sold best in urban America.

After a few decades, American consumers began to customize their large-bore Japanese muscle bikes to create a strong motorcycle with saddle bags and a trunk. Many riders jammed a small FM radio into the fairing.

Today, the lines between the European Café Racer and the American Iron Horse are so blurred, you have to look closely to determine where a motorcycle was built. Designers have incorporated the best of earlier designs into their newest models, and nearly all manufacturers build sportbikes, touring bikes, custom cruisers, and sport touring models. But regardless of where your bike was forged, the mountains of Virginia and West Virginia is where that pony should run!

RIDING SEASON

Riding through Wyoming, I was once warned not to ride to Utah because heavy snow was predicted. I told the waitress/meteorologist I would be just fine, pointing out that my destination, Salt Lake City, was lower in elevation and latitude than her town in Wyoming. She replied, "Son, people *ski* in Utah!" She was right. I spent three days in Wyoming, waiting for the snow to clear from the mountain passes.

West Virginia is home to dozens of ski resorts. Reread that sentence and consider the riding season as you plan your visit. A trick you can use to predict road conditions is to call one of the ski resorts listed in the back of this book and ask for a snow report. If they report fresh natural snow, you'd better delay your motorcycle tour of the area for a while. Generally speaking, you will find the roads free of snow and ice from early May to mid-October. If spring awakens the adventurous spirit in you, be sure to watch for road salt and gravel used to clear the roads in wintertime.

SHARE ROADS

In West Virginia, several county roads are known as "share roads," so called because that's what you'll be doing as you ride them—sharing them with oncoming traffic. These roads are a single strip of asphalt with gravel shoulders, wide enough for two cars to pass in opposite directions, with the right half of each car on the gravel. I found most motorists will yield completely to oncoming motorcycles, allowing us to occupy the asphalt section. But in order to yield, drivers must first be able to see you approaching, so keep as far to the right as you can when negotiating curves and hillcrests. These scenic roads are rarely used and traffic is light, but they come with that one warning—watch for the other guy.

WILDLIFE

While working on this book, I also shared the road with a bear, a horse, beaver, ground hogs, turkey, chickens, cattle, and countless deer.

Avoid riding in the twilight of dawn and dusk. I know it can't always be avoided, so if you ride during those times, cover your brakes, keep traffic off your tail, and watch closely for animals crossing the road. I love animals and I love my bike, but I'd hate to mix the two! Normally, in the animal-versus-motorcycle crash, the motorcycle loses. At night your field of vision is further reduced to the beam width of your headlight. Not much time to react to something, so ride defensively.

A FINAL WORD ABOUT THIS BOOK

As my bank account and waistline can attest, I've eaten plenty of meals to test the restaurants listed in this book, and I did it anonymously. I didn't accept free meals, and restaurants didn't pay to be included.

If I didn't like a certain place, I didn't mention it.

I rode every route listed in this book, usually several times. My bike has over a hundred thousand miles on its odometer, but so far, its mileages are spot on. Yours might show a slight difference. Generally, motorcycles will measure the same roadway with a difference of less than 10 percent, depending on your tires and the racing lines you cut along the ride.

You'll find the written directions and maps on facing pages because some riders are map-readers and some are direction-takers. Regardless of your style, don't try navigating one of these maps or reading the directions while you're riding. To check the map, stop for a few minutes at the next stop sign or scenic overlook.

Whether you're European, Japanese, red-blooded American, frosty Canadian, or a native of some other place in the world, you're sure to find some great curves in Virginia and West Virginia. I look forward to seeing you out there, carving up these adventures on whatever kind of Iron Horse you choose. Keep an eye peeled for animals, particularly Hawks! I'll be looking for you.

In these mountains, you never know what will be over the next rise.

Code of the Road

All over the world, motorcyclists share a camaraderie that bridges the gaps of social class, wealth, national origin, age, sex, and race. In their normal daily routine, two individuals might never meet, but introduce a powerful two-wheeled machine into the mix and they act like frat brothers and sorority sisters! The motorcycling community has millions of active members. Loosely knit and far-flung though it is, this community has distinct standards of behavior. I wouldn't dare call these rules. I think of them as tips or codes, passed down from rider to rider over the years. What follows is what I call the Code of the Road.

WAVES

Unless you're reading this in Braille, you've seen motorcyclists waving to each other. The reasons for waving are many, but the main one is to make those poor saps stuck in cars curious about what makes us so cool! Baseball players and coaches use hand signs to exchange game plans and strategy. Truckers have CB radios to pass the lonely hours behind the wheel. Motorcyclists use waves to communicate. Some waves say a simple "Howdy!" while others send a more complex message. Over the years, I've seen many different kinds of waves. Here are a few of them.

The "Goddess Durga Wave." If you're not up on your Hinduism, here's a quick lesson. The Goddess Durga is the golden, multiarmed Goddess who kills monsters. You'll see this humorous

wave when the passenger and rider of a passing motorcycle wave simultaneously on the same side of the bike, making it appear that the waving rider has several arms!

The "Hang Loose Wave." Taken from the surfers of Hawaii, this wave is used to denote the wild coolness of the rider. You can send it by extending the pinkie and thumb and twisting the wrist.

The "Long Wave." Use when waving at a passing group of motorcyclists, to make sure you don't leave anyone out. Keep your hand extended until the last bike in the line passes.

The "Bull Wave." This wave is usually displayed with the arm held straight up, fist in a ball with only the fore finger and pinkie extended. Occasionally, you'll see this wave sent with the arm bent toward the recipient, with a twisting motion as you pass, as if Toro is grinding his horns in a threatening manner.

The "Armpit Wave." It's easy to wave at a motorcycle passing in the opposite direction, but how do you wave at a motorcyclist travelling in the same direction? Sportbikers invented the Armpit Wave by reaching their left hand under their right arm to wave as they pass.

The "Sportbiker Commute Wave." Riding a sportbike over curvy mountain roads is fun; riding the interstate highways is another matter. Frequently you'll see sportbikers resting their shoulders, left elbow on the gas tank. Passing motorcyclists are greeted with a wave from the hand on the gas tank.

The "Vespa Wave." To wave or not to wave? The scooter riders of today don't know if they should wave or not, for fear of offending a motorcyclist who's a "real biker." Next time you see a rider aboard a scooter, wave. Their shocked response is sure to be the Vespa Wave, a clear but simple wave sent too late to see anywhere but in your left rearview mirror.

The "Stopped Biker Wave." As you ride along through the scenery of the Blue Ridge Parkway or any of the other scenic roads in this book, you're sure to see some motorcyclists stopped on the side of the road. It's only natural to wave at them. In response, you'll get the Stopped Biker Wave—a standard wave with the arm held upwards and hand extended, rider standing next to the motorcycle on its kickstand.

The "Top Gun Motorcycle Passing Wave." Stopped motorcyclists also send this wave, which mimics the motions of the deck launch crew of aircraft carriers, pointing in the direction of travel of the passing motorcycle, then spinning the other arm in that direction and dropping to one knee as if to allow your wing to pass harmlessly over him.

The sport of motorcycling won't suffer a deep loss if you don't wave. But out of respect for the traditions of the motorcyclists who made our sport what it is today, I urge you to wave at all brands and types of motorcycles. Besides, you never know when that guy you waved at will see you again. Maybe it'll be when a nail punctures your rear tire, or around the campfire while you're trading road lies. Either way, waving promotes camaraderie, and who doesn't want some of that? Sometimes we're too busy to wave, like when we're tearing through a hairpin turn. If you have a passenger, have him or her do it, and if you happen to both get a wave off, well, you can think of Goddess Durga! Wave at scooters, too. It'll give them a much-needed sense of coolness.

Waving promotes camaraderie— regardless of the style of motorcycle.

Tips for the Road

DEALING WITH THE LAWMEN

I spent nine years as a police motorcycle officer on the streets of suburban Atlanta. Most of the time my beat was the intersection of I-285 and I-75 during evening rush hour, and my primary responsibility was to quickly reach and clear traffic accidents. My motorcycle was well suited for this.

I also wrote my fair share of tickets, and let a few people go without one. What made me ticket some and let others off the hook? There were thousands of factors; a few of the reasons I let people go without a ticket are listed below. Whether or not these tips will get *you* out of a ticket is anybody's guess, but I offer them nonetheless.

Stop in a safe place. Many drivers who would later try to talk their way out of the ticket would get one regardless of their persuasive skills, because they stopped in a place that was dangerous to me and to them. Examples of places not to stop are: in the middle of the road (even if there is a center turn lane), on a curve, just over a hillcrest, and on the left side of the road (drivers who stopped on median walls were ticketed without exception). Examples of good places to stop are: scenic overlooks, gas stations, shoulders of interstate exit ramps, and well-lit businesses.

Be nice, but not ready. This one sounds counterproductive, but it isn't. When the officer makes it to the side of your bike, don't have your driver's license, registration, and insurance card ready. Make him ask you for those documents. The reason you want to make him ask you for them is so a conversation can begin. As you reach for your wallet or registration documents, tell the officer where you are reaching and what you're going to remove from there. "I'm going to have to open my saddlebag to get to the leather binder that has my registration in it." A simple statement like that lets the officer know that you're not just losing your mind and about to pull a gun or a knife on him.

Be polite. This one seems like a no-brainer, and drivers who aren't polite have no brains. Telling the officer you make enough money to buy and sell him, or some snappy comment about doughnuts, will only compound your problems. Officers won't be intimidated out of writing you a ticket, so it's important for you to understand your role on the traffic stop—the officer is in charge and you are his subordinate. Forget that stuff about "protect and serve." He or she is the boss and has the authority to tow in your bike, take your rude butt to jail, and generally ruin your day.

Talk to the officer. Bring up anything except a question about why you were stopped. Mention where you're going, or that you were distracted by the cute woman who just gave you the Vespa Wave. Better yet, say you've seen some beautiful scenery in his area and you're jealous of where he lives since your hometown offers nothing like it.

Know the officer. This one sounds impossible, but it's actually easy to pull off. I don't mean that you have to have dated the officer's sibling. I'm talking about addressing the officer by his or her correct title. If a State Trooper stops you, refer to him or her as "Trooper." If a Sheriff's Deputy has stopped you, refer to him or her as "Deputy." Police officers should be referred to as "Officer." Generally speaking, officers wear blue uniforms, deputies wear tan uniforms, and troopers might wear either or a combination of the two. In the event you see any rank insignia, refer to the official by that title. Two chevrons is a corporal, three chevrons is a sergeant, a gold or silver bar is a lieutenant. My father is an academic who put in a decade of study in institutions of higher learning to be awarded the privilege of the title "Dr. Hagebak." I, on the other hand, attended many classes and demonstrated years of leadership ability and professionalism for the privilege of being referred to as "Sergeant Hagebak." If you think referring to someone by their correct title is unimportant, consider this; if

You can always argue your case in court. And, hey, if it's in Parsons, WV, you'll get a tour of this historic place.

someone calls you "ma'am" and you happen to be a "sir," imagine how happy you'd be! I bet you'd give them a ticket if you could.

Flash some cleavage. Just kidding— don't even consider this one! Other major don'ts include offering a bribe ($100 clipped onto your driver's license won't do), crying, batting your baby blues at the officer, offering sexual favors, or arguing about the reason for the stop. Of the few good-looking women who left my traffic stops without a ticket, not a single one got a break because they were beautiful. They escaped with a warning because they told a funny joke or apologized for their infraction. In fact, I was much more lenient with drivers who did not flaunt physical beauty or wealth. To avoid a ticket, demonstrate to the officer that you are a regular person. To get a ticket, get uppity.

Drop your bike. To be honest, I have never witnessed this one, but I've heard of it a time or two. The story goes that a young woman was stopped for speeding and dropped her bike. The officer was so caught up in being chivalrous and assisting her with the motorcycle that he couldn't bear to write her a ticket. Whether it will work for you is anybody's guess. It'll be your chrome scratched and broken on the side of the road, but if you really want to try it...

Ask for a break. This sounds simple, and if the driver had followed the guidelines mentioned so far, I'd usually give him or her a break. I might write a ticket, but I'd reduce the speed noted on the citation, or I'd find something else wrong (like a turn light out) and ticket them for that nonmoving violation, or I'd just write WARNING across the ticket.

Sign on the dotted line. Okay, so none of these ideas worked for you. Remain polite and sign the ticket. I would often ask the driver to sign the ticket as a final check of their positive attitude, only to write WARNING on it in the end. Even if you get the ticket, even if you don't agree with it, remain polite. Snapping at the officer and telling him you'll see him in court, may cause him to make notes about why he stopped you, your demeanor, and violations he didn't cite you for in preparation for the court battle you have warned him about. If you are unremarkable, the chances he'll remember you in court are slimmer than if you make a spectacle of yourself.

Go to court. Even if you live out of town, it might pay for you to go to court. Pay through the mail and you are pleading guilty to the offense, so your license will likely have points added. The insurance industry uses

Plan ahead, study maps, and obey the law. It's always the best way to avoid a ticket.

these points to determine risk level of different riders. The motorcyclist who has no points pays less in premiums than the rider who has several points. When you go to court, meet with the prosecutor before trial and tell them you'll pay the fine but really want to keep the points off your license. What the prosecutor hears is, "I'm willing to settle this case without tying up the court's valuable time, and maybe you can make it home before your kids go to bed." If your request doesn't get a nibble, offer to attend a safe driving course (the Motorcycle Safety Foundation Rider's Edge or similar program can save you lots on your insurance, anyway). If the answer is still no, get ready to defend yourself. The judicial branch of government is there to listen after the executive branch of government has enforced the laws passed by the legislative branch. Explain to the judge that you intend to defend yourself (or hire an attorney if you want) and request his or her patience with you because you lack experience in that theater. This will tell the judge two things; one, you don't get in trouble a lot, and two, you are nervous but respectful about the court proceedings. When the proceedings start, remain professional and polite. Think of your questions and write them down as you think of them. Don't get flustered if the judge interrupts you; it's the judge's job to interrupt. Listen intently to what the judge has to say; chances are, in traffic court, he or she will have the final say about your guilt or innocence. To be found not guilty, all you have to do is introduce a reasonable doubt into the State's case against you. Whether you're found guilty or not guilty, thank the court for their time, pay your fine if you must, and get outta there!

Don't do anything wrong. This is the only sure-fire, never-fail way out of tickets. Page 19 lists some of the state laws pertaining to motorcycling in the

Central Appalachians. Watch your speed and abide by the rules and you should have few problems.

DEALING WITH THE LAWLESS

I have traveled around the globe and all across the United States. As yet, I have not been a crime victim. Although rare, thefts and assaults while motorcycling are not out of the realm of possibility. Unfortunately, many people with good personal safety habits in their own neighborhood seem to ignore those habits while on vacation. After all, "We're on vacation!" and it's only natural to relax.

In my many years as a police officer, I learned a thing or two about how the bad guy operates and how to avoid him. Generally speaking, criminals suffer from cowardice and mental and physical weakness. I have used my knowledge of these qualities to keep them at bay and prevent myself from becoming a crime victim.

Travel in groups. This will exploit the criminal's cowardice. He or she is less likely to victimize you if you have witnesses or someone who would potentially put up a defense against an attack or a theft. (I would recommend an actual defense only if you have extensive training, but criminals won't know if you're one of those "extensively trained" people or not.)

Have a winning attitude. Body language screams information to those around you—what's yours saying? Is your head down? Are your shoulders shrugged? Do you look like a dog that just wet the floor? Regardless of your stature, carry yourself confidently and criminals will fear you.

Lock your stuff—and your bike. By performing this simple task *every time*, you'll take advantage of a criminal's mental weakness. Unless he is particularly cunning, he will bypass your locked property to steal stuff that's an easier target. I have a friend who locks his bike with a huge snake-like chain through the front wheel every time he leaves the bike somewhere, even when just going into a restroom at an interstate rest stop. With the handlebar locked, the key out of the ignition and the chain through the front wheel, is my friend's motorcycle theft-proof? Nope, but who wants to go to the trouble to steal his bike? Maybe somebody will someday, but he's banking on the fact that the criminal will choose a softer target of opportunity.

Don't put all your eggs in one basket. What I mean here is, get into the habit of keeping money and credit cards in several places, not just in your wallet. That way, if the idiot criminal wants to steal your wallet, he's got your ID, $3 in cash, and a couple of credit cards (which you will *cancel* right away). Most criminals don't want your wallet—they want the money inside. Here's one idea: in case some assailant demands your wallet, pull some money out of your front pocket, throw it on the ground in front of him, and run. He'll go for the money, and you'll go for the phone!

Semper Paratus: *Always Ready.* Professional athletic teams, military combat units, and police officers all approach their adversary with a plan of action that in their minds will have them marching off the battlefield victorious. So try to think ahead. Don't be paranoid, but be vigilant, observant, and think of how you'd act in such a situation. Imagine yourself coming out unscathed and being a good witness to the police about the incident. Though the police might not

According to Murphy's Law, now that these motorcyclists are all decked out in rain gear, the weather will soon turn warm and sunny.

catch your criminal today, the information you give might prevent tomorrow's rash of crimes or point guilt at your bad guy in the future. For the record, please leave the butt kicking to the experts and the jury pools. Don't take matters into your own hands unless you want to get a sense of what handcuffs feel like.

DEALING WITH MURPHY'S LAW

Murphy's Law: "If it can go wrong, it will go wrong, and at the most inopportune time." With those words in mind, lets review a few of Murphy's Laws of Motorcycling.

New Rider Law. This law dictates that if you are taking someone on their first-ever motorcycle ride, it will rain—or your usually reliable motorcycle will burp and sputter like a toddler.

Bike Falling Law. This is the law that brings an unusual amount of gravity to the area under your motorcycle. This gravity field will be present when you're in front of a crowd (usually a crowd of the opposite sex), and will bring your bike down like a brick.

Rain Gear Dance Law. If it begins to rain and you're prepared enough to have brought rain gear, the more intricate and difficult your dance while donning your rain gear, the sooner the rain will stop once you've got it on.

Rain Gear Baking Law. You did the raingear dance to get your rain gear on, and it suddenly stopped raining. Now the sun comes out, baking you like a chocolate chip cookie!

Fuel Law. This law might strike as you admire the beautiful and remote scenery of Virginia and West Virginia from your bike. You'll check your fuel gauge and your trip meter and think, "I've got plenty of time to find a gas station." That's when you won't see one for the next 200 miles, and you'll be on the side of the road wondering where your next gallon of gas is coming from!

Motorcycle Reliability Law. Brag about your bike, and it'll break, guaranteed! If you happen to brag in front of a crowd, that crowd will be the one that will later stop to assist you in getting your reliable motorcycle taken to the shop.

Flat Tire Law. You will pick up a nail and flatten a tire only when you are far from home on a Saturday evening, just after the closest motorcycle shop has closed (of course it's 150 miles away and won't reopen until Tuesday), leaving you stranded and two days late for work.

BREAKING THE CURSE OF MURPHY'S LAW

Here's another chance for me to sling out the Coast Guard motto, *Semper Paratus.* If you're always ready, the pain of Murphy's Laws will be a minor inconvenience rather than a trip-ending disaster.

Prep your passenger. Keep your co-rider informed as to what's going on. Make them read this section, so they will be aware that a sudden downpour is their fault and have the opportunity to laugh it off. Let them know where they're going and what kind of road conditions to expect. Surprises are fun when they're wrapped in shiny paper, but not when they happen on the back of a motorcycle.

Carry an extra foot. I don't mean a good luck rabbit's foot, but a small block of wood or one of those hard plastic feet for sale at motorcycle shops. Use the wood or the foot under your kickstand when parking to prevent your steed from slowly sinking into the mud or hot asphalt.

Buy good rain gear. Many riders are miserable riding in the rain because they get wet and/or hot. Spend the extra money on some good rain gear that breathes, and for Pete's sake try it on before you ride with it! It's easier to learn the "rain gear dance" in the shop where you're buying the gear than on the road under a heavy downpour.

Fuel often and carry cash for gas. You may be really loyal to one fuel company, but the remote reaches of the region covered in this book is not the place to demonstrate those loyalties. Bring cash and buy fuel as you can. The mileage markers for gas stations are listed in each ride description. However, traveling late, you might find the one you need is closed. Especially in new territory, hedge your bets and fuel as often as you can.

Carry a cell phone. When your plans fall apart, you'll be able to call for some assistance. This tip comes with a warning, though—don't rely on it too heavily. Cells frequently don't work in West Virginia. The National Radio Quiet Zone prohibits certain frequencies and strengths in the area of eastern West Virginia to keep down interference for the National Radio Astronomy Observatory in Green Bank, and even outside the quiet zone, they sometimes just plain don't work in the mountains.

Bring a tire repair kit. These simple kits consist of plugs, a plug fid to jam the plug into the hole, CO_2 cartridges, and an air hose to inflate the tire. These tools provide a good temporary

Punctured tire—#@! Well, you're bound to get one sooner or later.

tubeless tire repair that will hold long enough to reach the motorcycle shop in the next town.

Use roadside service clubs. Most owner's clubs, and the American Motorcycle Association, offer a towing package as part of their membership. You might have to pay a few dollars extra for this service, but it more than pays for itself if you have to use it. And don't leave the phone number in the membership packet on your bedside table (like I do), carry it with you in your road-ready kit.

Pack a road-ready kit. Where does all this stuff go, and what about including some tools and a first aid kit? You don't have to buy anything fancy. I bought one of those insulated lunch bags for about $4. I loaded it with some first aid gear, my tire patch kit and a few tools, my club membership cards, and baby wipes, then topped it off with an energy bar (to tide me over while I push my bike out of the National Radio Quiet Zone so I can call for help). You can make this kit as simple or as complex as

you like. Just remember *you're* the one who'll be using it, so don't waste your time stuffing a widget into it if you don't know how to operate one.

PARTING SHOT

As you travel the highways and byways of this great land, remember to watch for the other guy. Support the sport of motorcycling by keeping up the camaraderie and mystique of motorcycling by sharing road lies, tips, and friendly waves. Will it matter if you don't contribute to this camaraderie and mystique? Probably not, but if enough people decide not to, motorcycling will lose its allure. Keep up the image by introducing someone new to the sport. You don't have to give them a ride, just plant the seed. You and I both know they secretly want to try it, anyway.

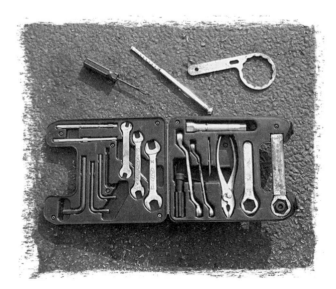

A good tool kit is worth its weight in gold.

Summary of State Motorcycle Laws

LAW	VA	WV	NC	TN	OH	MD
Helmets Required	Y	Y[1]	Y	Y	N[2]	Y[1]
Eye Protection	Y[3]	Y	N	Y[3]	Y[3]	Y[3]
Daytime Headlight	N	Y	Y	Y	N	N
Turn Signals	N	N	N	N	Y[4]	Y
Rearview Mirror	Y	Y	Y	Y	Y	Y
Headphones Permitted	Y	N	Y	Y	Y	Y[5]
Max. Handlebar Height (above seat)	U	15"	U	15"	15"	15"
Lane Splitting	N	N	N	N	N	N

Y = Yes
N = No
U = Unrestricted

[1] Reflectorization required
[2] Required if novice or under 18 years of age
[3] Not required if equipped with a windscreen
[4] Not required if manufactured before 1968
[5] Single earphone only

While there are certainly more laws relating to motorcycles than these, the most frequently questioned ones are listed here for convenient reference. This summary of state motorcycle laws was current as of July 2003.

NOTE: Virginia State Law prohibits the use or mere possession of radar detectors. All states listed permit modulating headlights.

The Shenandoah Valley

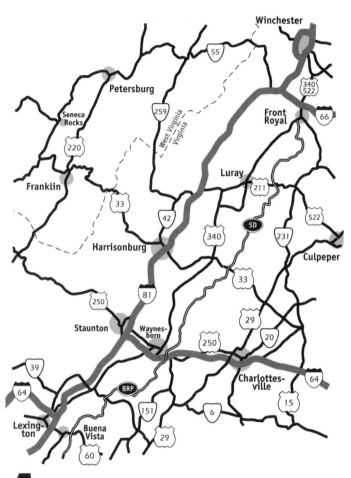

A wide river valley, a deep river gorge, a classic roadside diner, a 19th-century covered bridge, and the kind of roads all motorcyclists dream about—Virginia's Shenandoah Valley has it all.

Area Covered

Oh, Gosh, A Humpback Bridge!

Beautiful scenery, fun roads, and interesting sights. The interesting sights include the rapids of the Maury River; the mill of Gristmill Square in Warm Springs; the Homestead Resort, which opened first in 1766; a beautiful waterfall that cascades down 150 feet; the mammoth Westvaco Plant in Covington; and last but not least, the Humpback Bridge, built in 1835 of hand-hewn timbers. The roads on this tour keep you out of busy traffic and on the twisty two-lane ribbons that make this area popular for motorcyclists.

GAS

Gas is available at the start in Lexington and at miles 7.1, 20.1, 28.2, 33, 36.9, 43.7, 45.1, 45.3, and 51.9. There is also fuel available in Covington, near the end, but not directly on the route.

GETTING TO THE START

This ride begins in Lexington, VA, off I-64 just west of the intersection of I-64 and I-81. From I-81 take I-64 west to exit 55, US 11 (Lee Hwy.), and go north one block to VA 39. Reset your trip meter to zero as you turn left onto VA 39.

RIDE OVERVIEW

The first leg of this adventure from Lexington to the small town of Goshen is full of fun twists and turns. Leaving the comfort and convenience of Lexington behind, VA 39 leads over low hills and around small curves, just enough to get you warmed up for the ride ahead. Things really get interesting when you pass the last few homes on the outskirts of Lexington and enter the woods along the Maury River. Here you'll see fewer cars and more motorcycles. The Maury River flows south from Goshen toward Lexington, cutting through Goshen Pass. The Virginia Department of Transportation was kind enough to put VA 39 right next to the river, making it twisty, scenic, and popular among us biker types. There are several pullouts and scenic overlooks, and one that includes some information about Matthew Fontaine Maury, for whom the river was named. Mr. Maury was a seaman, and his memorial on the side of VA 39 is marked with a large ship's anchor (an odd sight, hundreds of miles from the sea).

With Goshen Pass in your rearview mirrors, you'll enter the town of Goshen. Small in size, Goshen is big on hospitality. Stop in at the Mill Creek Café, and you'll be treated like a neighbor, not an interloper. The Café will fill you with breakfast, lunch, or dinner and even offers fuel to fill your bike. If you're on a diet, do not sit at the bar. The pies are under glass behind it and the temptation to eat the whole pie is strong!

Leaving Goshen, you'll ride next to Calfpasture Creek. The road and the creek gently meander together through the woods and past farmland leading to the George Washington National Forest in a series of long sweeping curves. Just before entering the National Forest and climbing into the Alleghenies, you'll pass a massive plantation on the right side of the road. This plantation is surrounded by hundreds of acres of well-manicured fields and even has its own airstrip. The road then bends wildly up into the mountains, and you'll ride over several of them on your way to US 220 in Warm Springs.

VA 39 T's off into US 220 in Warm Springs. Turning left onto south US 220, you'll pass very close to what could be called the downtown section of Warm Springs. To tour this small town, turn right onto Courthouse Hill. The three minutes it takes to ride through town is worthwhile. Not only will you ride past the handsome Bath County Courthouse, you'll ride down from Courthouse Hill to Gristmill Square. The gristmill standing there today was built in 1900 to replace the one that had stood there since 1771. Today, the mill is home to the Waterwheel Restaurant. Open for dinner only (and closed on Tuesdays), the restaurant offers trout, steak, and veal dishes for $20 to $25 in a cozy atmosphere. Gristmill Square is also home to a very nice bed and breakfast inn, if you decide to make Warm Springs your base camp for western Virginia.

TOTAL DISTANCE
70.5 miles

TIME FRAME
2 hours. Add time to stop to eat and see the sights.

Riding south on US 220 between Warm Springs and Hot Springs, you'll see several stately homes along this gently curved section of roadway. In Hot Springs, you'll ride through a golf course (watch for little white balls flying onto the road) and then round a corner to see the Homestead Resort. The mammoth size of the Homestead seems not to correspond with its name. Most homesteads are homes. This homestead has 506 luxury rooms and towers over all other buildings for miles. Only the mountains are larger. Captain Thomas Bullett of the American Militia first opened the Homestead Resort in 1766. At the

The Humpback Bridge.

time, there was little money on hand to pay the militia officers and enlisted men. Instead, they frequently received land. Captain Bullett's remuneration was the 300 acres that is now the town of Hot Springs. In 1832, new owner Dr. Thomas Goode used the hot spring water to ease the suffering of his patients. The resort was purchased in 1888 by J.P. Morgan, and the Homestead became one of the first places in the country where guests would find running water, electricity (installed by none other than Thomas Edison), and phones in their rooms. Attracted to the amenities and the scenery, twenty-one U.S. Presidents have slept there, and hundreds of dignitaries, movie stars, and cool motorcyclists have stayed there as well.

Golf is the big summer draw to the Homestead. Sam Snead worked as a caddy there in 1919 and later became one of the world's best-known professional golfers. But there's more to the Homestead than golf. Activities range from horseback riding to snow skiing. If you do it, chances are you can do it at the Homestead. It's a hot spot for adventurers of all types.

From Hot Springs, US 220 gets curvier and a little rougher. You'll find some cracks in the asphalt and a bit more traffic. Take a break from the road at the roadside pullout near the town of Falling Springs. The overlook on the right side of the road has several picnic tables and a short, paved path next to the road leading you to a good view of Fallingwater Cascades. This waterfall is one of the most accessible in Virginia. As a matter of fact, you can see it from the saddle of your bike as you ride south on US 220. However, to get the full view, dismount and check it out. The stream falls about 150 ft. onto rocks below, then joins the Jackson River. There's another overlook past the Fallingwater Cascades overlook that gives a good view of the Jackson River Valley.

US 220 descends toward the city of Covington and to the large Westvaco plant that lies on the north side of town. Like the Homestead Resort, the enormous size of the plant seems to defy logic, considering how far it is from a major seaport or shipping center. Westvaco is the largest employer in western Virginia, and this plant is home to its bleached board division.

This route turns right onto US 60 West, also known as the Midlands Trail that stretches from Virginia Beach through Richmond into West Virginia and continues through the "midlands" of the United States. You'll still be riding in the shadow of the Westvaco plant as you near the western edge of Covington. Farther along, you'll find the Midlands Trail is lined with attractive older homes of nearly every design. Riding over a hillcrest, you'll be back into the country along the banks of Dunlap Creek.

Less than a half-mile from the end of the ride, you'll ride over Dunlap Creek on a "new" bridge where you'll see the signs directing you to the Humpback Bridge Wayside Park. Turn left and head down Rumsey Rd. under a railroad bridge to get to the well-manicured lawns and picnic tables of the Wayside Park. The Humpback Bridge itself is an amazing structure. It was built of hand-hewn timbers with a bow or "hump" in the middle to give it extra strength. Considering it was built in 1835, the designers must have known a thing or two about building strong bridges! It was used until 1929 when a new bridge was built nearby. In 1953, local civic and business organizations teamed up to create the park surrounding the bridge, and folks have been visiting the area ever since.

US 60 meets I-64 less than one mile from the Humpback Bridge. The ride ends there. Take I-64 east to head back toward Covington, Lexington, and I-81. Go west on I-64 to reach the adventures awaiting you in West Virginia.

RIDE ALTERNATIVES

In Warm Springs, at mile 42.1, you might want to consider a right turn onto Courthouse Hill to pass the Bath County Courthouse and ride down to the Gristmill Square to check out the gristmill built in 1900, replacing the one built in 1771.

Near the end of this ride, the route turns right onto US 60 West to avoid the busy downtown traffic of Covington. As you enter Covington and feel hunger pangs or need fuel, continue south on US 220 for a few blocks past US 60 West to reach fast food and fuel. US 220 will lead you to I-64, but by trimming the last few miles off this ride you'll miss the Humpback Bridge—and you really shouldn't miss it.

ROAD CONDITIONS

The first half of the ride on VA 39 is well paved and mighty twisty. Adequate signage warns of the sharpest curves. A few hairpin curves await you in the mountain passes, and those hairpins have a few asphalt cracks.

Don't let the fact that US 220 is a US route make you think it's a busy four-lane; it isn't. US 220 is a well-paved, two-lane road with sweeping curves. South of Hot Springs you'll find a few cracks and patches in the asphalt.

POINTS OF INTEREST

Goshen Pass, Warm Springs, Gristmill Square, the Homestead Resort, Fallingwater Cascades, Westvaco plant, Humpback Bridge.

RESTAURANTS

The town of Goshen is home to the **Mill Creek Café** (540-997-5228) in Goshen, VA. It's open Monday through Friday from 7 am to 9 pm, Saturday from 8 am to 9 pm, and Sunday 9 am to 9 pm for breakfast, lunch, and dinner. At breakfast you'll spend $1.25 for handmade biscuits, and the price ranges up to the steak and eggs for $6.50. Lunch items include the "econo sandwich," a 6-in. hoagie with meat, cheese, and lettuce for $3.29. A burger is just $2.50, and you can get a made-to-order sandwich (like a turkey sub) for around $4. For dinner, seafood and steak are offered for $11 and $14, respectively. You can dine on less expensive items for dinner, like a veggie plate for $6.

The Waterwheel Restaurant (540-839-2231) is in Warm Springs at the bottom of Courthouse Hill. It is open for dinner from 6 pm to 9 pm (until 10 pm Fridays and Saturdays) every day except Tuesday and open on Sundays for lunch. Here you will find elegant dining in a warm atmosphere. Dinner entrees include trout, salmon, duck, veal, and steak. Prices range from $20 to $24. Reservations are recommended. For lodging, the Inn at Gristmill Square offers 17 rooms, ranging in price from $90 to $150 depending on room amenities (like fireplaces) and the number of guests. Check them out on the web at www.gristmillsquare.com, or call the Waterwheel Restaurant, which has the same phone number.

At the **Homestead Resort** (800-838-1766) in Hot Springs you have eight restaurants to choose from. The restaurants and meals served represent a broad range of tastes, atmospheres and prices. Several require jackets for gentlemen (and they don't mean the latest in motorcycle leathers). One place that doesn't is the **Sam Snead Tavern**. Named for the legendary professional golfer and former caddy at The Homestead, this tavern is in the old bank building of Hot Springs (you'll see it from US 220). The menu includes dozens of grilled, blackened, fried, broiled, and roasted items. Expect to spend a little extra, with ribs for $20 and burgers for $11. Don't let the price get you down. Instead, consider your remote location as you bite into that delicious, melt-in-your-mouth entree. Reservations are not necessary at the Tavern, but for the fancier dining offered at the Homestead, you'd better call ahead, or find them on the web at www.thehomestead.com.

DETAILED DIRECTIONS

Mile 0—Turn left onto VA 39 West from US 11 North in Lexington, VA.

Mile 7.6—Fork to the left to stay on VA 39. *You'll follow the Maury River upstream into Goshen Pass. At mile 11 you'll enter Goshen Pass. There's a paved overlook at mile 13.4 that offers nice views down into the Maury River. You can learn about Matthew Fontaine Maury at a roadside marker at mile 13.7. You'll cross some railroad tracks at mile 18.6 and enter the town of Goshen.*

Mile 19.7—Turn left onto VA 39 Alternate (it's the main road through town). *VA 39 Alternate makes a sharp right turn at mile 19.9, crosses Mill Creek, and ends at VA 39.*

Mile 20.1—Turn left onto VA 39. *The Mill Creek Café is on the left at this intersection. The road follows*

Calfpasture Creek northwest, out of town. At mile 36, there's a large, handsome plantation on the right side of the road, complete with an airstrip. Enter the George Washington National Forest at mile 37.9 and you can enjoy a paved overlook of the nearby mountains at mile 39.7.

Mile 41.4—Turn left onto US 220 in Warm Springs, VA. *The Bath County Chamber of Commerce Visitor Gazebo is on the right side of the road. At mile 42.1 you'll pass Courthouse Hill Rd., which will lead you to the Bath County Courthouse and Gristmill Square. You'll ride through a golf course at mile 45.7; watch for errant golf balls. The Homestead stretches over the town of Hot Springs at mile 46.5. To reach the Sam Snead Tavern, turn right at mile 46.6. The main entrance to the Homestead is on the left at mile 47. Watch for golf balls again around mile 51 as you ride through another golf course. The Fallingwater Cascades is on the right at mile 58.5. There's an overlook of the Jackson River Valley on the right side of the road at mile 60.2. At mile 64.7, you'll see the huge Westvaco Plant on the right side of the road.*

Mile 65.2—Turn right onto west US 60 (Midlands Trail). *You'll cross some railroad tracks at mile 65.9.*

Mile 66.1—Turn right to remain on US 60 West. *You'll pass some nice homes around mile 66.4. To reach the Humpback Bridge, turn left at mile 69.6 onto Rumsey Rd.*

Mile 70.5—This ride ends at the interchange of US 60 and I-64. *Go west on I-64 to enter West Virginia; go east to head back toward I-81.*

Oh, Gosh...

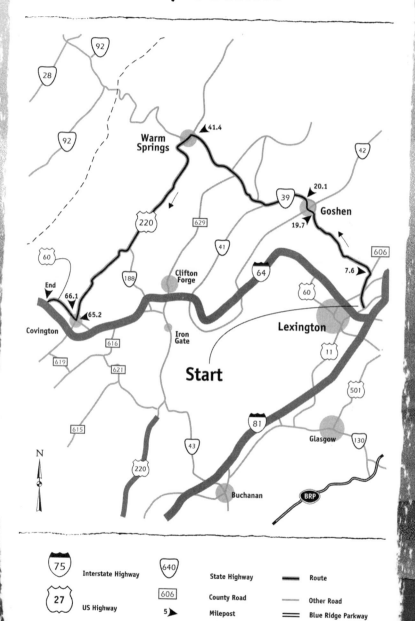

Great Big Thing Tour

The Great Big Thing, a.k.a. the GBT or the Green Bank Telescope, stands nearly 500 ft. tall. Its dish is larger than one and a half football fields. It cost almost $80,000,000 to build and is the largest land-based, moveable, manmade object in the world.

This ride is an all-day affair. Starting in Lexington, VA, you'll negotiate narrow Goshen Pass, take in some farm country, and possibly learn a thing or two about radio astronomy in Green Bank, WV. You'll return to Staunton, VA on a road designed and built by Napoleon's engineers, because U.S. engineers thought it was insane to bend a road through those mountains.

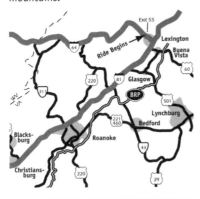

GAS

Gas is available at the start in Lexington; along the ride at miles 7.1, 20.1, 28.2, 33, 36.9, 43.1, 54.5, 81.4, 86.4, 93.3, 96.5, 119.4, 119.6, 128.7, 135.1, 144.9, and 155, and near the ride's end at mile 158.

GETTING TO THE START

This ride begins in Lexington, VA, off I-64 just west of the intersection of I-64 and I-81. From I-81 take I-64 west to exit 55, US 11 (Lee Hwy.), and go north one block to VA 39. Reset your trip meter to zero as you turn left onto VA 39.

RIDE OVERVIEW

From Lexington, ride VA 39 North toward Goshen Pass. Along the way, you'll bend and dip over hill and dale next to the Maury River. Motorcyclists come from far and wide to enjoy the well-paved curves of Goshen Pass. Following it upstream, you'll be able to better see the river's wild rapids and exciting falls. Pullouts and picnic areas offer a closer look at this section of river. The Maury River was named for Matthew Fontaine Maury, a seafaring gentleman who lived from 1806 to 1873. There's a small memorial to Mr. Maury on the right side of the road next to a large ship's anchor. Just beyond, an excellent paved lookout sits about 80 ft. above the river. Usually a couple of motorcycles are stopped there, with their riders sharing a few road lies.

Leaving Goshen Pass and entering the town of Goshen, this tour makes a left onto VA 39 Alternate to cut through town. If you stay on VA 39, you'll cross some rough railroad tracks and ride along a short stretch of roadway turning left just before the Groton Bridge. The Groton Bridge was erected in 1890 and is built with an iron superstructure on stone pillars. It's not very impressive-looking, but it's interesting, considering that most local bridges of the 1890s were covered bridges made of wood.

In Goshen, you'll cross Mill Creek and find the Mill Creek Café at the intersection of VA 39 Alternate and VA 39. Its mellow wood-panelled interior will warm your bones on a cold winter day (so will the 60-cent coffee). Waitresses there serve breakfast, lunch, and dinner with a roadhouse diner feel rarely found in today's fast food world. You can sit at the bar and stare out the window or ogle the homemade pies under glass behind the counter. An old cash register by the door adds ambiance. One more thing—the café sells fuel, too. It's not unusual to see travelers gas up and come in to pay, only to realize how hungry they are and sit down to enjoy a good meal.

From Goshen, you'll ride next to Calfpasture Creek. There's a large plantation on the right side of the road just before you enter the George Washington National Forest. Then you'll climb up and over two mountain passes before reaching Warm Springs, VA.

TOTAL DISTANCE
166 miles

TIME FRAME
5 hours from start to finish. Add a few minutes to look down into the chasm of Goshen Pass, an hour or two to dine in one of the fine restaurants along the way, and an hour to tour the National Radio Astronomy Observatory (home of the Great Big Thing).

In Warm Springs, the ride makes a left onto US 220 and then an immediate right back onto VA 39 West. In this little jog to the left, you'll see a large whitewashed building on the right side of the road, home to some of the warm springs from which the town gets its name. People come to the area to lie in the warm spring water to relieve their stress and heal physical maladies. If you were to continue south on US 220, you would reach the town of Hot Springs. The Homestead Resort was built in Hot Springs as a place for city dwellers to escape to the country without leaving the amenities of city

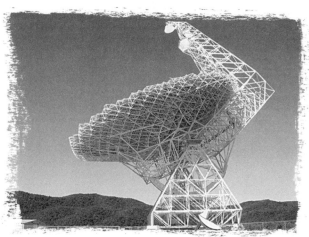

Standing 485 ft. tall and weighing 16,000,000 lb., the Green Bank Telescope is one Great Big Thing.

life behind. Today the Homestead Resort offers visitors luxurious accommodations, golf, tennis, and, of course, hot mineral baths. Both the warm springs and the hot springs flow between 2,500 and 5,000 gallons per minute, at a temperature between 77° F to 106° F, depending on location.

This tour makes a right onto VA 39 in Warm Springs and continues to wind through the George Washington National Forest. From Warm Springs, VA, to Minnehaha Springs, WV, the road is a wild set of twists and turns on tree-canopied asphalt. Watch for deer in this seldom traveled section of roadway. You'll pass through one heinous hairpin turn in Ryder's Gap and enter West Virginia. The road number remains the same. Unlike most states, which change road names and numbers as they cross state lines, Virginia and West Virginia were once one large state, so their road names and numbers rarely change at border crossings. Descending from Ryder Gap, WV 39 straightens out a bit and offers sweeping curves into Minnehaha Springs.

In Minnehaha Springs, fork to the right onto WV 92. At the fork in the road you'll find a map of Pocahontas County with most of the fun roads highlighted. A few years ago, leaders of Pocahontas County learned that motorcyclists enjoy great road conditions and fun curves, and that motorcyclists tend to spend money in the places they visit. They began to advertise in national motorcycle magazines in an effort to attract motorcyclists to the area. The advertising campaign has been a success, and more motorcyclists arrive monthly. Now, you're one of them!

WV 92 leads you north through a farm valley near Knapp Creek. As you ride, you'll notice high mountains on both sides of the valley and a feeling

of remoteness beginning to set in. So you won't be surprised to learn that this area is the heart of the National Radio Quiet Zone, where radio transmissions are controlled to prevent them from interfering with the radio telescopes here. If you have a radio on your bike, it probably won't be receiving much in this area, and cell phones are equally useless. Homes are few and far between, and cattle appear to be the only thing moving. You might hear the sound of a steam locomotive in the distance.

You haven't entered a time warp on WV 92, but you *can* go back in time by visiting the town of Cass, virtually unchanged from its heyday as a lumber town over one hundred years ago. Even its steam locomotives have remained. To reach Cass, turn off this tour onto WV 66 West and ride about six miles. However, be aware that this ride continues north on WV 92, and the feeling of traveling back in time will be shattered by the huge leap forward you'll take when you reach the National Radio Astronomy Observatory.

You'll find the National Radio Astronomy Observatory on the left side of the road in Green Bank, WV. The Observatory is home to seven operating radio telescopes, the largest of which is about two miles from WV 92. You aren't allowed to drive your bike to the Great Big Thing. It's not a security issue; you could walk the two miles to the GBT. The reason you can't ride is because the spark plugs on your motorcycle transmit an electric pulse that would interfere with the sensitive receivers of the telescope. To get a closer look, park your scooter in the Visitor Center parking lot and take the diesel-powered tour bus. The diesel motor has no spark plugs to cause electrical interference. Tour bus operators are very accommodating to visitors who want to stop along the

Inside the Visitor Center, a moving scale model of the Green Bank Telescope responds to computer controls and displays signal images on computer monitors.

two-mile ride and take photos of the GBT or other telescopes in the Observatory.

Once at the GBT, you'll be impressed with its mammoth proportions. It stands 485 ft. tall, weighs in at 16,000,000 lbs. (about the same as nineteen 747s) and its 2,004 metal panels cover an area larger than two acres. It cost $79,000,000 to build and cannot transmit—it can only receive. And the whole thing can move!

Open from 8 am to 7:30 pm, seven days a week, the Observatory Visitor Center is an educational and interesting place to visit. The tours, movies, and activities there are FREE. The hot dogs available at the snack bar are not free but are pretty cheap. There is a small gift shop in the Visitor Center where you'll be able to buy books, mugs, T-shirts, miniature GBTs, and freeze-dried ice cream. The gift shop also sells pieces of the old GBT, which suffered metal fatigue and collapsed a few years ago.

Leaving the National Radio Astronomy Observatory, continue north through the National Radio Quiet Zone as you near US 250, onto which the ride makes a right turn.

Back around 1830, when Virginia and West Virginia were one big state, Virginia advertised the job of designing and constructing a road that would cross the Allegheny and Shenandoah Mountain Ranges, connecting the towns of Petersburg and Staunton. American engineers quickly dismissed the project as too difficult. Napoleon's engineers, out of work since his defeat at Waterloo, were ready for the task. So it was the French who cut the road where US 250 is paved today. Enjoy the great curves, steep climbs, and spiraling descents as US 250 crosses dozens of mountains and passes through small towns in the valleys, entering Virginia and finally descending toward Monterey, the county seat of Highland County.

In downtown Monterey, you'll see the old courthouse on the right as you ride through town, and High's Restaurant is on the right about a block east. Here's a place where you'll want to fill your gut. High's offers good food seven days a week, preparing delicious dinners for a small amount of money. Monterey is also a good place for a fuel stop, and US 220 crosses US 250 perpendicularly. To reach Warm Springs, VA, turn right to head south on US 220; to ride into WV, and make a left onto US 220 North. This tour continues south on US 250, climbing out of Monterey back into the wild curves toward Staunton, where you'll enter the George Washington National Forest and reach an overlook in a gap on Shenandoah Mountain.

The gap on Shenandoah Mountain has a paved, scenic overlook with restrooms and some ruins of Confederate breastworks. The Shenandoah Mountain Trail crosses the road here, and part of the trail will lead you on a quick (200-ft.) hike to Civil War ruins that were built on April 1, 1862, to keep the Federal troops from entering the Shenandoah Valley. As it turned out, the Confederate breastworks afforded little protection, and the Federal troops spent little time defeating the outnumbered Rebel troops who guarded the gap. Descending from the gap toward Staunton, you'll ride through a few more mountain passes before leaving the George Washington National Forest.

Leaving the mountains behind, sweeping curves lead you through the western Virginia farmland. The tour turns left onto VA 275 a few miles north of Staunton, VA. If you want to ride through Staunton, don't turn on VA 275; continue south on US 250, which will lead you through the heart of Staunton. The new two-lane VA 275 takes you to I-81 with very little fanfare, avoiding the traffic and congestion of downtown Staunton. This long ride ends at the intersection of VA 275 and I-81. If you want to pack on more riding, head south on I-81 for a couple of miles to I-64 east for about 11 miles to Waynesboro, where the Blue Ridge Parkway and Skyline Drive begin.

RIDE ALTERNATIVES

In Goshen, this tour turns left onto VA 39 Alternate and rejoins VA 39 about a half-mile later. You can continue on VA 39 and ride that half-mile to rejoin the ride. In doing so, the mileage will be exactly the same. You'll miss the "downtown" section of Goshen, but you'll get a close look at the Groton Bridge, built in 1890 with an iron superstructure.

Near the GBT, you can make this already long loop even longer by turning left onto WV 66 and riding part of the *Time Travel* run (p. 172). Along the way you'll pass Cass Scenic Railroad State Park and Snowshoe Ski Resort. Turn right onto US 219 North, which will lead you to another right turn onto US 250. Once back on US 250, you'll rejoin this tour just north of the GBT. You'll add about two more hours to your ride by taking this alternative, and you'll miss the National Radio Astronomy Observatory, but you will get a good view of the GBT on WV 66 before entering the town of Cass.

The ride through Goshen Pass takes you high above the Maury River.

ROAD CONDITIONS

You name the road condition, and this ride has it. The tour begins with some well-banked, freshly paved sweeping turns through Goshen Pass, then bends slightly through farm country, then in a series of hairpin turns takes you up and over several mountain ranges before reaching the West Virginia farmland. Once in West Virginia, a twisty mountainous ride gives way to gently sweeping curves through farmland, but after turning on US 250 South back into Virginia, the twisties greet you again. Thank the crazy French, who took up the task of creating this beautiful stretch of road. All the roads on this tour are two-lane, with asphalt in pretty good shape. Watch for scrapes and an occasional chunk of gravel in the steepest turns. The other hazard you'll likely encounter is wildlife (as in deer, groundhog, and other species) that, if struck by your bike, would alter your schedule and maybe even your life. Watch for those pesky critters, particularly during hours of twilight when they are on the move.

POINTS OF INTEREST

Goshen Pass, Warm Springs, scenic overlooks, National Radio Astronomy Observatory (home of the GBT), Confederate breastworks, several mountain ranges and quaint towns.

RESTAURANTS

On this all-day ride, plan ahead to eat. Here's the "meal plan" for this tour.

For breakfast or an early lunch, stop at the **Mill Creek Café** (540-997-5228) in Goshen, VA. The café is open Monday through Friday from 7 am to 9 pm, Saturday from 8 am to 9 pm, and Sunday 9 am to 9 pm. Inside, you can sit at the counter, keep an eye on your bike parked outside, and watch traffic go by. Breakfast items are good biscuits for $1.25, steak and eggs for $6.50, and the two-egg breakfast for just $2.50. They don't make omelets but do offer up some delicious pancakes. For lunch, you can have the "econo sandwich"—a 6-in. hoagie with meat, cheese, and lettuce for $3.29. A burger is just $2.50, and you can get a made-to-order sandwich (like a turkey sub) for around $4. For dinner, seafood and steak are offered for $11 and $14, respectively. Or try a veggie plate for $6. If you are in Goshen for dinner, you'd better not attempt the rest of this tour until morning, because it's a long run to make in the dark.

Later in the ride, after passing the GBT and reentering Virginia, you'll probably be hungry again. **High's Restaurant** in Monterey, VA, offers delicious food at reasonable prices. They are open Monday through Saturday from 6 am to 8 pm and Sundays from 7 am to 6 pm. Unlike the Mill Creek Café, the bar at High's affords no view outside, so if you want to keep an eye on your scooter, you'll have to sit at a table or booth close to the door. The menu is comparable to that of the Mill Creek Café. For dinner you can dine on steak for $12 or mountain trout for $9, both served with a baked potato and a side salad. Lunch includes Buffalo-style hot wings for $6, burgers for $2.50, and sandwiches from $2.25. If you are at High's in time for breakfast, either you started this tour mighty early or you're riding it backwards. But just in case you need to know, for breakfast you can get a plate of pancakes for $2.25, two eggs for $3, and Southern-style grits as a side item.

The **National Radio Astronomy Observatory snack bar** offers hot dogs, sandwiches, and soft drinks. So if you really want to stretch out the day, you could have breakfast at the Mill Creek Café in Goshen, VA, lunch at the GBT in Green Bank, WV, and dinner back at High's in Monterey, VA.

DETAILED DIRECTIONS

Mile 0—Turn left onto VA 39 West from US 11 North in Lexington, VA.

Mile 7.6—Fork to the left to stay on VA 39. *You'll follow the Maury River upstream into Goshen Pass. At mile 11 you'll enter Goshen Pass. There's a paved overlook at mile 13.4 that offers nice views down into the Maury River. You can learn about Matthew Fontaine Maury at a roadside marker at mile 13.7. You'll cross some railroad tracks at mile 18.6 and enter the town of Goshen.*

Mile 19.7—Turn left onto VA 39 Alternate (it's the main road through town). *If you go straight and continue to follow the signs for VA 39, the mileage will be the same, but you'll miss the "downtown" section of Goshen. By going straight on VA 39, you'll get a good view of the Groton Bridge with its iron superstructure built in 1890. VA 39 Alternate makes a sharp right turn at mile 19.9, crosses Mill Creek, and ends at VA 39.*

Mile 20.1—Turn left onto VA 39. The Mill Creek Café is on the left at this intersection. *The road follows Calfpasture Creek northwest, out of town. At mile 36, there's a large, handsome plantation on the right side of the road, complete with an airstrip. Enter the George Washington National Forest at mile 37.9, and you can enjoy a paved overlook of the nearby mountains at mile 39.7.*

Mile 41.4—Turn left onto US 220 in Warm Springs, VA. *The Bath County Chamber of Commerce Visitor Gazebo is on the right side of the road.*

Mile 41.5—Turn right back onto VA 39 West. *There's a recreation area on the left at mile 51.3 offering picnic tables and restrooms. You'll enter West Virginia's Pocahontas County and the Monongahela National Forest at mile 59.1. VA 39 becomes WV 39. There's another recreation area with picnic tables and restrooms at mile 59.8.*

Mile 63.8—Fork to the right onto WV 92 North in Minnehaha Springs.

Mile 74—Turn left to remain on WV 92. *At mile 84.9, you could turn left onto WV 66 to get to the Cass Scenic Railroad State Park and the Snowshoe Ski Resort area. The National Radio Astronomy Observatory is on the left at mile 88.1 in Green Bank, WV. The parking area for the NRAO is near the road in front of the Visitors Center. At mile 88.3, there's a bank (with ATM) in Green Bank, but this banking institution is built of red brick.*

Mile 96.5—Fork to the right onto US 250 south.

Mile 98.6—Fork to the right again to remain on US 250 South. *Reenter Virginia at mile 105.8. At mile 112.7, there's a small overlook that gives good views of the valley below. You'll enter Monterey, VA, at mile 119, where you'll find High's Restaurant at mile 119.6, about a block past the county courthouse. Reenter the George Washington National Forest at mile 136.3, and you can check out the Confederate breastworks at mile 138.3 at an overlook with restrooms. There's a recreation area with picnic tables and restrooms at mile 140.5.*

Mile 160.5—Turn left onto VA 275 to bypass the busy downtown section of Staunton, VA.

Mile 166—The ride ends where VA 275 meets I-81.

Great Big Thing Tour

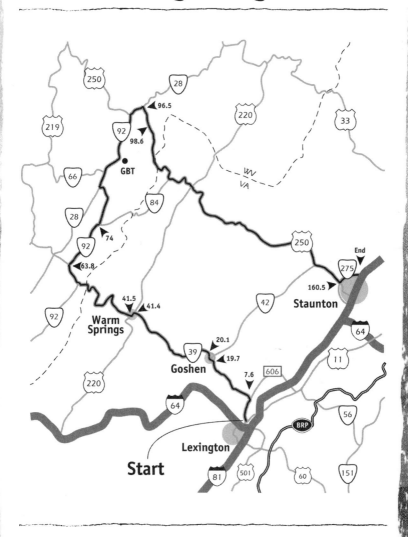

250   28

219   92   96.5

98.6

GBT

66   84

28   74

92

63.8

92   41.5   41.4

Warm
Springs

220   39   20.1

Goshen   19.7

7.6   606

64

220   BRP

Lexington

Start

81   501   60   151

220   33

250   End

275   160.5

42   Staunton

64   11

56

WV
VA

75	Interstate Highway	640	State Highway	Route
27	US Highway	606	County Road	Other Road
		5 ▶	Milepost	Blue Ridge Parkway

Tye Turnpike

This great adventure will lead you on a wild ride through incomparable scenery. You'll enjoy good road conditions, passing under the Blue Ridge Parkway twice while taking in the views. Off the bike, you can learn about early farm life on McCormick Farm and take a walk through the woods to see Crabtree Falls as they cascade down Pinnacle Ridge in the Crabtree Falls Recreation Area. Along the way, expect fresh, clean asphalt paved into beautiful sweeping curves—a motorcyclist's dream.

GAS

Gas is available at the start and at miles 10.2, 23.3, 25.4, 31.4, 41.2, 58.5, 58.7, 59.2, and 60.5.

GETTING TO THE START

This ride starts at I-81 exit 205 in Raphine, VA, heading onto CR 606 East toward the town of Steeles Tavern. Exit 205 is about an hour north of Roanoke. Reset your trip meter as you ride east from the northbound entrance/exit ramps for I-81.

RIDE OVERVIEW

After turning off I-81, you'll find CR 606 a four-lane divided road with businesses on both sides. As soon as you negotiate the first curve, the additional lanes and center median change to a more agreeable two-lane road sweeping through the countryside. On the left you'll see the McCormick Farm. Robert McCormick moved to the area in 1779 and built a farm on 450 acres. McCormick farmed wheat and corn and built a gristmill to grind his grains into meal. Early farming of wheat was done by hand, and the McCormicks owned many slaves to provide the labor required. Looking for a better way, Robert McCormick attempted unsuccessfully to build a reaper to harvest the wheat. He referred to his invention as a complete failure. Robert's grandson, Cyrus McCormick, took on the task of inventing a reaper that would work. In July of 1831, Cyrus's reaper was put to the task of reaping the McCormick farm wheat, and it was successful. Cyrus McCormick went to work in the family blacksmith shop to create iron parts for the reaper and sold a few to his neighbors. Soon he moved reaper production to Chicago. An astute businessman, McCormick extended credit to farmers who then bought his machine. He sold thousands of the devices. McCormick's business still provides farming tools, now known by the names Case and International Harvester. You can enjoy a free tour of this farm (now just five acres) seven days a week between 8:30 am and 5 pm. The McCormick family operated the gristmill until 1931 and lived on the farm until it was donated to Virginia Tech in 1956. Today, the farm is operated as a Virginia Agricultural Experiment Station.

Beyond McCormick's Farm you'll enter the town of Steeles Tavern. The Steeles were neighbors of the McCormicks and were one of the first farm families to buy one of Cyrus's reapers. They also operated an inn and restaurant, known at the time as a tavern. This ride makes a quick left and right onto and off US 11 onto VA 56 east.

From Steeles Tavern, you'll climb gently through the town of Vesuvius on the Tye Turnpike. This turnpike is a

TOTAL DISTANCE
62.4 miles

TIME FRAME
2 hours from start to finish. Add time to visit the McCormick Farm and a mile and a half hike up to the high falls overlook in the Crabtree Falls Recreation Area.

Virginia Byway, meaning the state recognized it as being particularly scenic. You'll cross some railroad tracks, and after that the road begins to climb steeply toward the Blue Ridge Parkway. About halfway up the mountain toward the Parkway you'll find the Tye River Gap Campground, the owners of which bill it as a "motorcycle-friendly" campground. The charge is $20 per night for campsites. Find it on the web at www.tyerivergap.com, or call at 540-377-6168.

Approaching the Blue Ridge Parkway, you'll enter the George Washington National Forest. Riding under the Parkway, the road begins to descend toward Crabtree Falls

Staying at motorcycle-friendly campgrounds like Tye River Gap is a great way to meet other motorcyclists.

The farm country along this route has sweeping curves and lots of barns.

Recreation Area. Inside the recreation area, ride along its paved driveway to a trailhead where a well-maintained four-mile loop trail with a really nifty wooden footbridge gives you a good view of the falls without hiking all the way there. If you stop at the overlook, you'll avoid the steepest part. Even if you don't make it all the way to the top of the falls, the views and fragrances you'll experience along the tree-canopied path are a strange and pleasant contrast to the wild twisties on VA 56. Leaving the Recreation Area, VA 56 follows the North Fork of the Tye River toward the town of Massies Mill, where both this ride and VA 56 make a right turn onto VA 151 south.

VA 151 South is as straight a road as could be built in the area. Don't panic, there are curves ahead. After VA 56 forks off to the left, VA 151 continues straight to the town of Shady Lane. Once in Shady Lane, you'll turn right onto CR 778, also known as Lowesville Rd. Lowesville Rd. has many more curves as you ride past Woodson's Mill on your way to the town of Lowesville. Woodson's Mill was built in 1798 and reconstructed in 1845. The Mill is a four-story post and beam structure with a large waterwheel that still spins today. While not open for tours, respectful visitors are welcome to view the mill from the grounds. One of the best views is from across the millpond, where the reflections of the rough wood of the mammoth mill structure make an interesting contrast with the smooth surface of the water.

Lowesville Rd. follows along Mill Creek until you reach Lowesville, where it makes a sharp left turn over Mill Creek and continues its narrow winding way through the Northern Virginia countryside. Lowesville Rd. ends at US 60, which is also known as the East Midlands Trail. This trail begins in

Charleston, WV and stretches east across Virginia. Along the way, it passes some interesting sites. You'll come to one of them before reaching the Blue Ridge Parkway on US 60 westbound. It's a heated bridge. Unremarkable except for a sign marking its significance, the site of Virginia's first heated bridge might seem a silly thing to some, but imagine attempting to stop a vehicle on a frozen bridge deck. On a heated bridge, the state Department of Transportation doesn't have to spread sand or salt, leaving its surface free of debris for springtime motorcyclists. A hundred years from now, motorcycle riders may marvel at this bridge much as we marvel at covered bridges today.

Leaving the bridge in your wake, you'll leave farm country and its sweeping curves behind as you enter the wooded George Washington National Forest and begin to enjoy its twisties, passing under the Blue Ridge Parkway. If you want to return to the Crabtree Falls Recreation Area, you can ride north on the Parkway for a few miles to return to VA 56. Continuing along this adventure, you'll bask in the glow of beautiful views as you descend steeply down into the city of Buena Vista (which translates as "beautiful views"). Entering the city, you'll find fast food, several motels, and even a city park along the banks of the Maury River. Try ordering fast food and taking it to the park for a meal with a view.

The ride ends at the intersection of US 60 and I-81 near the city of Lexington. Lexington is where the *Great Big Thing* ride begins. Read more about that ride starting on p. 28.

RIDE ALTERNATIVES

Near the end of the ride at mile 54.5, you can head north on the Blue Ridge Parkway a few miles to intersect the ride again on VA 56 and return to the ride's beginning or to reride some of what you've ridden.

ROAD CONDITIONS

Expect fresh, two-lane asphalt dominating this ride. Gravel has been thrown out onto the road in a few of the curves. There are an abundance of twists up and down the roads leading to and from the Blue Ridge Parkway, but the valley is full of sweeping curves punctuated with sharp, unmarked turns.

POINTS OF INTEREST

McCormick Farm, Blue Ridge Parkway, Crabtree Falls Recreation Area, Woodson's Mill, heated bridge deck, Maury River scenery.

RESTAURANTS

While the town of Buena Vista is home to dozens of fast food restaurants, the **Buena Vista Motel and Restaurant** (540-261-2138) might be a better choice if you're missing home cooking. The rooms go for between $36 and $66 nightly, depending on season and room size. The restaurant itself offers dishes much less expensive than the motel rooms. It's open for breakfast, lunch, and dinner seven days a week from 7 am to 9 pm and offers standard American diner fare, like the two-egg breakfast, burgers and sandwiches for lunch, and steak and fried seafood for dinner.

DETAILED DIRECTIONS

Mile 0—Take the Raphine exit 205 from I-81 and head east on CR 606 toward US 11 (Lee Highway). *The McCormick Farm is on the left at mile .07.*

Mile 1.5—Turn left onto US 11 (Lee Highway).

Mile 1.6—Make an immediate right onto VA 56 East. *At mile 3.3 you'll cross some railroad tracks in the town of Vesuvius and enter the woods on the way to the Blue Ridge Parkway. The Tye River Gap Campground is at mile 5.7. You'll pass under the Blue Ridge Parkway at mile 7.1. At mile 13.7 you can turn right to visit the Crabtree Falls Recreation Area.*

Mile 25.3—Turn right onto VA 56/151 South.

Mile 27.9—Fork to the right to stay on VA 151 (VA 56 forks to the left, heading east).

Mile 28.4—Turn right onto CR 778 (Lowesville Rd.). *At mile 31.1 you'll pass Woodson's Mill, established in 1794. Watch out for the sharp left turn over Mill Creek at mile 31.4 to remain on CR 778.*

Mile 38.2—Turn right onto US 60 (Eastern Midlands Trail). *At mile 40.1 enjoy the warmth of Virginia's first heated deck bridge. Twisties will have you working around mile 47. Pass under the Blue Ridge Parkway at mile 54.5. This is where the ride alternative begins. You can head north on the Parkway to return to the beginning of the ride on VA 56. Enter Buena Vista (fast food and fuel aplenty) at mile 58. At mile 61.4 there's a park on the banks of the Maury River.*

Mile 62.4—This ride ends at the intersection of US 60 and I-81.

Tye Turnpike

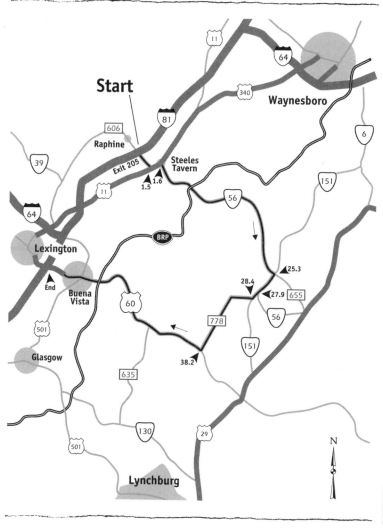

Start

Raphine

Waynesboro

Steeles Tavern

Lexington

End

Buena Vista

Glasgow

Lynchburg

1.5   1.6

25.3

28.4

27.9

38.2

	Interstate Highway		State Highway		Route
	US Highway		County Road		Other Road
			Milepost		Blue Ridge Parkway

N

Washington's Forest

This action-packed ride offers two-lane curves and twisties through rural Virginia and West Virginia. You won't encounter much in the way of vehicular traffic as you ride through the sparsely populated George Washington National Forest. In the forest's more than one million acres, you'll cross the Shenandoah Mountains twice, ride through several mountain passes, see a gristmill, take in some history at a Confederate defensive position, and enjoy some of the finest curves ever engineered. Food? Oh yeah, plenty of the good stuff!

GAS

Gas is available at the start in Harrisonburg and at miles 2.4, 30.7, 42.7, 52.2, 59.4, and 65.9, and at the ride's end in Staunton, VA.

GETTING TO THE START

This ride begins in Harrisonburg, VA at US 33 West off I-81. Take exit 247B from I-81 and reset your trip meter at the first traffic light west of I-81 (about one block).

RIDE OVERVIEW

Looking east from downtown Harrisonburg, you can see the tip of Massanutten Mountain. Looking west, Shenandoah Mountain looms on the horizon. US 33 leads this adventure west toward that horizon, but not before passing through the heart of Harrisonburg.

The first leg of the ride follows US 33 West. Along this stretch of road, there are several hazards to motorcyclists. These hazards include cross traffic from private driveways, a courthouse in the middle of the road, and several wild animal species. Cross traffic on this busy section is due to all the driveways of businesses, ranging from fast food restaurants to dry cleaners. Keep your head moving and your eyes peeled for the encroaching blind driver in a white Volvo station wagon (insert your personal nemesis here in place of the Volvo). A little over a mile into the ride, you'll come to the Rockingham County Courthouse. It sits in the middle of US 33 West. To get around it, you have to go around the block to the right. This involves a right turn, two left turns and another right turn, but you'll see the signs for US 33

West clearly posted throughout the town square. Once you've made it around the courthouse, the road becomes two-lane as you leave the town and the traffic in your rearview mirror. As you slip the bonds of Harrisonburg and enter some of Virginia's westernmost farmland, remember to watch for deer, bear, raccoons, and other animals that cross the road to reach food and the Dry River.

You'll enter the George Washington National Forest and begin a gentle climb up toward the pass on Shenandoah Mountain where US 33 enters West Virginia. Yes, it is Shenandoah Mountain (part of the Alleghenies) that you'll ride over in the George Washington National Forest. In the Blue Ridge Mountain Range to the east, there is the Shenandoah National Park and then there's the Shenandoah River. If that weren't confusing enough, George Washington National Forest was once known as Shenandoah National Forest. Luckily, the name was changed, and the confusion has abated.

From US 33 West, you'll only catch glimpses of this amazing National Forest. With over a million acres, there are 900 miles of hiking trails (60 of which are the Appalachian Trail, connecting Georgia to Maine), 400 tree species, 2,000 shrub species, and thousands of animals. Once the home of the Sioux, Shawnee, Delaware, and Catawba Indians, the area was settled by French, English, and Scottish immigrants in the late 1700s. These new residents took what they needed from the land with little concern for conservation. By the early 1900s, the mountains were barren of trees. Erosion caused creeks to fill with silt and flooding resulted. Land values plummeted, and the Federal government began buying it up for pennies an acre. Soon, the George

TOTAL DISTANCE
112.2 miles

TIME FRAME
3 hours from start to finish.
Add time for dining and for checking out the Confederate breastworks.

Washington National Forest rivaled the nearby Jefferson National Forest in size. The two National Forests were later administratively combined, meaning that the left hand would know what the right hand was doing. Today, about 39 percent of the land in the Washington National Forest is managed, resulting in an annual crop of timber worth 3.4 million dollars.

US 33 continues west along the bank of the Dry River in a nearly straight course toward the pass that enters West Virginia. The rise in elevation is not too noticeable on a motorcycle, but if you were bicycling, you'd notice your elevation has nearly doubled since leaving Harrisonburg. Just before reaching the mountain pass that tosses you into West Virginia, the road makes a wild curve to the left and the right. You're 3,450 ft. above sea level as you cross over the top of Shenandoah Mountain.

It has been said of WV that if you were to flatten out its mountains, it would be as big as Texas. Keeping that in mind, the roads make some wild twists and turns through the Mountain State. The previously mentioned "relatively straight" part of US 33 West is behind you; in West Virginia, US 33 West is full of switchbacks, hairpin turns, rapid climbs, and descents. You'll get the sensation of piloting a WW II Spitfire locked in air combat.

The 1847 McCoy's Mill on Thorn Creek is now a bed and breakfast.

Touching down in the town of Brandywine, West Virginia, US 33 makes a right turn. Immediately after that, you'll see Fox's Pizza on the left side of the road. More than just a pizza place, this restaurant is also a small motel, offering rooms for weary motorcyclists-*cum*-fighter pilots. North from Brandywine, you'll ride in the shadow of the Alleghenies, which tower over the valley to the east. Turning west again toward the town of Franklin, US 33 takes in a few more curves, but watch your speed here. There is a West Virginia State Police barracks on the right, and the West Virginia State Police will be happy to watch your speed if you are unwilling to.

In Franklin, WV, make a left turn onto US 220 South. If the aroma of the pizza in Brandywine got your taste buds demanding some pizza, make a right turn at the T intersection in downtown Franklin and go one block north on US 220 to reach another Fox's Pizza/Motel. If you want quick food, stop in at the gas station at the intersection of US 33 and US 220. Believe it or not, the little restaurant in this gas station serves up some tasty biscuits and good lunch items, particularly if you like Southern fried foods! Turning south on US 220, you'll ride through the center of Franklin,

passing a few businesses before leaving the quiet and remote Mayberry-esque town.

On US 220 South, you'll be led through a valley with little noticeable change in elevation. The curves sweep through the countryside in this part of the adventure, and the scenery is mostly low-lying farm country. Despite the fact that the area has been farmed for centuries, the soil remains fertile. The river valley floods every few years, bringing new minerals to the topsoil, making farming this remote location possible. In this valley the South Fork of the Potomac River flows, and several smaller creeks also feed the river that eventually flows through the Nation's capitol. One of them is Thorn Creek.

At the confluence of Thorn Creek and the South Branch of the Potomac River, you'll see McCoy's Mill on the left side of the road (about 3.4 miles south of Franklin). The first mill was built there in 1759 but was replaced in 1847 because the first one was too small to keep up with the demands of local farms. Despite flooding every few years, the mill stands today. The worst damage occurred in 1985 when a flood took out a stone wall, but it was quickly rebuilt. The mill isn't used anymore for grinding. Today, McCoy's Mill is a bed and breakfast inn, offering three rooms from $65 to $75. Of the amenities mentioned by the innkeeper, the words "phone, television, and computers" were conspicuously absent. If you're looking for a hideout, call 304-358-7893 to make your reservation in this historic structure.

Continuing south on US 220, you'll pass two rock quarries that were abandoned after the Civil War. You'll continue to glide through sweeping curves, passing the farms of the valley on your way back into Virginia and the town of Monterey.

In Monterey this adventure makes a left turn onto US 250 East. However, to get some good grub, make a right turn onto US 250 and ride about a block to High's Restaurant. At High's you'll find your momma's home cooking at breakfast, lunch, and dinner. With a full fuel tank and a full belly, head east on US 250.

From Monterey, US 250 climbs and descends a few mountain passes before reentering the Washington National Forest. The road now known as US 250 was built in 1830 by French engineers who were the only engineers who would do the job. Other engineers refused the road project because it appeared impossible to lay a road across the steep Shenandoah and Allegheny Mountains. The French, desperate for work, traveled to the area to complete the job. The asphalt you'll ride on today is paved over the same single-lane road cut by those crazy French engineers.

In the narrow and twisty pass over Shenandoah Mountain, you'll find an overlook, restrooms (outhouses), the Shenandoah Mountain Hiking Trail,

and the Confederate breastworks. The breastworks were built on April 1, 1862, to prevent the advancing Union roops from entering the Shenandoah Valley. The battle for this mountain pass lasted only days, and the Union eventually defeated the Confederacy, making the loss of life in these hills pointless. Intended to last only months, the breastworks stand today as a silent memorial to the lives taken by the War Between the States.

From Shenandoah Mountain, US 250 descends in twists and turns, giving way to sweeping curves in the lower elevations toward Staunton, VA. Before reaching the busy section of downtown Staunton, this adventure makes a left turn onto VA 275 to avoid the heavy traffic. VA 275 leads you to I-81, where the ride ends.

RIDE ALTERNATIVES

There are no alternatives for this ride.

ROAD CONDITIONS

This adventure begins on a busy section of five-lane roadway, but after you survive the first three miles and escape from Harrisonburg, you're home free on two-lane asphalt that starts straight, then adds some gently sweeping curves before throwing you into wild twists and turns up and over Shenandoah Mountain. The asphalt is well maintained, but watch for small gravel in the curves (particularly in early spring) left over from snow clearing.

POINTS OF INTEREST

George Washington National Forest, towns of Brandywine & Franklin, McCoy's Mill, the town of Monterey, Confederate breastworks.

RESTAURANTS

There's enough fast food in Harrisonburg to clog your arteries several times over, but if you can hold your hunger pangs for a few miles, try one of these places:

Fox's Pizza offers delicious pizza and delightfully warm motel rooms as well. You'll find two Fox's Pizzas along this ride. The first is in Brandywine (304-249-5136) just after you make the right turn at mile 30.7 to stay on US 33 West. In Franklin (304-358-2118), you'll have to turn right onto US 220 North and go one block up the hill to reach this restaurant. As the name suggests, you'll find pizza on the menu as well as sandwiches, and homemade pies for dessert. Expect to spend about $12 for a large pizza with a couple of toppings. The motel rooms run from $38 to $45 depending on the size of the room. Both of these establishments are open from 10:30 am to 9 pm and until 10 pm on Friday and Saturday.

If you need something quick and warm, stop in at the **gas station** at the intersection of US 33 and US 220 in Franklin. Even if you have a rule against eating where you buy gas, make an exception here. The handmade biscuits for breakfast are worth the trip, and the tastes of the sandwiches, fried chicken, and other lunch and dinner items will make you forget you're in a gas station.

In Monterey, VA, just about one block to the right of where this ride turns left onto US 250 East, is **High's Restaurant**. At High's you can dine on steak for $12 or mountain trout for $9; both are served with a baked potato and side salad. Lunch includes Buffalo-style hot wings for $6, burgers for $2.50, and sandwiches from $2.25. If you are reaching High's in time for breakfast, a plate of pancakes is just $2.25, and two eggs are $3 with Southern-style grits as a side item. High's is open Monday through Saturday from 6 am to 8 pm, and Sunday 7 am to 6 pm.

DETAILED DIRECTIONS

Mile 0—Continue west on US 33 at the first traffic light west of I-81 in Harrisonburg, VA.

Mile 1.3—You have to ride around the Rockingham County Courthouse by making a right, an immediate left, another immediate left, and then another immediate right to remain on US 33 West. *You'll enter the George Washington National Forest at mile 11.2. At mile 17.5, the road gets busy with twists and turns. You'll enter West Virginia at mile 23.6 on the back of Shenandoah Mountain at 3,450 ft.*

Mile 30.7—Turn right to remain on US 33 West in Brandywine. *Fox's Pizza and Motel is on the left at mile 30.8. Check your speed at mile 39 as you pass the West Virginia State Police Barracks.*

Mile 42.7—Turn left onto US 220 South. *If you turn right for one block, you'll find another Fox's Pizza/Motel. At this intersection, in the gas station to the left, is the "you'll-forget-the-food-came-from-a-gas-station" restaurant. There's an old rock quarry on the right at mile 44.9, and at mile 46 you'll see the McCoy's Mill across the creek on the far side of the valley. Some good curves await you at mile 52.2.*

Mile 66—Turn left onto US 250 East. *To reach High's Restaurant, turn right— it's one block west. You'll reenter the George Washington National Forest at mile 82.5 and reach the Confederate breastworks (overlook, hiking trail, restrooms) at mile 84.5. There's a recreation area on the right at mile 86.7.*

Mile 106.7—Turn left onto VA 275.

Mile 112.2—This adventure ends where VA 275 meets I-81.

Washington's Forest

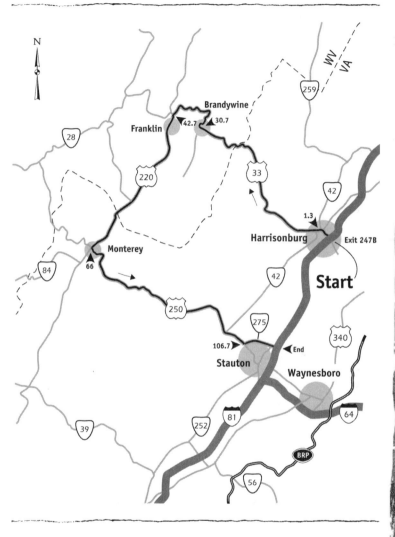

Franklin

Brandywine
42.7 30.7

259

WV / VA

28

220

33

42

1.3

Harrisonburg

Exit 247B

Monterey

66

84

42

Start

250

275

340

106.7 End

Stauton

Waynesboro

39

252 81

64

BRP

56

N

---

75 Interstate Highway

27 US Highway

640 State Highway

606 County Road

5 ▶ Milepost

━━ Route

━━ Other Road

═══ Blue Ridge Parkway

Shenandoah Valley Run

Meandering like a giant serpent between Massanutten Mountain and the Blue Ridge Mountains, the Shenandoah River has attracted people to its banks for thousands of years. On this adventure, you'll cruise through rolling farmland and small towns on gentle sweepers. Take a few minutes to get off your bike and check out the stalactites and stalagmites in Skyline and Luray Caverns. These two privately owned parks are worth the visit for anyone curious about the geologic history of the area. You won't find any wicked twisties on this ride, only graceful curves.

GETTING TO THE START

This ride starts at the intersection of the north end of Skyline Drive and US 340 South. From the south, take exit 99 from I-64 and follow Skyline Drive north for 107 miles. From the north, take I-66 to exit 6 at US 340 South, and ride about a mile through Front Royal, VA. Zero your trip meter at the intersection of Skyline Drive and US 340 as you continue south on US 340.

RIDE OVERVIEW

Think of this ride as a counterpart to the *Skyline Drive* ride (p. 54) because Skyline Drive and this adventure connect Front Royal with Waynesboro. While the mountaintop vistas of Skyline Drive are spectacular, this ride is spectacular in its own right. Passing through the historic and scenic Shenandoah Valley, along the Shenandoah River, between the Blue Ridge Mountains and Massanutten Mountain, this route takes in some interesting sights. The Shenandoah Valley also offers two caverns and several small towns along the way.

From the intersection of Skyline Drive going south on US 340, the road quickly turns from a four-lane highway back into a two-lane blacktop. At the end of the first mile, you'll see signs on the left side of the road directing you to the Skyline Caverns, open everyday from 9 am to 6 pm in the summer months, closing an hour earlier in the spring and fall, and closing at 4 pm in the winter. It costs just $14 for adults to visit these caverns with their

---

GAS

Gas is available at the start in Front Royal and at miles 8.6, 20.3, 25, 34.6, 41.8, 42.6, 46.6, 47.5, 63.9, 70, 71.9, 78.4, and 79.6, and at the ride's end at mile 82.

---

stalagmites, stalactites, and unusual anthodites in a constant 54° Fahrenheit. The cool temps are reason enough to check out the caverns on hot summer days. While taking the guided tour, you'll see three underground streams and one 37-ft. waterfall. To learn more, or for group rates and other discounts, check the web at www.skylinecaverns.com or call 800-296-4545.

South of Skyline Caverns the road is hilly, crossing over several tributaries to the Shenandoah River. Water flows from streams (both above and below ground) originating in the Blue Ridge and Allegheny Mountains into the Shenandoah River. The Shenandoah River flows north into the Potomac River. The fact that the river flows north made it invaluable for transporting goods and people. After the railroad came to the valley, lumber, copper, and other natural resources were transported by rail, leaving the river free for recreation. Today, the town of Front Royal, VA calls itself the "Canoe Capital of Virginia." After emptying into the Potomac River, the same water you saw flowing over the waterfall in Skyline Caverns makes its way through Washington, DC, and into the Atlantic Ocean by way of Chesapeake Bay.

If you didn't stop to see the water flowing through Skyline Caverns, fear not—a few miles ahead in Luray is Luray Caverns, which is "wet" as well. In the town of Luray, this ride makes a right turn to remain on US 340 South. If you care nothing about seeing Luray Caverns, consider taking ride alternative #1. Continue straight on the two-lane section of US 340 Business through the town of Luray. It will lead you to a T intersection where you'll turn left back to US 340 South.

Staying on this route, you'll turn right onto interstate-like US 340

South/211 West. On the right you'll see a huge sign inviting you into the parking lot for Luray Caverns. These caverns are similar to Skyline Caverns in that they also have water flowing through, but there is no waterfall. Luray Caverns are much larger than Skyline Caverns, a difference you'll feel as you walk for over 45 minutes underground. In Luray Caverns you'll see the "Great Stalactite Organ." The haunting sounds of this unusual instrument are produced by hammering the stalactites hanging from the ceiling. Different tones are

You'll always know what time it is in Front Royal.

The Shenandoah Valley **49**

A tour of Luray Caverns includes both the caverns and a car museum. Wow, look at those stalactites hanging down!

produced because the stalactites are of various length, thickness, and composition. A visit to Luray Caverns will set you back $17 for the guided tour of the caverns and a self-guided tour of the adjacent car museum (no motorcycles on display). The Caverns are open from 9 am until 7 pm in the summer, closing an hour earlier in spring and fall and at 4 pm in the winter. On weekends the last tour begins at 5 pm. Contact Luray Caverns on the web at www.luraycaverns.com or by phone at 540-743-6551.

From the caverns, US 340 South continues west for a couple of miles with US 220 West. The ride makes a left turn to stay on US 340 South. Here you can opt for ride alternative #2. Continue straight on US 220 West over Massanutten Mountain and into the town of New Market where you'll find I-81.

After turning left from US 220 West to remain on US 340 South, you'll find the four-lane divided road a distant memory as US 340 South rolls over the hills of the Shenandoah River Valley. Shortly after passing where US 340 Business rejoins the ride, you'll see the St. Paul Lutheran Church. This church was built of stones cut from the nearby mountains. Its small, neat

appearance will remind you of simpler times, when people rode horses to services. Today, "Iron Horses" are welcome to tie up outside as you walk the church grounds, discovering its history or attending a Sunday morning service.

Continuing south you'll pass through the town of Shenandoah (home to several fast food restaurants and gas stations) before reaching Elkton at the intersection of US 340 South and US 33. If you want to take in some of the curves offered by Skyline Drive, head east on US 33 and ride up to Swift Run Gap where you can enter the Shenandoah National Park and Skyline Drive. If you head west on US 33, you'll ride past the southernmost tip of Massanutten Mountain, under I-81 in Harrisonburg, where the *Washington's Forest* ride begins (p. 42).

This ride continues south on US 340, crossing some railroad tracks before reaching a mammoth Coors Brewery on the left. The welcome, sweet aromas of the hops and yeast used in the brewing process waft across the valley, like the offensive odor of a paper mill, except this is the good odor of beer being born! As a matter of fact, since the brewery opened in 1987, the brewery's 500 employees have created an average of 5,000,000 barrels of beer annually. Unfortunately, there are no public tours of this brewery, so you'll just have to be content with the odor of the Killian's, Coors Light, and Keystone beers that are produced there.

A few miles past the brewery is the town of Waynesboro. US 340 South becomes a four-lane street. You'll see Wayne's Cycle Shop on the left, offering motorcycles, apparel, accessories, and service (Honda, Kawasaki, Suzuki, and Yamaha). Near the heart of town, you'll see signs indicating that US 340 South forks off to the right. However, this ride continues straight south on Main St. You'll cross the Shenandoah River and see a large park on the right side of the road. This park is home to a farmer's market on warm weekend days. The ride makes a left onto Broad St., which will lead you to the ride's end at I-64, where there are several hotels and motels and national chain bar and grills.

The ride ends at the intersection of US 340 South and I-64. Take I-64 west to reach I-81, or head east on I-64 to reach the southern end of Skyline Drive.

RIDE ALTERNATIVES

There are two ride alternatives. Alternative #1: In Luray, VA, this ride makes a right turn onto the interstate-like US 340 South to pass the Luray Caverns. If you don't care to see the caverns, continue straight at that intersection (mile 22.7), follow US 340 Business through town, and meet up with the ride later (mile 34.2). You won't shave off any mileage, but you will avoid the four-lane divided section.

Alternative #2: Also in Luray, instead of continuing the run all the way south into Waynesboro, you can follow US 340 South and continue straight onto US 211, crossing Massanutten Mountain and heading into the city of New Market, where you'll find I-81.

ROAD CONDITIONS

Other than the eight-mile section of US 340 that merges with US 211 in Luray to create a four-lane divided highway, US 340 is a gently banked, two-lane road, with well-maintained asphalt rolling over the hilly countryside along the Shenandoah River.

POINTS OF INTEREST

Skyline Caverns, Luray Caverns, Massanutten Mountain, St. Paul Lutheran Church, and the Coors Brewery.

The Daily Grind serves both breakfast and lunch items seven days a week.

RESTAURANTS

At the beginning of the ride, two restaurants really stand out. Both are on Main St., which runs off of US 340 about a mile north of the start of this run. To get to Main St., take US 340 into Front Royal and turn east onto Main St. at the Warren County Courthouse.

On the right side of the narrow Main St., about a block from the Courthouse, you'll find the **Daily Grind Coffee Shop** (215 E. Main St.; 540-635-3556). The name is a bit misleading, considering breakfast and lunch items are served as well. You'll find the Daily Grind open for business from 7 am to 9 pm every day and until 10 pm on Tuesdays and Fridays.

Two blocks farther down, across from the town commons, is **Grapes and Grains** (401 E. Main St.; 540-636-8379). The menu is an eclectic mix of well-prepared dishes ranging from steaks for carnivorous bikers to vegetarian dishes for those not willing to dine on bovine. As the name would suggest, there is an extensive wine list as well. Expect to spend between $8 and $20 per entree. Reservations are encouraged for large groups. Grapes and Grains is open for lunch and dinner Tuesday through Saturday. Hours are Tuesdays and Wednesdays 11 am to 5 pm, until 7 pm on Thursdays and Saturdays, and until 9 pm on Fridays. Groups of four are easily accommodated without reservations.

DETAILED DIRECTIONS

Mile 0—From its intersection with Skyline Drive, head south on US 340, away from the town of Front Royal. *Skyline Caverns is on the left at mile 1.0.*

Mile 22.7—Turn right onto the entrance ramp to the interstate-like US 211 West/340 South. *Ride Alternative #1: Don't turn right onto the entrance ramp, continue south onto US 340 Business—it will lead you back to the ride in a few miles. Turn left when US 340 Business ends at US 340 to continue this route towards Waynesboro. At mile 24.4, Luray Caverns invites you to turn right into its large parking area to take in a tour of the caverns and car museum (no motorcycles on display in the museum).*

Mile 30.4—Turn left to remain on US 340 South. *Ride Alternative #2: To reach I-81, don't turn left onto US 340 South, but continue west on US 211 over Massanutten Mountain through the town of New Market. At mile 33.8, US 340 Business rejoins US 340 South toward Waynesboro. The St. Paul Lutheran Church is on the left at mile 36.8. There's some Italian food at mile 42.8: Mamma Mia Pizza, Pasta & Subs. You'll Cross US 33 at mile 47.8 in Elkton. Pay attention to the road at mile 52.2 as US 340 South passes over some railroad tracks. At mile 53.5, the odor of beer fills the air as you ride past a Coors Brewery. This adventure enters Waynesboro at mile 75.8 (where you'll pass Al Gore Ln.—no kidding!).*

Mile 78.4—Continue straight ahead onto Main St., ignoring the signs directing you to turn right to stay on US 340 South.

Mile 80—Turn left onto US 340 South.

Mile 83—This ride ends at the intersection of US 340 and I-64. Head west on I-64 to reach I-81, or east to reach the Skyline Drive and Blue Ridge Parkway (both at exit 99).

Shenandoah Valley Run

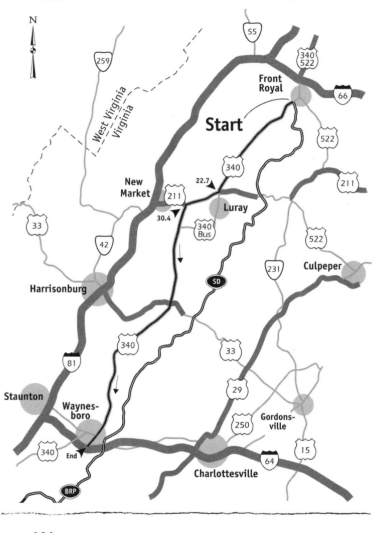

N

259

West Virginia
Virginia

55

340
522

Front
Royal

66

Start

340

522

22.7

211

New
Market

211

340

Luray

30.4

33

340
Bus

42

SD

522

231

Culpeper

Harrisonburg

340

33

81

29

Staunton

Waynes-
boro

250

Gordons-
ville

340

End

15

BRP

64

Charlottesville

75 Interstate Highway	640 State Highway	▬ Route
27 US Highway	606 County Road	— Other Road
	5 ▶ Milepost	═ Blue Ridge Parkway

Skyline Drive

This adventure leads you north on Skyline Drive, following the top of the Blue Ridge Mountains through the Shenandoah National Park. As on the Blue Ridge Parkway, there are no red lights, stop signs, commercial vehicles, or rush hour traffic on its entire 107-mile length. Only two roads enter (or rather, merge with) the Skyline Drive. You ride on well-maintained and deliciously curvy asphalt. But it's more than just a pretty ribbon of blacktop. Expect amenities including fuel, lodging with a view, dining on mountain outcroppings, wilderness hiking, and wildlife. Lovely vistas abound.

GAS
Gas is available at miles 26.5, 55.2, and 82.7, and at the end of the ride in Front Royal, VA.

GETTING TO THE START

Follow I-64 East from I-81 to the Rockfish Gap exit 99. The exit ramp will take you back under I-64. At the T intersection at the bottom of the ramp, turn right onto US 250, which will lead you about 100 yd. to the right turn onto the driveway to Skyline Drive/ Blue Ridge Parkway. At the top of the driveway, turn left (turning right would lead you south on the Parkway). Reset your trip meter as you turn left onto Skyline Drive.

RIDE OVERVIEW

Measured from I-64 on the south end to US 340 on the north, Skyline Drive stretches 107 miles along the ridge of the Blue Ridge Mountains, bisecting the Shenandoah National Park. Road construction began about a billion years ago and was completed just prior to World War II. Along this ancient path, you'll see the foothills of the Appalachians rolling like giant waves toward the ocean. To the west, the Alleghenies form the next series of waves.

First, a history of the Park. There was once one great continent known as Pangaea. Things started looking up for the Blue Ridge Mountains about 200 million years ago, after Pangaea broke apart and North America slammed into Africa for a (relatively speaking) brief period, pressing the tectonic plate upward, creating the Appalachian Mountains. Ice ages came and went, dinosaurs roamed the land, and it wasn't until about 10,000 years ago that humans began to inhabit the area. There were about 2,000 Monacan and Manahoac Indians in the Blue Ridge Mountains when Captain John Smith explored the area in 1608. Other explorers followed: John Lederer in 1669 and Governor Alexander Spotswood in 1716. The natives and white men traded everything. Unfortunately, the friendly natives got smallpox, measles, and tuberculosis out of the deal, and by 1730 most of them were gone, having died or moved away, leaving the area ripe for the new settlers. By 1790, 67,000 Europeans lived in the Shenandoah Valley and surrounding mountains. Industry began to move to the area, attracted to the apparently limitless supply of natural resources. In the late 1800s a lumber camp called Stonyman Camp was built where Skyland Lodge stands today. Early lumberjacks and copper miners who worked at the camp returned home to rave about beautiful views. In the 1890s, the idea of a resort was born. People came from far and wide to relax in the fresh mountain air of Stonyman Camp. Among the frequent visitors were President and Mrs. Herbert Hoover, who built a vacation home nearby. Others included the

TOTAL DISTANCE
107 miles

TIME FRAME
4 hours from start to finish. Add time for the 35 mph speed limit and taking in several overlooks and amenities.

Washington elite, who quickly saw the need for a National Park in the Blue Ridge Mountains. Congress authorized the establishment of the Shenandoah National Park, and groundbreaking ceremonies for Skyline Drive were held on July 18, 1931, in the midst of the Great Depression. President Franklin Delano Roosevelt dedicated the park on July 3, 1936. Skyline Drive was completed on August 29, 1939. You'd think the early engineers were motorcyclists, given the fun, sweeping curves and distant vistas they gave us to enjoy. It costs just $5 per person on a motorcycle to enter and $10 per car. The money is used to improve the road and amenities along the way.

The Skyline Drive is in the Shenandoah National Park.

The history lesson is over; let's go for a ride! This ride begins where the Blue Ridge Parkway ends and Skyline Drive begins, on the bridge over I-64. The National Park Service measures the mileage of Skyline Drive from the Front Royal Entrance Station south to the Rockfish Entrance Station. Mileposts on this ride go from the bridge over I-64 to US 340, which adds a couple of miles to the Park Service's official 150.4 miles. Within the first mile, you'll stop at the Rockfish Entrance Station and pay the $5 per person. You'll be given a small booklet about the Shenandoah National Park and a very flimsy receipt that will serve as your week-long pass to the Shenandoah National Park and Skyline Drive. You might want to ask the friendly Park Ranger for a piece of tape. Use the tape to affix that flimsy receipt to your bike somewhere (the leeward side of the windshield or near the front of your gas tank) so that if you do want to reenter the park, you'll know where your pass is, and the ranger working the entrance station can see it. Leaving the entrance station, you'll see the first of several signs warning you of deer. Heed these warnings, because there are over 5,000 deer in the park. Because of hunting and settlements, there were no deer in the area in 1926. Then in 1933, 13 white-tailed deer were released. With no hunting allowed in the park and strict law enforcement, the deer population has rebounded to an almost intolerable level. Your chances of seeing deer are 100%, particularly if you are traveling in the winter months when deer are attracted to the rye grass growing on the roadside. Keep your speed down to make your encounter with wildlife a good one.

You'll begin to climb out of Rockfish Gap in a series of fun, sweeping curves before reaching the first of dozens of scenic overlooks.

The Park people are there to help.

These overlooks will be on the left and right sides of the road because Skyline Drive is built as near to the ridge crest of the Blue Ridge Mountains as is practical. From one of the first overlooks on the left side of the road you'll see the rocky slopes of nearby mountains. These talus slopes are made up of football-sized stones that were once a solid mass of stone which shattered due to natural forces at work. You'll spot these slopes for most of the rest of the ride, and now you'll know what they are. Aren't you just smart?

Here's another fun fact to know and tell. During the Civil War, Confederate General Stonewall Jackson used these mountains to hide 17,000 Rebel troops to repel over 45,000 Federal troops in a series of raids and attacks in 1862. The Dundo Overlook tells about the Civil War in the Shenandoah Valley.

Soon you'll reach the Loft Mountain Wayside. This seasonal Wayside is closed from early November to mid-April. When open it offers fuel, camping, gifts, information, food (to go) and restrooms. There are several hikes that begin nearby. Since motorcycle boots are usually a suitable substitute for hiking boots, you may want to check out some of these hikes at the information center.

Leaving the Wayside in your rearview mirrors and continuing north on the ride, you'll see the Allegheny Mountains to the west (left side of the road) about 30 miles away. Between the Blue Ridge Mountains and the Alleghenies is the Shenandoah Valley. No sooner do you become accustomed to this view while you down shift, up shift, and lean into the curves, than Massanutten Mountain appears in the valley. Massanutten stretches for 50 miles north through the valley. Considering its size, it has an odd name, which sounds like "mass o' nuttin." Maybe the name should be changed to reflect its mammoth size, something like "mass o' rock" or "mass o' dirt." Anyway, the view of Massanutten Mountain and the Alleghenies beyond is a good measure of air quality. If you can clearly see the Alleghenies, the air quality is pretty good; if you can't even see Massanutten, better strap a breathing mask to your helmet!

In just 10 miles you'll come to the Swift River Gap entrance station at the intersection of Skyline Drive and US 33. Traffic coming from US 33 merges onto Skyline Drive after passing this station. There is no cross traffic on this ride. If you wish to leave Shenandoah National Park, US 33 is one of only two ways to do so until the end of the ride. If you were to take US 33 West, you'd arrive in the town of Elkton in about four miles. Riding east, you'd reach Standardsville in about 10 miles.

From Swift Run Gap, Skyline Drive begins to climb toward Big Meadows, but not before passing Lewis Mountain Wayside. This wayside is closed between November and May and does not offer fuel, but there is camping, a small store, and a few cabins.

You'll climb through a series of sweeping curves to the unusual panorama of a large meadow on the right side of the road atop a mountain. Here's a name that makes sense. It's known as Big Meadow. On the right side of the road is the big meadow, on the left is the Big Meadow Wayside—information center, museum, lodge, cabins, restaurant, and fuel. This area is seasonal; closed from November to late March. In the Byrd Information Center (newly renovated in the winter of 2003) you'll discover a bookstore, restrooms, and a museum. The museum chronicles the history of the area and some of its more famous residents. From Big Meadow, the road continues to climb.

Near the apex of the road is the entrance to the Skyland Lodge on the left. Once known as Stonyman Camp, Skyland Lodge gets its name from the fact that it was built on the highest part of the Shenandoah National Park or "up in the sky." It began as a logging and mining camp. In the late 1800s, the area of Skyland was rich with copper and lumber. Men came from the valley to remove these natural resources to build the growing nation. After the area had been mined out and all the lumber that was needed had been removed, Stonyman Camp owner George Pollock transformed it from a rustic working logging camp to a recreation area for the nearby Washington, DC elite. Visitors flocked to the area and have been visiting ever since. Stonyman Camp became Skyland Lodge when the park was formed. Today, Skyland Lodge offers fine amenities with views second to none in the area.

Just past the entrance to Skyland Lodge is the sign marking the highest point of the Skyline Drive. At 3,680 ft. above sea level, you won't need an oxygen mask, but the beauty might make you light-headed.

For the rest of the ride, you'll be traveling down. You'll descend toward US 211, reaching it only after passing though the Mary's Rock Tunnel. The only tunnel on the Skyline Drive, it was carved out of Mary's Rock in 1932. Stay to the right half of your lane—oncoming cars tend to ride over the center line to avoid the interior wall of the tunnel. There are frequently icicles hanging from the entrance and exit, particularly on the north side where the sun doesn't shine.

US 211 passes harmlessly under you at the Panorama Information Center in Thornton Gap. If you have a desire to see the town of Luray and Luray Caverns, head west on US 211 for about 12 miles. If you wish to visit Sperryville, head east on US 211 for about eight miles. The traffic entering Skyline Drive from US 211 has to yield to you.

Continuing your descent, you'll see the foothills of the Appalachian Mountains to the right. They seem to flow east like tumbling waves crashing on a beach. In a geologic sense, that's exactly what is happening to them. Over thousands of years, these waves will eventually flatten. But for now, "surf's up!"

You'll reach another wayside with a funny name as you continue your descent toward the end of the ride.

The Elkwallow Wayside is closed from November to April. When open, it offers fuel, gifts, groceries, and meals to go.

One of the best views of the Shenandoah Valley is the last view on Skyline Drive. At the Dickey Ridge Visitor Center there is an observation deck at the base of a grassy hill. From that observation point, you can see south through the Shenandoah Valley between the Blue Ridge Mountains and Massanutten Mountain. Those previously mentioned "waves" are plainly visible, if you only imagine the mountains being filled with sea foam instead of lush green forests. In the Visitor Center there is a museum and gift shop. And there's an added bonus for chilly motorcyclists—a bun-warming fireplace!

You'll enjoy a few more sweeping curves as you complete this ride down into the town of Front Royal. About a mile before this ride ends, you'll pass the Front Royal Entrance Station. Where the Skyline Drive ends in a T at US 340, the Shenandoah Valley Run (p. 48) begins by turning left. You might want to take a break from your scooter for a while by turning right and heading into Front Royal for a cup of coffee at the Daily Grind Coffee Shop or a delicious meal at Grapes and Grains Restaurant. Both of these restaurants are in the historic district on Main St. To get there, turn right onto US 340 and ride straight toward the Warren County Courthouse and turn right onto the well-marked, but unusually narrow, Main St. Both establishments are on the right two and three blocks down, respectively.

RIDE ALTERNATIVES

This ride leads you north. The mileposts on the Skyline Drive begin with zero at its northern end, making this ride a countdown to zero as you head north. Heading south from Front Royal, VA' the mileage of the ride will roughly match that of the Skyline Drive mileposts. Either way, the Skyline Drive is a blast, and the scenery is equally breathtaking.

ROAD CONDITIONS

The Skyline Drive is two lanes of gently banked, sweeping curves of well-maintained asphalt. The winters can be a little rough in the Shenandoah, causing a few cracks in the pavement. Part of the $5 you'll pay (per person) to enter the park goes to repairing the road, so smile as you hand off that Lincoln!

Wildlife! The 35 mph speed limit might seem ridiculously low, since a skilled rider could easily handle the curves of the Skyline Drive much faster. However, mix high speed with abundant wildlife, add distance from medical facilities, and the 35 mph limit begins to make sense. The Park has over 5,000 deer, hundreds of bear, and many smaller animals no less harmful in a crash. Take your time to

Watch carefully for deer on the road.

enjoy the scenery and the wildlife— don't let the critters ruin your day.

POINTS OF INTEREST

Wildlife, Loft Mountain Wayside (with restaurant, fuel, lodging), Lewis Mountain Wayside (cabins, gift shop, camping), Big Meadows Wayside (visitor center, gift shop, museum, lodge, restaurant, cabins, fuel), Skyland Lodge (restaurant, horseback riding, lodging, taproom), Elkwallow Wayside (groceries, carry-out food, fuel), Dickey Ridge Visitor Center, dozens of scenic overlooks.

RESTAURANTS

There are two sit-down restaurants along Skyline Drive, and they are seasonal—one at **Big Meadows**, the other at **Skyland**. The restaurant at Big Meadows is closed October to mid-April; Skyland closes in November and reopens in March. The meals served at these two restaurants are similar in taste and price. Hours for breakfast are 7:30 to 10:30 am, lunch from noon to 2:30 pm, and dinner from 5:30 to 10:30 pm. Each restaurant has a taproom, or pub, open from 2:30 to 10:30 pm, offering bar food. At Big Meadows and Skyline, breakfasts run from $2.50 to $8 depending on the size of your early morning appetite (muffins are pretty cheap, while the three-egg omelets with all the trimmings are filling and more expensive). The lunch menu is full of sandwiches, personal pizzas, soups, and barbecue dishes. Lunch prices range from $6 to $12. Dinner can be as simple as fried chicken for $10 or as elaborate as ribs for $21. Both restaurants offer an extensive wine list, and the taprooms have nightly entertainment.

There are **snack bars** at **Loft Mountain** (closed November to mid-April), **Lewis Mountain** (closed November to May), and **Elkwallow** (closed November to April). These snack bars offer prepared box lunches for you to stuff into a saddlebag and chow on at one of the many scenic overlooks or picnic areas. Expect to spend about $5 for a roast beef sandwich, chips, and juice or milk.

Front Royal has two really cool places to eat on Main St. From the end of the ride, turn right onto US 340, which becomes Royal Ave. as you continue straight through two major intersections heading into town. When you reach the Warren County Courthouse, turn right onto Main St. Both restaurants are on the right a couple of blocks down from the Courthouse.

Coffee connoisseurs will want to stop in at the **Daily Grind** (540-635-3556), 215 E. Main St. While the coffee is mighty tasty and satisfying, the sandwiches, muffins, and bagels there will fill you up. It's open from 7 am to 9 pm every day and until 10 pm on Tuesdays and Fridays.

If you want to dine more elegantly after a long ride, try **Grapes and Grains** (540-636-8379) at 401 E. Main St. It's open for lunch and dinner Tuesday through Saturday, 11 am to 5 pm on Tuesdays and Wednesdays, until 7 pm on Thursdays and Saturdays, and until 9 pm on Fridays. The menu is an eclectic mix of dishes ranging from steaks for carnivorous bikers to vegetarian entrees for those who decline to dine on bovine. As the name suggests, there's also an extensive wine list. Expect to spend between $8 and $20 per entree. Groups of four are easily accommodated without reservations.

DETAILED DIRECTIONS

Mile 0—Turn north onto Skyline Drive crossing over I-64. *Have your Lincoln ($5 bill) ready at mile 0.6 as you reach the Rockfish Entrance Station.The old entrance station is at*

mile 0.9. Around mile 10, the asphalt worsens for a few miles. You can see the first of the talus slopes on the left side of the road and learn what they are at the overlook at mile 13. At mile 26.5, you'll find the Loft Mountain Wayside with its seasonal fuel, souvenirs, food to go, and lodging. The site of the 1986 Big Run Forest Fire is at mile 27. You'll pass over US 33 at mile 40.7. US 33 West will lead you into Elkton, while US 33 East takes you into Standardsville.

At mile 48.8 the Lewis Mountain Wayside offers seasonal lodging, groceries, and camping. You'll begin to see Massanutten Mountain to the west beginning at mile 50. The Big Meadows Wayside at mile 55.2 offers fuel, dining, ATM, museum, visitor center, taproom, lodging, and camping. On the left at mile 63.9 is the Skyland Lodge. Skyland offers dining with a view, lodging, camping, horseback riding, gift shop, and groceries. The highest point on Skyline Drive is at mile 64.7 (3,680 ft. above sea level). Keep to the right half of the northbound lane at mile 74.3 as you pass through the Mary's Rock Tunnel. You'll cross over US 211 at mile 75.1 in Thornton Gap. Thornton Gap is also home to the Panorama gift and snack shop. Take US 211 West to reach the town of Luray, or go east to reach Sperryville.

The Elkwallow Wayside is at mile 82.7, with fuel, groceries and gift shop. The Dickey Ridge Visitor Center is on the left at mile 102.3. At mile 106.6, you'll pass through the Front Royal Entrance Station.

Mile 107—The ride ends at the intersection of Skyline Drive and US 340. *Take a right and ride less than a mile to the heart of Front Royal, or turn left to begin the* Shenandoah Valley Run *(p. 48).*

Skyline Drive

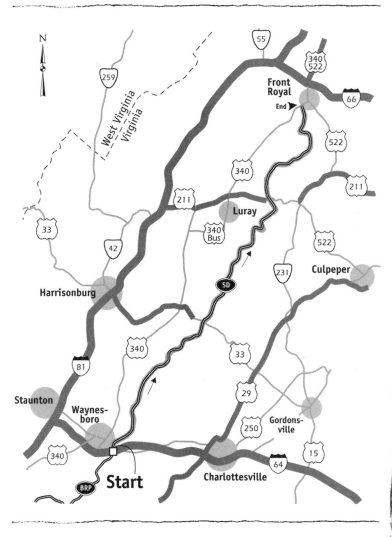

Roanoke Area

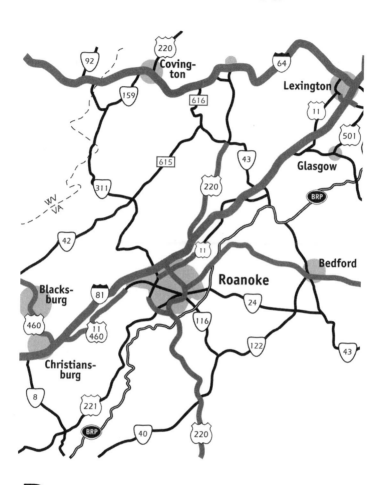

Roanoke, star city of the South. This small-town big city will surprise you with its easy access, busy market square, restaurants both historic and hip, attractions of all kinds, and sights just plain fun to look at.

Area Covered

Exploring Roanoke

At the bottom of a deep valley between the Catawba Mountains and the Blue Ridge Mountain Range, on the flatland next to the Roanoke River, Europeans first saw the Roanoke Valley in 1671. Agriculture brought permanent residents in 1740. In 1882, the town really got a boost when it became the terminus of the Norfolk and Western Railroad. Before the year's end, 500 residents chartered the town of Roanoke.

Today, the Roanoke Valley is home to nearly 300,000 people. With all the great scenery, restaurants, attractions, and a low altitude (which helps to moderate the cool winter temps), it's no wonder Roanoke is a great place to live. It's also a motorcyclist's dream. On one side there's an interstate highway, making for easy access, and on the other is the internationally acclaimed Blue Ridge Parkway. Roanoke is a fun little town wrapped up in a big city. There's no way this chapter could include all Roanoke has to offer, but it will serve as a good primer to the area. Ride safe, and enjoy Roanoke!

GAS
Fuel is available throughout Roanoke.

GETTING TO THE START

The city of Roanoke, VA, can be found on I-81 about 145 miles north of the Tennessee state line. You can also reach Roanoke by following I-64 and I-77. No need to fiddle with your trip meter for this ride, because it really isn't a ride at all. This chapter is a motorcyclist's guide to downtown Roanoke.

COOL PLACES TO VISIT

The city of Roanoke uses well-placed blue signs to aid your navigation of the city. You'll see these signs at nearly every intersection, bearing a distinctive star (Roanoke is the "Star City of the South") and arrows indicating the best way to the coolest sites. You can visit the Roanoke Valley Convention and Visitors Bureau at 114 Market St. (next to Awful Arthur's Seafood), check them out on the web at www.VisitRoanokeVA.com, or call 1-800-635-5535.

In the heart of downtown is the Roanoke Farmers Market at Market Square. Surrounded by good restaurants, fresh produce, and flowers, the aromas of Market Square are unforgettable. Since it opened in 1882, the market has been open year-round, every day of the week except Sundays. The actual City Market Building was built in 1922 and the art-deco flavor of the neon sign bearing its name is a stark contrast to its historic brickwork. To check out the Market before you get there, surf the web to www.downtownroanoke.org or call 540-342-2028.

Next to the Farmers Market is the Center in the Square. This is in the heart of downtown Roanoke and is home to three art museums, a theater, several specialty shops, and the History Museum of Western Virginia. It costs nothing to visit the Center itself, and only $2 for adults and $1 for children to visit the History Museum. Open Tuesday through Saturday from 10 am to 4 pm and Sundays from 1 to 4 pm, the museum chronicles life in the Roanoke Valley from prehistory to modern times. For a more hands-on museum, check out the Virginia Museum of Transportation.

The Virginia Museum of Transportation is in the historic freight station that once brought goods to the people of Roanoke. Today, this museum showcases several trains, trucks, fire engines, and even an airplane. Sorry, no motorcycles are included in the exhibition, but you can usually get a tour of downtown Roanoke in a classic car (like a Ford model T) for just a few bucks. Outside, there's even a rocket on display. You can check out the Virginia Museum of Transportation on the web at www.vmt.org or call 540-342-5670. The Virginia Museum of Transportation is open Monday through Saturday 10 am to 5 pm and Sundays noon to 5. Admission is $7.40 for adults and just $5.25 for kids 11 and under. Senior riders (60+) get a discount at $6.40.

Another downtown icon is the Hotel Roanoke, built by the Norfolk and Western Railroad. It's the large Tudor Revival building across the railroad tracks from downtown. Reach the Hotel via the walkway over the railroad tracks. Built in 1882 with only 34 rooms, it was expanded in 1898 and 1938 to 384 rooms. It fell into disrepair before being donated by the railroad to Virginia Tech in 1989. It reopened in 1995 as the polished gem you see today and is home to the

Roanoke Conference Center. You can contact the Hotel Roanoke and Conference Center at 1-800-222-TREE or 540-985-5900, or find it on the web at www.hotelroanoke.com.

If you are in Roanoke during nighttime hours, you're sure to see the Roanoke Star. Atop Mill Mountain, the great neon star shines brightly over the city. So brightly, in fact, that it serves as a navigation aid to aircraft passing within about 30 miles. Built in 1949 as a symbol of the progressive spirit of the city of Roanoke, it is made of several multicolored neon tubes and glows 17,500 watts. Standing 100 ft. high, 88.5 ft. wide, and weighing in at 5 tons, it's the largest man-made star in the world. Visiting the Roanoke Star is free. You may do so during the day or at night, but be aware it's a favorite evening spot for teenage trysts.

Next to the Star is Mill Mountain Park—also free, with nice views of Roanoke from several trails that trace the crest of Mill Mountain through well-manicured gardens.

Next to the Roanoke Star and Mill Mountain Park is the Mill Mountain Zoo. Open from 10 am to 5 pm seven days a week, it costs just $6.92 for adults and $4.53 for children (11 and under). Seniors pay just $6.23 to visit the 171 animals who call the zoo home. Some of the animals are as rare as the Amur tiger and snow leopard, others as common as a prairie dog. The money you spend at the zoo goes

The Hotel Roanoke is a downtown icon.

right back into it. It's a great break for the road weary and educational, too! You can access the zoo on the web at www.mmzoo.org or by phone at 540-343-3241.

On the eastern side of Roanoke, just off the Blue Ridge Parkway, are two great destinations. The first is Roanoke Mountain. A four-mile loop road leads up to an elevation of 2,161 ft., about 1,000 ft. higher than the city. It is free to ride up the paved, one-way road, which has two really nice overlooks. The first one offers a view of Mill Mountain, which overlooks Roanoke. The second is atop Roanoke Mountain, where you'll find a short trail leading to the summit. Don't bother with the hike unless you want bragging rights for having scaled Roanoke Mountain; the trees of the summit obscure the views.

Further north on the Parkway is Virginia's Explore Park. Here you'll learn about life in the Roanoke Valley during 1671, 1740, and 1850 from people dressed in period clothing performing the daily tasks of days gone by. Admission is $8 for adults, $4.50 for children 11 and under, and $6 for seniors (60+). The historic area

is open from early May to the first days of November, Wednesday through Saturday 10 am to 5 pm and Sunday from noon to 5 pm. For more info, call 540-427-1800 or find it on the web at www.explorepark.org.

PLACES TO EAT

Roanoke has lots of great places to eat. To enjoy the many restaurants in downtown, park your bike at Market Square and explore on foot. There's sure to be something close by to please your palate.

For a good cup of coffee, stop in at **Mill Mountain Coffee & Tea** (540-342-9404), 112 Campbell Ave. near the Market Square. Inside, you can sip some gourmet coffee or espresso while taking in the energy of the young crowd who frequents the shop, discussing their "problems du jour."

If seafood is in your diet plan, try **Awful Arthur's** (540-344-2997), 208 Campbell Ave. Dinner entrees run between $13 and $24, and appetizers from $6 to $10. There's a well-attended bar inside as well.

Across the street from Awful Arthur's is **Saltori's Café and Spirits** (540-343-6644) at 202 Market Square. Saltori's is home to delicious Italian food authentically prepared with dining available next to the sidewalk, just like in Rome! You'll spend between $9 and $20 for dinner entrees.

The first of the trio of local icons to be mentioned is the **Roanoke Wiener Stand** (540-342-6932), 25 Campbell Ave. on the Market Square. The wiener stand is a local landmark. Conversation topics ranging from local politics to personal successes fill the air inside, as does the aroma of the best hot dogs in the region.

For modern *haute cuisine,* check out **Metro!** (540-345-6645), 14 E. Campbell Ave. just east of Market Square. This is the place to come to celebrate a special event. Dinners are served in several courses, and you'll pay dearly for them. Expect to drop about $100 per couple for dinner here. Even if you don't dine there, you can still appreciate the chefs' artfully prepared meals, because you can watch them at work. The kitchen was built next to the sidewalk, with large windows that allow passersby to look in and the chefs to see out. When the kitchen gets really hot, the doors leading from the kitchen to the sidewalk are opened, and the delicious aroma drifts onto the sidewalk and into the noses of passersby.

You can have dinner, share some beers with a friend, play some billiards, and sit outside overlooking downtown Roanoke from the deck of **Corned Beef and Co.** (540-342-3354),107 S. Jefferson St. near the intersection of Jefferson St. and Campbell Ave. The menu of Corned

Beef and Co. offers everything from steak to pizza to sandwiches (hot wings, too!), and its narrow storefront belies its large, two-story interior.

For a taste of Ireland, stop in and visit Kara at **Kara O'Caen's Irish Pub** (540-344-5509), 303 Jefferson St. You'll probably see the Irish Flag flying proudly above the door of this fine establishment. Inside, you'll experience a cozy Irish pub, complete with shepherd's pie and the redheaded Irish lass, Kara, serving Guinness Stout to jolly patrons. You don't have to be Irish to enjoy Kara O'Caen's Irish Pub, but you'd better be hungry!

For a tasty burger without a crowd, try the **Texas Tavern** (540-342-4825), 114 W. Church Ave. Never closed, the Tavern is a town favorite and is the second in the trio of local icons. With only ten seats, the atmosphere in the Tavern has led to many a compromise in local politics, grand plans, and

The Blue Ridge Parkway is a great way to get to Roanoke.

minor schemes. "Serving thousands, ten at a time," is the Texas Tavern's slogan. Check out their menu on the web at www.texastavern-inc.com.

The last (but not the least) to be mentioned in the icon trio is **The Coffee Pot** (540-774-8256), 2902 Brambleton Ave. This place has been serving up good grub, cold beers, and acclaimed entertainment since it opened its doors in 1934. As you look at the building, you'll see how it came to be known as the Coffee Pot—there's a huge coffee pot sticking out of the roof! The Coffee Pot used to be more than a restaurant, once offering cabanas for nightly rental, although most of them were used only for a few hours. It was a favorite haunt for local politicians. Today, the Coffee Pot offers no rooms for rent, but plenty of southern hospitality and good eatin'. There's a lunch buffet (steak on Mondays), and the dinner menu is more extensive than one might think could be produced from a Depression-era log cabin, which is how this restaurant began.

MAJOR ROADS

The Blue Ridge Parkway. Stretching through the eastern side of Roanoke, the Blue Ridge Parkway meanders 469 miles from Waynesboro, VA, down to Cherokee, NC. Roanoke is close to the "top" of the Parkway, between its mileposts 105 and 125.

THE INTERSTATES

I-81: unless you get to Roanoke by way of the Blue Ridge Parkway, chances are you rode I-81 to get into town. I-81 is situated in the northwestern suburbs of Roanoke and runs in a northeast-southwest direction.

I-581: I-581 starts at exit 43 on I-81 and slices through downtown, just north of the center of town. It will lead you from the interstate in the western suburbs into downtown. Along the way there are several well-marked exits for sights of interest mentioned earlier in this chapter.

US Route 220: I-581 ends without fanfare in downtown Roanoke, but US 220 continues on the path I-581

The City Market building marks the location of Market Square in Roanoke.

started. Continuing away from I-81, US 220 flows like an interstate all the way out of town on the eastern side, crossing under and providing access to the Blue Ridge Parkway.

VA 419: If you're accustomed to perimeter highways like the beltway circling Washington, DC, you might be disappointed to learn that Roanoke doesn't have one of those. Instead, Roanoke has VA 419. You'll find VA 419 by following US 220 to the southeast corner of town. From there, it flows west-northwest back to I-81, skirting the western side of town (and Salem, VA). VA 419 is a busy four-lane divided road that has several stoplights and businesses (including Tanglewood Mall).

US 11 (a.k.a. Williamson Rd.): This four-lane surface street traverses the business district, linking the downtown area with the airport. You can reach Williamson Rd. from I-581 by taking exit 5. If you go south on Williamson Rd., you'll arrive immediately at the city center. Head north on Williamson Rd., and you'll ride through a business district with motorcycle shops, restaurants, and used car lots. Williamson Rd. is a "cruising road," that is, kids and adults alike cruise it to see and be seen.

Center of Town Surface Streets: The city center of Roanoke is laid out in a convenient grid. Generally speaking, avenues run north-south and streets run east-west. The major surface streets of Roanoke are: Williamson Rd., First, Second, Third, and Fourth Streets flowing north-south, with Williamson Rd. being the farthest east and Fourth St. being the farthest west. The streets crossing

A narrow road climbs to the top of Roanoke Mountain.

perpendicular to these are: Salem Ave., Campbell Ave., Kirk Ave., Church Ave., Luck Ave., and Franklin Rd., with Salem Ave. at the top of the grid near the railroad tracks. These roads run east-west, but some are one-way, so watch for signs.

OTHER IMPORTANT SURFACE STREETS

Walnut Ave. climbs away from Jefferson St. and up Mill Mountain toward the Roanoke Star, ending at the Blue Ridge Parkway at the foot of Roanoke Mountain. Along the way, Walnut Ave. changes names to J. P. Fishburn Pkwy. and Mill Mountain Parkway.

US 221 (a.k.a. Brambleton Ave.) is like the other avenues mentioned earlier in that it flows east-west through the city. You can reach Brambleton Ave. by following the signs for US 221 through the center of town (it starts as Franklin Rd. and becomes Brambleton Ave. after several turns) or more simply, by following the interstate like US 220 (extension of I-581) to the south side of town to VA 419 north. You'll find Brambleton Ave. 2.2 miles to the northwest.

Colonial Ave. is a thriving business district that's home to a few motorcycle shops and can be reached easily by following US 220 south to VA 419 north. You'll ride VA 419 for about 1.7 miles and turn right onto Bent Mountain Rd., which becomes Colonial Ave. in a couple of blocks.

Peters Creek Rd. is home to a Harley-Davidson dealership and a Honda/Kawasaki/Suzuki/Yamaha dealership. To reach these shops, take exit 143 from I-81 onto I-581. Then take the first exit onto Peters Creek Rd. (VA 117) and follow that south (*away* from the airport) for about 1.5 mi. to the Harley dealership and about two miles to the other shop.

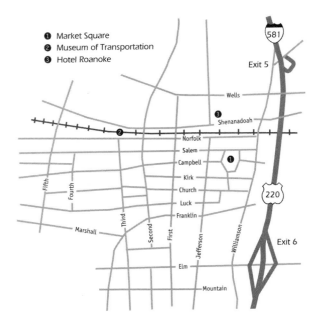

❶ Market Square
❷ Museum of Transportation
❸ Hotel Roanoke

Detail of important streets and attractions in downtown Roanoke from map on p. 71.

Exploring Roanoke

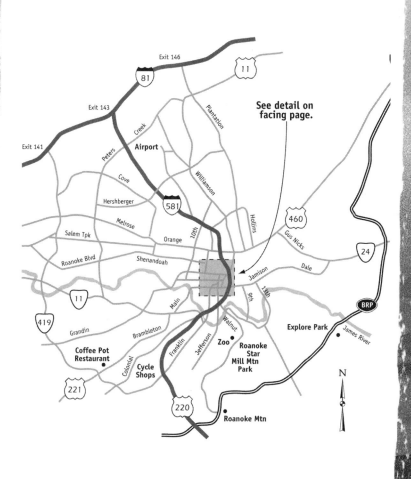

See detail on facing page.

Map labels:

Exit 146 · 81 · 11
Exit 143 · Creek · Plantation
Exit 141 · Peters · Airport · Williamson
Cove · 581 · Hollins · 460 · Gus Nicks · 24
Hershberger · 10th
Melrose · Orange · BRP
Salem Tpk · Shenandoah · Dale · Jamison
Roanoke Blvd · 11 · Main · 13th · 9th · James River
419 · Grandin · Brambleton · Walnut · Explore Park
Coffee Pot Restaurant · Franklin · Jefferson · Zoo · Roanoke Star Mill Mtn Park
Colonial · Cycle Shops
221 · 220 · Roanoke Mtn

N

Legend

75 Interstate Highway	640 State Highway	— Route
27 US Highway	606 County Road	Other Road
	5 ▶ Milepost	Blue Ridge Parkway

Roanoke Star

The world's most famous cities are known for their famous landmarks. Paris is known for the Eiffel Tower; London for Big Ben; New York for the Statue of Liberty; Marietta, GA for the Big Chicken. Now you can put Roanoke, the "Star City of the South" on that list, with its big neon star. This adventure takes you to the soaring elevation of Roanoke Mountain, then drops you down to the Mill Mountain Overlook with its famous Roanoke Star, before finally leading you down into the city center. In the center of Roanoke, you'll find friendly people, interesting museums, great restaurants, and cool sights. This adventure ends at the Virginia Museum of Transportation.

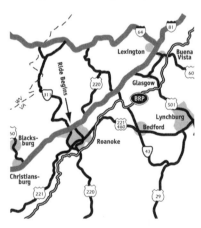

GAS

Gas is plentiful. You'll find it at miles 1.7, 3.2, 3.9, 7.7, 9.3, 9.7, 10.3, 23.4, and 23.6.

GETTING TO THE START

You'll begin this ride near Roanoke from I-81 by turning south on VA 419 (exit 141). Zero your trip meter as you make the turn on to VA 419 South from I-81.

RIDE OVERVIEW

After leaving I-81, ride along VA 419 South through part of the town of Salem, VA. If you're worried about witch-hunts, don't panic—that was Massachusetts. Salem, VA is a friendly town with plenty of fast food and lots of fuel available. Further along the four-lane divided section of VA 419, you'll come to US 221. If you have the time to take a short side trip, turn left onto US 221 North here, to reach the famous slice of Americana known as the Coffee Pot Restaurant. Located just over a mile from VA 419, the Coffee Pot was built by Jack Kefauver between 1934 and 1936. He kept his fledgling business alive during the depths of the Great Depression by building a large coffee pot sticking out of the roof on one end of the cabin-like building, and people have been spending money there ever since.

Back on VA 419, you'll pass the Tanglewood Mall as you near US 220. Turn right onto the ramp to US 220 and head up the hill toward the Blue Ridge Parkway. Along the way, you'll pass several more fast food outlets, but if you can stave off your hunger for just a little while longer, there's great food at the end of this ride in downtown Roanoke.

Exit US 220 to the right and continue up to the Blue Ridge Parkway. This route takes in only a small section of the Parkway, but the asphalt is in great shape and the view of Roanoke Mountain on the right side of the road is spectacular. In just a few minutes, you'll be atop the mountain, looking down on the city of Roanoke and surrounding area.

Watch for the signs directing you to turn right off the Parkway onto Roanoke Mountain Rd. Advertised as a four-mile loop, this single lane, mostly one-way road climbs up Roanoke Mountain and has two excellent overlooks. The first is on the left just a little over a mile from the Parkway. While the view from the paved pullout is good, the stone overlook itself is attractive. On a clear day, look toward the city of Roanoke to see the Roanoke Star, situated above the city, between where you're standing and the tall buildings of downtown. In a few minutes, you'll be standing at the base of that star. Until then, keep riding up Roanoke Mountain toward the 2,161-ft. summit. As you near the top, the road becomes two-way for a few hundred feet. There's another great view from the parking lot near the summit, but you won't see Roanoke from here, nor from the summit itself—just all the beauty of nature from the north side of Roanoke Mountain. The best views are from these two overlooks. Lucky you! The road down Roanoke Mountain quickly becomes single lane and one-way again, with a couple of fun hairpin turns. When you reach the Blue Ridge Parkway, turn left. Pass the entrance to Roanoke Mountain Rd., then take your first right onto unmarked Mill Mountain Rd.

Riding away from the Parkway and entering the city of Roanoke, turn left into Mill Mountain Park and ride less than a mile up Mill Mountain to the

Roanoke Star. The parking area behind the Star itself is large enough to accommodate several cars and motorcycles. If you can't find a space there, park in the lower lot near the Zoo and Park Headquarters.

Take a minute to walk to the front of the star to take in the view of downtown Roanoke and the star's mammoth proportions. It's the largest man-made star in the world. Built in 1949, it stands 100 ft. tall, is 88.5 ft. wide, and weighs 5 tons. Its multicolored neon tubes consume 17,500 watts when powered up every

The neon Roanoke Star is the largest man-made star in the world.

night from sunset to midnight. The Roanoke Star was built as a symbol of the progressive spirit of Roanoke, the "Star City of the South." If you want to see it up close and personal at night, the park is open for you to do so, but be forewarned, nighttime is the right time for teenage love at the Roanoke Star. Just down the hill from the Star is the Mill Mountain Information and Visitor Center. Next door, the Roanoke Zoo is open 10 am to 4:30 pm every day of the year except Christmas. Tickets are $6.92 for adults, $4.53 for children 11 and under, and $6.23 for seniors. Why the unusual pricing? Beats me, but the prices include sales tax.

Descending from the Roanoke Star, you'll turn left to continue down Mill Mountain toward the city center. You'll enjoy a few more sweeping curves before entering the bustle of downtown traffic. Leaving the tree-covered roadway behind, you'll cross the Walnut Ave. Bridge with its antique-style lampposts on either side. Turn right onto Jefferson Ave. where you'll begin to see directional signs (blue with white stars) indicating the way to all of the coolest attractions in the downtown area. Most of the downtown attractions are near Jefferson Ave.

Getting to Market Square is as easy as following the signs, which will direct you to turn right onto Campbell St. You'll be there in just one city block. At the Market, park in any space (in Roanoke, motorcycles may share a single parking space).

By day, the Market Square really *is* a market. You'll walk among the office workers and farmers who mingle without a thought of the bizarre-looking difference in their clothing. Farmers offer fresh produce for sale on tables under the yellow canopies that line the square. If you prefer your

Take the loop road to the overlook.

food cooked, fear not, biker buddy—the Market Square also has just about any kind of meal you desire.

This adventure continues down Jefferson Ave. toward the Virginia Transportation Museum. When Jefferson Ave. ends at Salem Ave., turn left and go just three blocks to Third St., then turn right into the parking lot for the Virginia Museum of Transportation. As you ride down Salem Ave., you'll pass through the building which houses the *Roanoke Times*. The Museum itself was built from a restoredd train depot; it costs just $7.40 to enter (less for seniors and children). The museum is open weekdays from 11 am to 4 pm, Saturdays 10 am to 5 pm, and Sundays from 1 to 5 pm. Inside, you'll see many locomotives and rare vintage automobiles. Unfortunately, no motorcycles are yet on display. Near the front entrance, you can hire a Ford Model T to give you a tour of the Market Square for $2, or ride all the way up to the Roanoke Star for just $8 per person.

The museum is where this adventure ends. You might want to ride back to the Market Square to enjoy some tasty food and cool scenery. Or ride back to Jefferson Ave. and turn right onto Franklin Rd. (US 221) to take in the sights of the *Roanoke Valley Run* (p. 78), or try out the *Invading Normandy* ride that also begins in downtown Roanoke.

RIDE ALTERNATIVES

Near the beginning of this ride at mile 7.7, you may want to turn left onto US 221 to visit the Coffee Pot Restaurant. It's just over a mile up on the right. While on the Parkway, look up to see the summit of Roanoke Mountain. If you can't see the top due to clouds, don't spend your time riding up the narrow one-way road to the top of Roanoke Mountain—unless you need the bragging rights, in which case, go for it!

ROAD CONDITIONS

Part city riding, part wilderness riding. The roads of this ride range from four-lane divided highways to narrow, single-lane paths. The asphalt throughout is in excellent condition, but you'll find a few spots with gravel on the road.

POINTS OF INTEREST

Blue Ridge Parkway, Roanoke Mountain, Mill Mountain Park, Roanoke Star, Roanoke Zoo, Downtown Market, Transportation Museum.

RESTAURANTS

The Coffee Pot (540-774-8256) is a Roanoke culinary icon. Named for the huge coffee pot rising through the roof at the end of the building, it offers a lunch buffet (steak on Mondays) and dinner with entertainment nearly every night. Expect to spend $7 for the lunch buffet and about $8 for the Killer Burger—a tasty mix of peppers cooked in a slab of ground beef served with anything you'd ever want to put on or near a hamburger. Beer, wine, and mixed drinks flow freely at the Coffee Pot.

In downtown Roanoke, park your bike at Market Square and walk around the block to get a feel for what's offered here. For a taste of Irish Pub food (like shepherd's pie or fish and chips for between $6 and $8 per entree), try **Kara O'Caens's Irish Bar**. It's a block away from Market Square on Jefferson Ave. at Church Ave., open from 5 pm to 2 am every day. Just down Jefferson Ave. is **Corned Beef & Co.**, with some of the best hot wings in the downtown area. In the mood for *haute cuisine*? Try **Metro!** (540-345-6645) on Campbell Ave., for delicious European-style meals. Expect to spend about $50 on a dinner for two. **Awful Arthur's** (540-344-2997), at 208 Cambell Ave. has a full bar and dozens of different kinds of fish excellently prepared in dozens of ways. Prices run from $6 for a sandwich to $20 for lobster. **Saltori's Café** (540-343-6644), across from Awful Arthur's, serves tasty Italian food for dinner from $7 to $18 per meal. And don't miss the **Roanoke Wiener Stand** (540-342-6932), open Monday through Saturday from 8:30 am to 7 pm at the corner of Market Square and Campbell Ave. Every day this downtown landmark is packed with office workers, construction crews, and political leaders who come to enjoy the best dogs south of Chicago. Try the two-dog/soft drink/fries meal for just $4.95. For 24-hour dining, go down Church Ave. between First and Second Streets to find the **Texas Tavern** (540-342-4825). The

Texas Tavern has just ten seats and boasts they "serve thousands, ten at a time." Impress them by ordering some "Chili With" (which is chili with onions) and a "Cheesy Western" (a cheeseburger with an omelet in it). Find the Texas Tavern on the web at www.texastavern-inc.com.

DETAILED DIRECTIONS

Mile 0—From I-81 take exit 141, which is VA 419, and turn left at the top of the ramp to head toward Salem, VA, on VA 419 South. *At mile 7.7, you'll cross US 221; turning left here and riding just 1.3 miles down the road will take you to the famous Coffee Pot Restaurant.*

Mile 9.9—Take the exit for US 220 South (this exit is across from Tanglewood Mall).

Mile 11.9—Exit from US 220 onto the ramp to the Blue Ridge Parkway, and at the top of the ramp, turn right (north). *You should see Roanoke Mountain ahead to your right. If you can't see it due to fog or rain, don't bother climbing up Roanoke Mountain Rd.*

Mile 13.3—Turn right onto the Roanoke Mountain Rd. This road is generally a one-way, narrow, winding road, so use caution. *There's an overlook on the left at mile 14.4. The road briefly becomes a two-way at mile 14.9, and the summit overlook is at mile 15.2. Coming down from the summit, the road curves right and becomes one-way again at mile 15.5.*

Mile 14.9—Turn left (south) onto the Blue Ridge Parkway.

Mile 17.1—Turn right onto Mill Mountain Rd.

Mile 17.7—Turn left into Mill Mountain Park. *The Roanoke Star at*

mile 20.8 is where you'll have to turn around and begin descending Mill Mountain. Descending from the Roanoke Star, you'll find the Visitor Center and Zoo on the right at mile 21.

Mile 20.1—Turn left from Mill Mountain Park onto Mill Mountain Rd. (it becomes Walnut Ave.) *You'll start seeing homes at mile 23.1 and cross the Walnut Ave. Bridge at mile 23.5.*

Mile 21.5—Turn right onto Jefferson Ave. *You'll be in downtown multilane traffic for the remainder of this ride. To get to the Market Square, turn right onto Campbell Ave. at mile 24.4 to see the open air market and dine in one of the many restaurants offered there.*

Mile 24.5—Turn left onto Salem Ave. This section of Salem Ave. takes you through the Roanoke Times Newspaper Building.

Mile 24.8—Turn right into the parking lot for the Virginia Transportation Museum. This adventure ends here. *For more riding try out the* Roanoke Valley Run *(p. 78) or* Invading Normandy *(p. 86).*

Roanoke Star

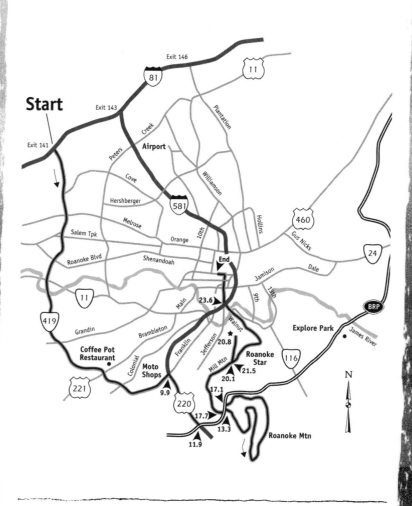

Start

Exit 146

Exit 143

Exit 141

81

11

Creek

Plantation

Peters

Cove

Airport

Williamson

Hershberger

581

Melrose

10th

Hollins

460

Salem Tpk

Orange

Gus Nicks

24

Roanoke Blvd

Shenandoah

End

Dale

11

Jamison

9th

13th

BRP

419

23.6

Walnut

Explore Park

James River

Grandin

Brambleton

Main

Franklin

Jefferson

20.8

★

Roanoke
Star

116

Coffee Pot
Restaurant

Colonial

Moto
Shops

Mill Mtn

21.5

20.1

N

221

9.9

220

17.1

17.7

13.3

11.9

Roanoke Mtn

Roanoke Valley Run

*T*his ride will lead you through and out of the Roanoke Valley along a superb stretch of roadway, into the town of Floyd, home to several hip places to eat and be entertained, then up to the Blue Ridge Parkway. You'll then follow the scenic, internationally famous Parkway north back into the Roanoke Valley. Filled with curves, twisties, and fun things to do, this run is a blast for any motorcyclist.

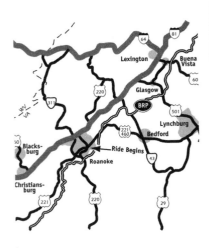

GAS

Gas is available at miles 4.5, 5.4, 5.7, 16.6, 22.9, 25.9, 26.9, 31.4, 35.5, 40.1, 43, 95.7, and near the end of the ride in Roanoke at mile 96.1.

GETTING TO THE START

This ride begins and ends in downtown Roanoke at the intersection of US 221 and I-581. To get there, take I-81 to I-581 through town, then take exit 5. Zero your trip meter as you turn south on US 221 from I-581.

RIDE OVERVIEW

Immediately after exiting I-581, you'll be headed south on US 221 toward downtown. On the right is a tall Tudor-style structure, the Hotel Roanoke, which had only 34 rooms when the Norfolk and Western Railroad opened it in 1882. The Hotel was expanded to 384 rooms but eventually fell into disrepair. In 1989, the railroad donated the hotel to Virginia Polytechnic Institute. After an extensive refurbishment, it reopened and was placed on the National Register of Historic Places. Today, the hotel hosts thousands of visitors a year, and because it is home to the Roanoke Conference Center, it hosts hundreds of events annually as well.

Crossing the bridge over the railroad, you'll see two classic neon signs on the right side of the road, advertising a brand of coffee and a still-popular soft drink. Beyond the bridge, you'll see signs directing visitors to the center of town and the market square. Don't go in that direction just yet. The ride covers about 96 more miles before returning to downtown Roanoke.

Following the signs to US 221 South, turn right onto Franklin Rd., which will take you over Jefferson Ave. and into a section of town known as Old Southwest. This neighborhood has suffered a bad case of mid-70s urban blight. The residents of Old Southwest fled the downtown area into the relatively less expensive and apparently more secure suburbs. The homes that were left behind lost value, and the neighborhood declined. Crime skyrocketed where kids once played stickball, and classic homes with broken windows sat empty. Vagrants moved in, serving only to affirm the past residents' decision to move away. All of that began to change in the late 80s and 90s when new residents discovered large houses near downtown that needed a little fixing up. For their square footage and convenience to downtown, the homes of Old Southwest were a steal. Today, well maintained, stately residences shine brightly next to houses that appear to be rotting in place. The neighborhood of Old Southwest is on the rebound, but still has a ways to go.

The ride forks onto a bumpy section of Elm Ave. Leave Old Southwest after crossing the Roanoke River and fork to the right onto Main

TOTAL DISTANCE
97 miles

TIME FRAME
4 hours from start to finish. Add time to eat in Floyd or to explore the many overlooks on the Blue Ridge Parkway.

St. Watch closely for the signs indicating US 221 South. On Main St. and later on Brambleton Ave., you'll pass through another neighborhood filled with beautiful homes on larger lots than those in Old Southwest. On this side of the River urban blight never set in, so these houses and gardens need much less time and money to restore. Another good example of restoration stands on the right. A handsome, two-story brick schoolhouse stood on the hilltop there. The children who once attended there were long gone, and a business needed lots of office space. Rather than tear down the school, the business simply moved in, changing the building's outward appearance

Don't forget to stop at the Coffee Pot roadhouse. It's easy to recognize—just look for the giant coffee pot.

Cruising along the Blue Ridge Parkway makes almost any outing more enjoyable.

very little with only a sign indicating the name of the business.

After turning left onto Brambleton Ave. you can begin to breathe easier—no more turns until you get to Floyd, VA, in about 38 miles. Whether you eat there or not, check out the Coffee Pot on the left side of the road about a mile after turning off Main St. The Coffee Pot is the red and black, single-story log cabin on the left with the huge coffee pot sticking out of its right side. A snapshot of you with your bike in front of the sign will prove to the world that you have been to Roanoke. Inside, you'll find a friendly staff serving up good food amidst billiard tables, dart boards, and a small music stage. Apparently, if you are a rock star you must play the Coffee Pot at some shining point in your career, as evidenced by the photos on the wall of the internationally famous rock and blues musicians on stage at the Coffee Pot.

Past the Coffee Pot, US 221 becomes a four-lane for the next few miles, and the businesses with traffic threatening to pull out on either side will keep your eyes and brakes busy. After crossing VA 419 you'll enter the town of Cave Springs, and as you roll through it, the road changes back to two-lane.

Riding the southern end of the Roanoke Valley, you'll get a glimpse of some pre-Civil War architecture. In the town of Poages Mill, you'll see a few old homes and businesses as you ride over the hilly valley floor to get to the southern rim. US 221 is well-paved in this area and there is little on the road to worry about except the seams in the bridges. As you approach a bridge, brace yourself and your bike to handle a sharp bump or maybe even a dip. The asphalt meets the bridge deck with an inch or more difference! Don't get surprised by these rude bumps. Having survived the bridges, you'll begin to notice that the downhill part of "hilly" is gone. The up-and-down rhythm of the road becomes a steady climb as the road bends up through Bent Mountain. Fortunately, the traffic engineers realized there would be motorcycles on this stretch of beautiful road, and they built passing lanes so we can overtake the heavier traffic lumbering up the mountain. Over your left shoulder there are some great views of Roanoke and the Roanoke Valley. Once at the top of Bent Mountain, you'd expect a sharp descent on the other side, but not here. US 221 stretches its legs by replacing the tight twists and turns it took to get out of the Roanoke Valley with the long sweeping curves of the Virginia farmland. You'll ride with Poor Mountain towering on your right side and the crest of the Blue Ridge on your left. The section of Parkway running atop those mountains on the left will take you back to Roanoke on this ride.

At the little town of Floyd, make a left turn onto VA 8. Floyd is so small you might be tempted to just make the left and ride out of town without experiencing its charms. Don't you dare miss this cool spot. Floyd is full of eclectic residents and businesses; you're as likely to see a Rastafarian in a leisure suit as you are a farmer in bib overalls. There seems to be some kind of buzz in town at all times. There is usually some live music (rock, blues, bluegrass, country, you name it) being performed at one of the many clubs within the city limits. Two of the best are the Pine Tavern Restaurant and Odd Fellas Cantina. In the evening, you can count on finding some music to your liking and a tasty dinner to boot at one of these establishments. The relaxed and easy-going atmosphere of the town will quickly grab hold of you and shake the stuff that stresses you right out. Floyd is one of those places where watches don't have much importance. So, park your scooter at the Pine Tavern or in front of the Floyd County Courthouse and walk to Odd Fellas Cantina (to the left of the courthouse), or stop in the billiard parlor across the street. Whatever you do, stop in Floyd—your therapist will think you've had a breakthrough!

After chillin' in Floyd, make the left turn onto VA 8 South and ride up to the Blue Ridge Parkway. On the way, you'll feel the increase in altitude as you near Tuggles Gap. In Tuggles Gap, this run makes a left onto the ramp to the Blue Ridge Parkway and another left onto the Parkway heading north. If you need fuel, or if you *will* need fuel in the next 45 miles, continue on VA 8 south under the Parkway to Tuggles Gap Gas Station/Restaurant/Motel. This little store has a reputation for delicious desserts, so fill your tank with gas and your gut with a delicious homemade dessert; after all, you won't reach another restaurant for about an hour.

Few roads are as nice as the Blue Ridge Parkway, and as you ride north from Tuggles Gap, you'll be reminded why. With clean asphalt, scenery that can't be beat, and no commercial traffic, this road was made for motor touring—literally. There are dozens of scenic overlooks and sites of interest on the way to Roanoke. One of the first you'll come to is Rakes Mill Pond. Rakes Mill is long gone, but the dam he built to create a millpond still stands, leaving the pond and some falls for us to enjoy. To see an old mill still in operation, turn south on the Parkway to reach Mabry Mill in about a half an hour.

This run continues north on the Parkway toward Roanoke. You'll find the Smart View Motor Trail on the right side of the road. Ride its one-mile paved loop under a thick canopy of trees to get a view of an old cabin—you won't even have to get off your bike! If you take this motor trail, add a mile to the detailed directions on p. 84.

You'll know you're nearly back in the Roanoke Valley when you reach the Poor Mountain Overlook. Earlier in this run you rode past Poor Mountain after climbing out of the valley. The Parkway won't actually drop you down into the Roanoke Valley, it keeps you riding on the crest of the Blue Ridge on the valley's eastern rim. The distant vistas from the Poages Mill Overlook are stunning. Once you see the sign for Roanoke Mountain, get ready for the left turn. Cross US 220, then ride up a hill with a large field and Roanoke Mountain on the right side of the road. Near the top of the hill, turn left onto Mill Mountain Rd. Mill Mountain Rd. will take you down into the Roanoke Valley and into Roanoke itself. For a good view of downtown Roanoke, turn left into the well-marked Mill Mountain Park and ride up to the Roanoke Star. The Star is the largest neon star in the world and glows every night until midnight. By day, the views from its base are amazing.

Head back down Mill Mountain Rd. and into the heart of downtown. You'll cross an old bridge with a set of street lamps posted like sentries, welcoming you to the city. Then turn right onto Jefferson St. and ride into the heart of downtown. This adventure ends at the intersection of Jefferson St. and Salem Ave., just two blocks from the Virginia Transportation Museum, the Roanoke City Market, and dozens of good places to eat. Check out *Exploring Roanoke* (p. 64) for more info about downtown Roanoke.

RIDE ALTERNATIVES

This run ends in downtown Roanoke, so get the *Exploring Roanoke* ride (p. 64) ready. There are no alternatives to this ride, but if you're staying in an area south of Roanoke, you can use this route to guide you to and from the city.

ROAD CONDITIONS

The first several miles of this run are on the bumpy two-lane city streets of Roanoke. Once leaving town, the road improves a bit, becoming a four-lane. South of town, US 221 becomes two-lane again as it climbs in a series of twisty cutbacks out of the Roanoke Valley. Once out of the valley, you'll roll over hills through farmland into Floyd. In Floyd, the twisty and well-banked curves of VA 8 South head up to the Blue Ridge Parkway's legendary curves, clean asphalt, and absence of commercial traffic. Other than a very bumpy bridge crossing near mile 11, the only hazard to warn you about is the wild animals crossing the roads on this urban-to-rural-to-urban run.

POINTS OF INTEREST

Scenery of the Roanoke Valley, town of Floyd, Pine Tavern and Odd Fellows Cantina, Tuggles Gap, Rakes Mill Pond, Smart View Motor Trail, the Roanoke Star on Mill Mountain.

RESTAURANTS

While Roanoke offers literally hundreds of restaurants, this run features restaurants not in the downtown area. To read about the restaurants in downtown Roanoke, flip to the *Exploring Roanoke* ride (p. 64).
The Coffee Pot (540-774-8256) is technically in the city of Roanoke, but it's far enough from the downtown area to get a mention here. The Roanoke Star may be the symbol of the city, but the Coffee Pot is *the* local meeting place. At some point, everyone in Roanoke goes there. It was built in the depths of the Great Depression. Owner Jack Kefauver knew he'd have to do something unusual to draw customers into his business, so he built a huge coffee pot sticking out of the top of one end of the building. It served as a watering hole for politicians, thieves,

judges, and lawyers (some of whom were one and the same), and important decisions about local politics were decided at the tables inside. Carroll Bell bought the place in 1979 and began serving up entertainment nearly every night. The house specialty is the lunch buffet that includes steak on Mondays. You'll spend about $7 for lunch ($2 more with a beer), and about $12 for dinner ($4 more for a glass of wine). Call ahead to see who's on the playbill.

Just north of Floyd is the **Pine Tavern**. Since 1927 the Pine Tavern has been inviting its guests to escape from whatever monsters chase them. Today, you can escape to the Pine Tavern for delicious dinners served Wednesday through Sunday, 5 pm to 10 pm. The tavern proper is open late, but the kitchen quits serving around 10 pm. The menu lists ethnic treats from Greece, Mexico, Italy, and the Middle East. If you're not that adventurous, you can order American fare like a Cornish hen for $14 or a New York Strip for $21. There're even some vegetarian choices available. Dinner goes for between $10 and $21, depending on what you order, and you can expect some good musical entertainment while you dine. To learn about who's playing and see what's on the menu, check out www.thepinetavern.com, or call 540-745-4482. Had too much to drink? Check into the Pine Tavern Lodge (not affiliated with the Pine Tavern Restaurant) by calling 540-745-4428.

In downtown Floyd, next to the Courthouse, is the **Odd Fellas Cantina** (540-745-3463). As its name suggests, the Cantina offers Tex-Mex dishes. Actually, the term "Tex-Mex"

doesn't quite fit. "Appalachian-Latino" is probably more accurate. Open daily except Mondays, it serves lunch from 11 am to 3 pm, then closes until 5 pm, when it reopens for dinner served until 9 on Wednesday and Thursday, and until 10 on Friday and Saturday. Sunday is brunch day at Odd Fellas, with a good buffet from 10 am to 3 pm. During dinner and Sunday brunch, expect to be entertained by local musicians whose talents would indicate they play in Floyd not because they have to, but because they choose to. Performers and customers alike come to Odd Fellas to enjoy the small-town atmosphere and eclectic mix of patrons. You'll spend between $5 and $7 for lunch and between $8 and $18 for dinner (most items are cheaper than $18; that's for the cooked-to-order steak). The menu changes frequently, as does the entertainment. For the latest, check out Odd Fellas on the web at www.oddfellascantina.com.

DETAILED DIRECTIONS

Mile 0—Exit I-581 at exit 5 onto US 221 South (also known as Williamson Rd.). *On the right, pass the Hotel Roanoke. Cross the railroad tracks to see the Dr. Pepper and coffee neon billboards.*

Mile 0.4—Turn right onto Franklin Rd. to stay on US 221 South. *Ride through the downtown section.*

Mile 1.1—Fork to the right onto Elm Ave. to stay on US 221 South. *Riding through the neighborhood known as Old Southwest, you'll cross the Roanoke River, which flows through downtown.*

Mile 2.5—Fork to the right again onto Main St. to stay on US 221 South.

Mile 2.7—Turn left onto Brambleton Ave. to stay on US 221. *You'll pass the Coffee Pot at mile 4.4 as the road stretches to become four-lane. US 221 becomes two-lane again at mile 7.5. Around mile 13.4, you'll begin to climb out of the Roanoke Valley in a series of nice steep turns that (thankfully) have passing lanes. Check out the view of Roanoke at mile 14.3—it's a doozey! You'll ride through hilly farm country until you reach the Pine Tavern on the right at mile 38.5, just north of Floyd, VA. You'll enter Floyd and be at the center of town at mile 40.2. Park in front of the courthouse and walk to the Odd Fellas Cantina (to the left of the courthouse) to enjoy music, well-prepared meals, or a drink.*

Mile 40.3—Turn left onto VA 8 South

Detail of downtown Roanoke from map on facing page.

and begin to ride up to the Blue Ridge Parkway.

Mile 46.3—Turn left onto the access ramp to the Blue Ridge Parkway and then left again (mile 46.4) onto the Parkway northbound. *If you need fuel, better not get on the Parkway before you stop in at Tuggles Gap to top off your tank. There's no fuel on this ride for the next 45 miles. At mile 49.2 on the left is Rakes Mill Pond. You can turn to the right at mile 56.5 and ride the mile-long Motor Nature Trail around the Smart View area (log cabin and good scenery). There are several good overlooks along this section of the Parkway. One of the best looking onto the Roanoke Valley is the Poages Mill Overlook on the left at mile 82.5. You'll cross US 220 at mile 90.3. Use US 220 as a reminder of your next turn.*

Mile 91.4—Turn left onto Mill Mountain Rd. (see p. 77) *To get a close-up look at the Roanoke Star, or to visit the Mill Mountain Zoo and Mill Mountain Park, turn left at mile 93.8 into Mill Mountain Park.*

Mile 96—Turn right onto Jefferson St. and ride it into the center of town. This ride ends at mile 97 where Jefferson St. intersects with Salem Ave. *Quickly flip to the Exploring Roanoke ride (p. 64) to figure out what you're going to do next!*

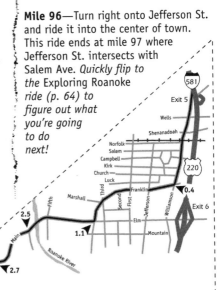

Roanoke Valley Run

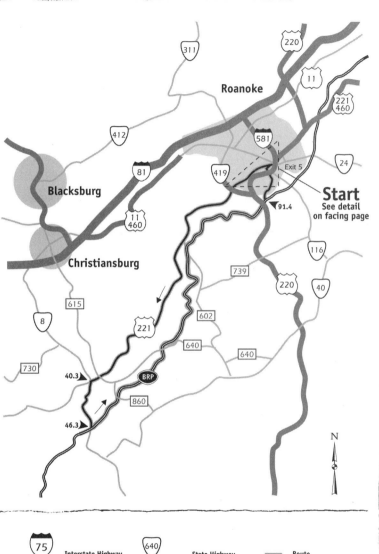

Roanoke

Blacksburg

Christiansburg

Exit 5

Start
See detail
on facing page

91.4

40.3

BRP

46.3

N

 75 Interstate Highway

 640 State Highway

— Route

 27 US Highway

606 County Road

5 ▶ Milepost

— Other Road

═══ Blue Ridge Parkway

Invading Normandy

This ride leads you to the National D-Day Memorial in Bedford, VA. Along the way, you'll get a glimpse of what the brave young men of Bedford were fighting for. You'll ride sweeping curves through rolling farm country, surrounded by beautiful mountains. Having lost a greater proportion of its young men than any other city or town in the nation, Bedford was chosen as the location for the National D-Day Memorial. The Memorial itself is a staggering sight. In the faces of the statues of soldiers fighting for the freedom of people everywhere, you'll see bravery and determination, and their boyish looks as well. The people of Bedford know all too well that freedom isn't free, and you, my biker brother and sister, will be reminded of that as well.

GAS

Gas is available at miles 2.6, 7.8, 9, 10.7, 24.8, 25.3, 29.4, 33.3, 39.2, 39.5, 44.3, 46, 49, and 51.3.

GETTING TO THE START

This ride starts at the intersection of the Blue Ridge Parkway and VA 24, about four miles east of downtown Roanoke. You can reach the start by taking exit 6, VA 24 East, from I-581 in downtown Roanoke. From the Blue Ridge Parkway, ride to mile 112.2 of the Blue Ridge Parkway and exit onto VA 24. At the bottom of the exit, turn right onto VA 24 East. Reset your trip meter to zero as you cross under the Parkway or turn off it heading east on VA 24.

RIDE OVERVIEW

In the morning hours of June 6, 1944, the citizens of Bedford, VA sent their best young men to the remote beaches of Normandy, France, in the first salvo to remove the Nazis from Europe. By the end of that fateful day, nineteen letters of regret were being sent to mothers and wives of Bedford soldiers who gave their all. Within weeks, four more letters had to be sent to Bedford addresses. Given that the total population of Bedford was only 3,200, this was not only a catastrophic loss for the families but for the community as well, not to mention the Nation. History has proven that the sacrifice made by the men of Bedford was for a righteous cause—the Nazis were defeated and Europe was rebuilt. The town of Bedford carried its grief, and on June 6, 2001, the citizens of Bedford and dignitaries from around the world dedicated the National D-Day Memorial in remembrance of men who died on that fateful day. You are free today because of the valor and sacrifice of the men from Bedford and towns like it all over the world, who participated in Operation Overlord. Visit the National D-Day Memorial and pay respect to those who served their country and the world to defeat tyranny.

This ride begins on a four-lane section of VA 24 heading east. Don't let the four lanes discourage you—the road narrows to two lanes in a couple of miles. Paved with clean asphalt, the hilly ride begins with several well-banked, sweeping curves rolling through the western Virginia farm country.

If you have been to France, you might be struck by the similarity of the Virginia landscape to that of northern France. In fact, Virginia and France have more in common than landscape. Both have tranquil vineyards and agricultural fields stretching out over rolling hills. The men of Bedford could have easily imagined that the war they were fighting was in their own backyard.

The ride makes a left onto VA 122. Be careful when turning left from VA 24 onto VA 122, because the traffic on VA 122 does not stop, and it travels at a high rate of speed. After turning, you'll see A.J.'s Country Store and Restaurant on the left side of the road. A.J.'s is one of those places you can buy a gallon of milk, some fishing tackle, and a chicken biscuit all in one stop. A.J.'s can only seat about twenty-five people at a time, but it serves good food at a good price. From A.J.'s, VA 122 will take you north toward Bedford. Along the way, you'll ride past a few more farms before crossing US 221/460 into Bedford.

Once in Bedford, you'll turn left onto Tiger Trail, which is the road to the town elementary school and the National D-Day Memorial. Fork to the right, enter through the gate, then ride up the hill to the 88-acre Memorial overlooking a peaceful scene that also takes in the Peaks of Otter to the north. The mileage for this ride includes the long driveway to and around the Memorial, so you won't have to sweat the math later. The Memorial is open from 10 am to 5 pm seven days a week, but is closed on Christmas Day, New Year's Day, January 2, and Thanksgiving. You'll pay a $10 parking fee to the guard, who will likely direct you to the motorcycle parking. An asphalt parking area for cars and buses circles the Memorial, but the intelligent designers figured that motorcyclists

would visit, too, so they constructed a concrete parking pad just for us. Because it's on the far side, you'll have a chance to view the entire thing from all angles before dismounting and walking around. Once parked, the real adventure begins.

As soon as you take off your helmet, you'll hear the mysterious swooshing sound that seems to come and go with sporadic frequency; head over to the Triumphal Arch to investigate. The Arch towers above the beach invasion tableau and all the others as well. Inscribed at the top is the word OVERLORD, which was the name of the D-Day invasion operation. Behind it is the Final Tribute, a bronze statue of the inverted rifle and helmet marker commonly used as a temporary tombstone during battle. Looking toward the wall over the beach, you'll see the determined young face of a soldier hoisting his weapon as he nears the top of the wall. In the distance behind him are the buildings of the town square of Bedford—a strong reminder of what they were fighting for. Beyond the wall, you'll notice there are three other soldiers on the wall itself. One is falling, but each is giving his all so that one can reach the top. Farther down toward the beach, you'll see several soldiers receiving fire. They've just left the

relative safety of the landing craft, and the incoming rounds splash water around them. The swooshing sound is from the splashes created by the "bullets." In the water, soldiers are fighting, drowning, dying, and reaching for victory—all of which was done on D-Day.

Away from the beach, flags of the 12 nations of the Allied Expeditionary Force fly in Victory Plaza. At the base of each flagpole is the story of what that nation sacrificed on D-Day to assist in the invasion. Turning away from the beach and looking through the Arch, you'll see the haunting, faceless statue of a WWI French Freedom fighter. Her face was blown off during the WWII liberation of the village she happened to be in. No one knows whether the Allies or the Nazis were responsible. The statue was donated by some very appreciative French residents of the town who fled into Allied territory during the Nazi occupation.

On the far side of the beach is the English Garden, the design of which was inspired by the shoulder patch worn by the invasion force. The Supreme Commander's Order of the Day for 6 June 1944 is inscribed nearby. On either side of the beach a display area hosts revolving exhibitions; a U.S. Coast Guard bell and a small propeller-driven scout plane were on display in 2003. The beach itself is quite large, offering great views from all angles; the one from the polished marble landing craft is particularly haunting.

After taking in the views of the statues and memorial, stop in the gift shop to buy a shirt or some other souvenir to commemorate your visit and promote the memorial. For more information about the National D-Day Memorial, log onto the web at www.dday.org or call 800-351-DDAY. You might also want to spend another

$10 to pay a visit to the National D-Day Museum in New Orleans, LA. Check it out at www.ddaymuseum.org or call 540-527-6102.

When you're ready to leave the National D-Day Memorial, follow the same long driveway back through the entrance gate and left onto Tiger Trail. The ride makes a right onto VA 122 and an immediate right onto the ramp to US 221/460.

Following US 221/460 West toward Roanoke, you'll be surprised how much fun this four-lane divided roadway can be. Filled with sweeping curves and views of the Peaks of Otter on the right side of the road, it's a real treat. Watch for some gas tanker trucks as you pass a "tank farm" before riding between Coyne and Porter Mountains (Coyne Mountain will be on your right side).

You'll enter the business section of Roanoke, and the ride ends where US 221/460 meet I-581. About a block before this ride ends, you can make a turn onto Williamson Rd. Turning to the right will lead you to a good motorcycle shop, the airport, and several restaurants; turning left will lead you toward the center of Roanoke. To reach I-81, go north on I-581 and ride about four miles. Regardless of what direction you travel, remember the men of Bedford and thousands of others like them who gave everything so that you could enjoy your days. Remember the sacrifice of these brave souls by celebrating the freedom *you* have, and getting out there for a ride!

RIDE ALTERNATIVES

Once in Bedford, instead of returning to Roanoke on US 221/460, you can take VA 43 North through downtown Bedford up to the Peaks of Otter, and ride part of the *Peaking at Dinosaurs and the Natural Bridge* ride, which begins on p. 98.

ROAD CONDITIONS

On a map, VA 24 looks like a straight road. Don't be fooled; the first four miles of VA 24 are four-lane, but it changes to a well-paved section of sweeping curves as you near VA 122, which continues the good road

Soldiers receiving enemy fire as they land at Normandy Beach is just one of the life-like historical details shown at Bedford, Virginia's National D-Day Memorial.

conditions and sweepers, leading you through Virginia farm country. After visiting the Memorial, ride the four-lane divided US 221/460 back into Roanoke. This ride has no twisties, and is a good one for riders who long for an easy cruise.

One place to be cautious about: at the intersection of VA 24 and VA 122, you'll be turning left. The traffic on VA 122 DOES NOT STOP, so use extreme caution when turning left onto it.

POINTS OF INTEREST

The National D-Day Memorial.

RESTAURANTS

While there is much to choose from in Roanoke, there is little along this short ride. One place that stands out is **A.J.'s Country Store and Restaurant**. You'll find it on VA 122 just north of VA 24 on the left. Open Monday through Saturday from 6 am to 9 pm and Sunday from 8 am to 8 pm, this little diner serves a lumberjack-sized plate of flapjacks for $1.79 and omelets with all the trimmings for $5. For lunch you get a salad, burger, or sandwich for about $5. Dinner is cheap, too—menu items start at $6, and steak cooked to order is $12, or try the house specialty, chicken livers. There's only seating for about 25 in A.J.'s, so arrive early on weekend nights.

DETAILED DIRECTIONS

Mile 0—Head east on VA 24. *You'll lose the 2 extra lanes of VA 24 at mile 3.8, changing the road to a more comfortable two-lane ride.*

Mile 17.4—Turn left onto VA 122 North. **Use caution at this intersection: the traffic on VA 122 does not stop!** *A.J.'s Country Store and Restaurant is on the left at mile 17.7.*

Mile 25.6—Turn left onto Tiger Trail (signs direct you to the Elementary School and Memorial).

Mile 25.7—Turn right into the National D-Day Memorial. *You'll ride the long driveway to the guard shack at mile 26.2 where you'll pay your $10. The motorcycle parking is at mile 26.7, on the left after you circle the Memorial. You'll leave the Memorial along the same long driveway.*

Mile 27.4—Turn left from the Memorial Driveway onto Tiger Trail.

Mile 27.5—Turn right onto VA 122 and then take an immediate right onto the ramp to US 221/460 West. *There's a gas tank farm on the left side of the road at mile 39.5, so watch for gas tankers pulling out onto the road.*
You'll ride between Coyne and Porter Mountains at mile 43.5. At mile 46, you'll begin to see some of the businesses of Roanoke.

Mile 52—The ride ends where US 221/460 meets I-581 in Roanoke. *Williamson Rd., at the intersection just one block before the end of this ride, is a good way to get to downtown Roanoke (turn left onto Williamson Rd.), or turn right to get to a motorcycle shop, the airport, and a few popular restaurants.*

Invading Normandy

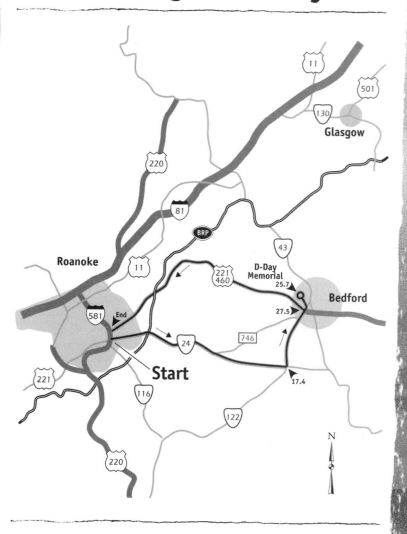

Roanoke

Glasgow

Bedford

D-Day Memorial

Start

End

BRP

25.7
27.5
17.4

Legend

Interstate Highway

US Highway

State Highway

County Road

5 ▶ Milepost

━━ Route

Other Road

═══ Blue Ridge Parkway

Covered Bridge Run

I f the beautiful scenery and excellent road conditions of this adventure are not enough to satisfy your wanderlust, maybe two covered bridges will do the trick. Need more reasons to try this route? How about the Eastern Continental Divide, great food, abundant fuel, and close proximity to downtown Roanoke?

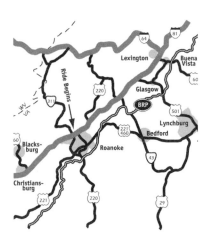

GAS

Gas is available at miles 1.2, 7.9, 10.4, 16.1, 16.9, 20.3, and 20.6, and near the end of the ride on US 460 south (just a couple of miles south).

GETTING TO THE START

This ride starts just southwest of Roanoke on VA 311 off I-81 at exit 140. Regardless of which way you're travelling on I-81, turn left onto VA 311 North at the bottom of the exit ramp. Zero your trip meter as you turn left. The mileage for this ride begins under I-81.

OVERVIEW

You'll be amazed how fast you'll leave the bustling city life of Roanoke behind once you turn onto VA 311. This well-paved stretch of road will carry you through a series of sweeping curves before reaching the Moose Lodge which, ironically, marks the eastern edge of the Havens State Wildlife Management Area. For the record, moose are not native to the area, but as you climb the twisty section of VA 311 up Catawba Mountain, do watch for deer and other potentially trip-ending wildlife. Mowing down a deer or bear would surely be bad for you and might even scratch the animal.

As you near the top of Catawba Mountain, the road composition changes from freshly paved asphalt to some older, cracked asphalt. The road is still a pleasure to ride, giving you little to worry about other than observing the scenery on the left side of your bike. Near where the road reaches the crest of Catawba Mountain, the Appalachian Trail crosses the road. Wave at the hikers trekking from Georgia to Maine, then descend toward the town of Catawba and enjoy the scenic views off to your right. Soon the town of Catawba welcomes you with straight roads and a couple of interesting sights.

In Catawba you'll see signs indicating the location of the Catawba Hospital. This Public Mental Health Facility was built on the grounds of what was originally the Roanoke Red Sulphur Springs Resort. The resort opened in 1858 to accommodate residents of Roanoke who wanted to escape city life for the healthy air and water of Catawba. At the time, many patients suffering from consumption (later known as tuberculosis) came to be treated at the resort. In 1908, the resort was sold to the State of Virginia and it became a tuberculosis sanitarium. By the mid 1920s, TB was easily treated; by 1940 the disease was all but wiped out. Shortly thereafter, the sanitarium began serving the mental health community. Not just a storage place for the mentally ill, this modern facility helps to liberate its patients from the grip of illness and become more independent. While some might point and flippantly refer to the hospital as a "nut house," most motorcyclists know or have heard of a fellow rider who has suffered a brain injury and could benefit from the treatment available in Catawba.

On the far side of town after a sharp left turn, you'll see a home place on the left about 150 yards from the road, surrounded by mountains and green pastures. That home place is exactly that—the Homeplace Restaurant. The paved driveway will deliver you to some of the finest home cooked meals you can consume without your grandma around. Serving dinner only Thursday through Sunday, it offers hospitality that will remind you of home, regardless of how far

TOTAL DISTANCE
51.6 miles

TIME FRAME
1½ hours from start to finish. Add an hour to eat and a few minutes to explore the Sinking Creek and Links Farm covered bridges.

away from home you actually are. Continuing north on VA 311, you'll enter the Jefferson National Forest and ride a few fun turns on the back of Broad Run Mountain on your way to the town of New Castle. The town of New Castle is a sleepy community with several Victorian houses restored to their original condition and adorned with bright colored paint. These houses make for interesting scenery through the relatively straight ride through town.

For fine homecooked meals, be sure to stop at the Homeplace Restaurant.

The old Sinking Creek Covered Bridge was built in 1916.

If you need to eat, you'd better stop at the Bread Basket. The Bread Basket is on the right side of the road about a block before you have to turn left onto VA 42 to continue this route. It's open seven days a week and offers three meals every day except Sunday, when they don't serve breakfast because they don't open until 11 am. If you need fuel, better top off in New Castle; there isn't any available for the rest of this ride.

Making the turn onto VA 42 from VA 311, you'll immediately climb past more Victorian homes and up to the gap between Johns Creek Mountain and Sinking Creek Mountain. On the left side of the road a poorly maintained overlook offers good views of the valley below. Past the overlook the road winds along Meadow Falls Creek and through the gap. You might think that after all that steep climbing the road would descend, but it doesn't. Apparently the phrase "what goes up must come down" doesn't apply here. The road simply levels out and takes you through the sweeping curves, rolling hills, and cattle ranches of the Sinking Creek Valley. With asphalt in excellent condition, the urge to crack open the throttle might tempt you to thunder through this valley. Don't get going too fast, you might have to stop to avoid a loose cow or a tired hiker. Tired hiker? Oh yeah, the Appalachian Trail crosses in this valley.

You'll see the sign on a hillcrest on the left side of the road marking the Eastern Continental Divide. If you're not familiar with this divide, consider this: the rain that falls on one side of it rolls into the Gulf of Mexico, and what falls on the other side flows into the Atlantic Ocean.

You'll leave VA 42 by turning right onto Clover Hollow Rd. (CR 601). Clover Hollow Rd. was recently paved and follows Sinking Creek about a half-mile away from VA 42 before reaching the Sinking Creek Covered Bridge. Just before crossing the new bridge over Sinking Creek, you'll spot the 70-ft. covered bridge built in 1916. Bridges were covered to minimize the wear and tear wrought on early bridges whose driving surfaces were exposed to weather. There's a small park (picnic tables included) next to the bridge, and a brick walkway leading to the bridge. The walkway was paved with bricks bearing the names of covered bridge lovers from all over. You can add you name by ordering one from the Newport Village Council for $25. Proceeds from brick sales go toward the upkeep of the bridge and park. There are order forms for bricks, a register for you to record your visit, and some history of the bridge on display inside the bridge itself. And while the bridge is big enough to accommodate a motorcycle, no motorized vehicles are allowed to cross it. This and the Links Farm Covered Bridge are both "modified Howe truss"-style bridges that have iron uprights in their construction to make them sturdier than their all-wooden timber brethren.

Heading toward Links Farm Covered Bridge, you'll turn left onto Zells Mill Rd. (CR 604) and enjoy a few more minutes of riding next to Sinking Creek before Zells Mill Rd. ends, where you'll turn left onto Mountain Lake Rd. (RC 700). If you were to turn right you'd enter Mountain Lake Resort, and a short ride would take you to Mountain Lake, which was featured in the movie Dirty Dancing. There's no dancing on this ride, so turn left and cross Sinking Creek. You'll see the 55-ft. Links Farm Covered Bridge on the right side of the road as you cross the new bridge. Unlike the Sinking Creek Covered Bridge, the Links Farm Bridge is privately owned and maintained. Fortunately, the property owner is realistic about the motoring public's desire to get a closer look. To help maintain future access, be respectful to the property owner by staying close to the bridge, keeping noise to a minimum, and leaving the place in better condition than when you arrived.

The ride ends at the intersection of Mountain Lake Rd. (CR 700) and US 460. Turn left onto this interstate-like, four-lane divided super-slab to reach a gas station in less than a mile and I-81 in about 18 miles, or turn right to follow the New River into West Virginia.

If you want to see more covered bridges, there are two on the *Mabry Mill* ride that begins on p. 114.

RIDE ALTERNATIVES

If you care nothing about the covered bridges at the end of this ride, continue straight on VA 42 into the town of Newport, where you can end the route at the intersection of VA 42 and US 460. In doing so, you'll save only five minutes of riding time, and you'll miss some of the best scenery in the area.

ROAD CONDITIONS

Riding over Catawba Mountain and between Sinking Creek Mountain and Johns Creek Mountain, this route is dominated by gently sweeping curves on well-paved roads. There's also a couple of tight twisties to grab your attention. You'll find only a couple of cracks in the asphalt, and the really tight turns have signage to warn you of their approach. Most of the time county roads are in worse shape than their state-maintained brethren, but not here. The county roads at the end of this ride are freshly paved but have few, if any, paint markings.

POINTS OF INTEREST

Catawba Mountain, Eastern Continental Divide, Sinking Creek Covered Bridge, Links Farm Covered Bridge.

RESTAURANTS

There are two dining establishments along this route. The first you'll come to is the **Homeplace Restaurant** (540-384-7252), open Thursday through Saturday, 4 pm to 8 pm, and Sunday 11 am to 6 pm. As the name suggests, the Homeplace Restaurant is in an old farmhouse, surrounded by pasture land in the middle of the Catawba Valley. The name also accurately indicates the type of food served here. You'll get huge portions of homemade food just like Mamma used to make, with plenty of veggies and meats to fill your stomach. You can expect to spend about $9 for dinner.

If you don't happen to be taking this ride during the short hours the Homeplace Restaurant is open, you might want to stop at the **Bread Basket Restaurant** in New Castle. This small-town diner is complete with colorful locals and moves with the pulse of the town. If you want to know what's going on in New Castle, look no further than the Bread Basket. In addition to the town gossip, you'll also find breakfast, lunch, and dinner. The Bread Basket is open from 6 am to 8:30 pm, Monday through Thursday, on Friday and Saturday 6 am to 9 pm, and Sunday from noon to 8 pm. A breakfast of two eggs, a waffle, and coffee will set you back just about $4, as will a sandwich and chips for lunch. Dinner is cheap, too—under $5 for only one or two items per meal (there is no dinner menu; if you don't like what they serve for dinner on a particular day, check back the next day).

DETAILED DIRECTIONS

Mile 0—Take exit 40 from I-81 and turn left onto VA 311. This adventure's mileage begins under the I-81 bridge.

Mile 1.2—Turn left to remain on VA 311 (it's well marked). *You'll start a curvy ride up Catawba Mountain at mile 4.3. Keep an eye peeled for hikers crossing the road at the intersection with the Appalachian Trail at mile 6. You'll find the Homeplace Restaurant on the far side of the town of Catawba at mile 8. At mile 20.4, the Bread Basket Restaurant will be on your right in the town of New Castle.*

Mile 20.6—Turn left onto VA 42. *You'll find a poorly paved overlook on the left side of the road at mile 22.3 offering views of the town of New Castle. The Eastern Continental Divide is marked on the left side of the road at mile 28.7.*

Mile 36.4—Fork to the right to remain on VA 42 (this is well marked). *Watch for a sharp right turn at mile 39.4.*

Mile 49.1—Turn right onto Clover Hollow Rd. (CR 601). *The Sinking Creek Covered Bridge and park will be on the right at mile 49.7.*

Mile 49.9—Turn left onto Zells Mill Rd. (CR 604).

Mile 51.3—Turn left onto Mountain Lake Rd. (CR 700). *On the right at mile 51.4, you'll see the Links Farm Covered Bridge.*

Mile 51.6—This adventure ends at the intersection of Mountain Lake Rd. and US 460. Turn left onto this 4-lane, hilly slab of highway to get back to I-81 in just over 18 miles. Turn right onto US 460 to follow the New River into West Virginia about 22 miles away.

Covered Bridge Run

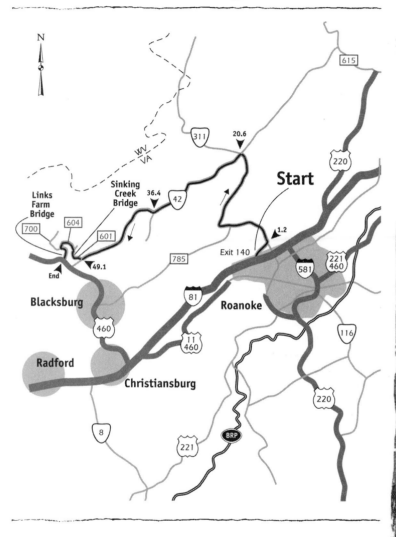

N

615

311   20.6

220

Start

WV
VA

Sinking
Creek
Bridge   36.4   42

Links
Farm
Bridge

700   604

601

785   Exit 140   1.2

49.1   221
460

End   581

Blacksburg   Roanoke

460

81

116

11
460

Radford

Christiansburg

8

220

221   BRP

---

75   Interstate Highway   640   State Highway   ▬▬▬ Route

27   US Highway   606   County Road   ─── Other Road

5 ▶ Milepost   ════ Blue Ridge Parkway

Peaking at Dinosaurs and the Natural Bridge

The name of this adventure is not a misprint; it's called Peaking at Dinosaurs and the Natural Bridge because that's what you'll be doing. This ride will take you on the Blue Ridge Parkway over the Peaks of Otter, then release you from the Parkway to the town of Glasgow where you'll see full-size dinosaurs on nearly every building, and it won't end until you get a glimpse of the geologic wonder that is the Natural Bridge. The roads are wonderful, the scenery inspirational, and the towns divine. Near the start of the ride is the town of Buchanan, whose residents remind visitors of nearly forgotten hospitality with delicious food and walks on a swinging bridge traversing the James River.

GAS
Gas is available at the start and at miles 2.2, 3.7, 4.6, 14.4, 48.7, 48.8, 49, 51.4, and 56.1.

GETTING TO THE START

This ride begins at exit 162 from I-81 north of Roanoke, VA. You'll turn onto US 11 North and head toward the town of Buchanan. Don't be fooled by the fact that US 11 parallels I-81 through western Virginia; this ride starts on US 11 at exit 162. Reset your trip meter as you turn north onto US 11.

RIDE OVERVIEW

After turning off I-81, you'll be traveling on Lee Hwy., also known as US 11. Before I-81 was built, Lee Hwy. served the area as the direct route between large cities. Today I-81 has taken much of the traffic, and some of the older hotels and attractions abandoned the older road for the more lucrative exit ramps of the newer one. There is still much to see on Lee Hwy., though. The first two sights of importance are the James River and Purgatory Mountain, which you'll see on the left before reaching the town of Buchanan.

Buchanan has restaurants, a swinging pedestrian bridge (it's the bridge that swings, you don't have to be a swinger to enjoy crossing it), a rock quarry, a couple of gas stations, and finally, the scenic byway of VA 43, which cuts through the center of town. Near the intersection of US 11 and VA 43 are two of the best restaurants in the area. Fanzarelli's Pizzeria Ristorante and the Sunflower Grill couldn't be more different; as a matter of fact, they are on opposite sides of the road. The Sunflower Grill is on the right before you reach VA 43 on US 11. This little café-style restaurant offers breakfast, lunch, and dinner every day except Tuesday, with large portions at small prices. Fanzarelli's Pizzeria Ristorante is on the left at the intersection of US 11 and VA 43. As the name implies, this eatery offers pizza and Italian food, served inside or on the deck near the river. The swinging pedestrian bridge to the left of the US 11 bridge was built where an old stretch of US 11 once crossed. Take a walk—about 300 ft. across—to get a good view of the river.

You'll turn right onto VA 43, a Virginia Byway. You may be surprised to see so many dumptrucks and so much stone dust on the first mile or so of this supposed scenic and wild road. It seems particularly odd when you consider the sign warning large trucks about the tight twists and turns of the road ahead. But all those trucks disappear into the rock quarry before the fun section of VA 43 winds its way up toward the Blue Ridge Parkway. Enter the Jefferson National Forest and climb the back of Cove Mountain

TOTAL DISTANCE
56.4 miles

TIME FRAME
2 hours from start to finish. Add time for eating and tourist-style combat sightseeing.

in a series of hairpin turns on smooth asphalt. Soon you'll turn north onto the Blue Ridge Parkway.

Taking in a few sweeping curves of the Parkway, head toward the Peaks of Otter. Flat Top, Sharp Top, and Harkening Hill are the three peaks that make up the Peaks of Otter. There are no otters within hundreds of miles, so the name is a bit of an anomaly. Some people say the name came from the early Scottish settlers who believed the Peaks resembled Ben Otter, a mountain in Scotland. Others theorize the mountains were named by the Cherokee Indians well before then. The Cherokee word *Ottari* translates to "high places." Because the words ottari and otter sound similar, this

Virginia's Natural Bridge has been attracting tourists for generations.

In Glasgow, dinosaurs show up most anywhere!

theory holds as much water as the Scottish one, so the choice is yours.

To reach the Peaks you'll have to hike, but if reaching the summit of just one peak will satisfy you, take the Sharp Top bus. You'll find the bus schedule in the information center. This bus will drive you to Sharp Top Mountain's panoramic views at an elevation of 3,865 ft. above sea level. There are many amenities nearby—a gas station, an information center, a camp store, a lodge, and a restaurant. Built on the shore of Abbott Lake, the restaurant and lodge are open year-round. Room rates for the lodge change with the seasons, but menu prices are the same year round—breakfast, lunch, and dinner at reasonable rates. There's even a small coffee shop to warm your bones and give jolt for the curves ahead.

Riding north away from the Peaks of Otter, enjoy several scenic overlooks and the classic lines of the Blue Ridge Parkway. You'll descend toward the James River, and after crossing it, you'll come to the Otter Creek Visitor Center. Otter Creek itself has been dammed to create a small but scenic lake. A wooden deck juts out over the lake, offering a floating perspective of the pond. Take a moment here to say goodbye to the Blue Ridge Parkway; you'll be turning off the Parkway just north of Otter Lake.

Make a right turn to exit the Parkway to get to VA 130, then turn right again to head toward the banks of the James River. Commercial traffic is rare on this section of VA 130 because trucks over 36 ft. in length are prohibited. Those trucks will leave you to enjoy the curves on your own for a few miles, but will meet back up with you where US 501 joins VA 130.

Just past the merge of VA 130 and US 501 you'll see a narrow bridge, built just a few feet above the James—it's what Appalachian Trail hikers use to cross this mighty river. Beats swimming!

Turn left at the fork in the road to remain on VA 130, cross the Maury River, and enter the town of Glasgow. Be forewarned that Glasgow has a pest problem. The townspeople have learned to live with these pesky critters, and in return the pests who tower over the town eat very little and rarely cause damage to property. Glasgow occupies only about a mile of VA 130, but that mile takes a long time to ride when you're watching for huge dinosaurs on the roadside. In case you're wondering just why dinosaurs grace Glasgow, here's what I know. A local artist created and installed them there as a kind of kitschy tourist attraction. It worked. I just had to see those dinos with my own eyes.

VA 130 straightens out for several miles before taking you through a couple more fun curves near the Natural Bridge Park at the intersection of VA 130 and US 11. This privately owned park packs a lot into a busy little intersection. The Park is home not only to the Natural Bridge but also a toy museum, a wax museum, a haunted house, and the Natural Bridge Caverns. To visit the Natural Bridge itself, enter the Welcome Center and pay just $10 at the ticket window. From the ticket window you'll be directed down a flight of stairs and out of the building. Outside, take the shuttle bus down to Cedar Creek or walk the 137 steps that follow Cascade Creek through the woods down to Cedar Creek. Once at Cedar Creek, give your ticket to the greeter at the Summerhouse Café, then follow the well-paved path around the corner for a stunning view of the Natural Bridge.

Billed as one of the seven natural wonders of the world, the Natural Bridge stands 215 ft. high, 90 ft. wide, and 40 ft. thick and is 500,000,000 years old. It was once surveyed by a young man who would later become our nation's first President, and is inscribed with the initials, "G.W." about 30 ft. up from the creek. Thomas Jefferson purchased the Natural Bridge and the surrounding 157 acres from the King of England on July 5, 1774 for the

sum of $2.40. The area near the Natural Bridge is still home to the Monacan Indians.

After satisfying your curiosity of the Natural Bridge, walk back to the Summerhouse Café . You won't find any *haute cuisine* on the menu, but if a burger and chips will fill the void in your stomach, a stop at the Summerhouse Café will do. Get back to the Welcome Center in one of two ways. The easy way is the free shuttle bus that leaves the Café every few minutes. Or take the exercise-machine-like 137 steps up the side of Cascade Creek. For information on all the park's attractions and lodging at the Natural Bridge Inn, call 800-533-1410 or check the web at www.naturalbridgeva.com.

Back on the ride, turn left from VA 130 onto US 11 South. You'll actually cross the Natural Bridge on pavement. As you cross you won't be able to take in any scenery; a tall privacy fence

The swinging pedestrian bridge in Buchanan. Luckily, you don't have to be a "swinger" to use it.

serves as blinders to prevent drivers and riders from becoming distracted by the scenery and running off the bridge. US 11 offers one or two more sweeping curves before this ride ends at the intersection of I-81 and US 11, just two miles from the Natural Bridge itself. Turn south on I-81 to head toward Roanoke, or turn north to reach Lexington.

RIDE ALTERNATIVES

To extend this ride a few miles, don't get on I-81 at the end. Instead, make a loop by turning left onto US 11 and heading back south into Buchanan.

ROAD CONDITIONS

This route has straight sections, tight twisties, sweeping curves, and all kinds of good road conditions— enough to please sportbikers, cruisers, and touring bike pilots alike. With the exception of the first mile or so which is four-lane, two-lane blacktop dominates. The roads are in pretty good shape with a few cracks in the tight twists of VA 43 and VA 130. In fact, VA 43 and VA 130 are so twisty that trucks over 36 feet are warned to avoid those stretches. The Blue Ridge Parkway is in great shape and the section covered on this ride offers dozens of sweeping curves and scenic overlooks. On weekdays, watch for heavy truck traffic on the first half-mile of VA 43 near Buchanan, where the quarry dumps gravel into dump trucks for construction in the area. Don't worry, those trucks wouldn't dare attempt to climb the steep twists and turns of VA 43 toward the Parkway; those curves are reserved for you!

POINTS OF INTEREST

The Swinging Bridge in Buchanan, the Blue Ridge Parkway, Peaks of Otter, Otter Lake, the Dinosaurs of Glasgow, the Natural Bridge (with monster museum, wax museum, toy museum, and caverns).

RESTAURANTS

Three restaurants really stand out on this ride. The first two are in Buchanan, and the third is at the Lodge in Peaks of Otter. A fourth is mentioned only because it is so convenient.

If you're hungry for a well-prepared and inexpensive meal, try the **Sunflower Grill** (540-254-1515) in Buchanan. It's a two-story storefront on the right side of the road, before you reach VA 43. The Sunflower Grill is closed on Tuesdays, but open 7 am to 8 pm other days except Sunday, when it's open from 11 am to 3 pm. Inside, omelets are just $3, and a cheeseburger is $4. Breakfast items include handmade Southern biscuits, eggs, and waffles. Lunch items include burgers, sandwiches, and salads. For dinner, expect large portions, but the price still won't exceed $10.

The **Fanzarelli's Pizzeria Ristorante** (540-254-3020) stands next to the swinging footbridge at the intersection of US 11 and VA 43. Fanzarelli's is closed on Mondays, but open for dinner Tuesday and Wednesday 4 to 9 pm and open for lunch and dinner Thursday through Sunday from 11 am to 9:30 pm (closing at 10 pm on Fridays and Saturdays). Fanzarelli's occupies a whitewashed single-story building surrounded by a white picket fence with ample outside seating on a huge wooden deck. This restaurant originally offered gourmet Italian dishes with a gourmet price. Discovering that the people living in and around Buchanan didn't want a pretentious atmosphere, the Fanzarellis changed their menu to meet the tastes of their customers. Today, simple but delicious pizzas can be custom-ordered as mild or wild as you like. Expect to spend $8 to $22 per pie.

In the **Peaks of Otter Lodge** (540-586-1081), the restaurant is open from 7 am to 8 pm. Expect to spend $3 for eggs cooked to order and coffee. For lunch you'll drop about $6 for a sandwich, and dinner gets a bit pricier, with shrimp and pasta dishes added to create the dinner menu. Dinners range from $6 to $11. The restaurant also has an impressive wine list. If you want to stay in the lodge, plan to spend $65 to $120 for a room, depending on the season. Reservations are recommended.

In the Natural Bridge Park near the end of the ride is the **Summerhouse Café**. Actually a snack bar on the bank of Cedar Creek, the menu lists what can best be described as baseball park food—classic American cuisine like hot dogs, hamburgers, and yes, the coveted nacho cheese on round corn chips served in a plastic tub. And because it's the only food available in the park, you'll pay a little extra. You'll find the Café open any time the Natural Bridge Park is open—8 am until dark.

It may take a while to get used to Glasgow's lunch crowd welcoming committee.

DETAILED DIRECTIONS

Mile 0—Take exit 162 and ride north on US 11 (Lee Hwy.) toward Buchanan. *As you ride toward Buchanan, you'll see Purgatory Mountain on the left side of the road across the James River.*

You'll enter Buchanan at mile 3.8, and find the Sunflower Grill on the right at mile 4.4, and Fanzarelli's Pizzeria Ristorante on the left at mile 4.6. Next to Fanzarelli's is the swinging pedestrian bridge which was hung where the old section of US 11 once crossed the James River.

Mile 4.6—Turn right onto VA 43. VA 43 is a Virginia Byway. *Don't worry about those large trucks in the road, they disappear into the rock quarry when you make a hard right turn at mile 5.2. You'll enjoy a few hairpin turns as you enter the Jefferson National Forest near mile 6.5.*

Mile 9.3—Turn left onto the ramp to the Blue Ridge Parkway, and then take another left at the top of the ramp onto northbound Blue Ridge Parkway toward the Peaks of Otter. *At mile 14.4 you'll be among the Peaks of Otter. To learn more about the Peaks and the surrounding area, stop in at the Information Center on the left at mile 14.4. This is also where VA 43 turns off the Parkway to the right and descends down into the town of Bedford (home of the World War II Memorial). The Park Camp Store is just south of the Parkway on VA 43. You'll see the Peaks of Otter Lodge on the right at mile 14.8. You'll cross the James River at mile 37. After crossing the James River, you're invited to check out the Otter Creek Visitors Center (restrooms). Just past the Visitors Center is the Dam on Otter Creek that creates Otter Lake.*

Mile 39—Turn right off the Blue Ridge Parkway, then right again onto VA 130 North. *Shortly after turning, you'll see a sign that reads, "Trucks Over 36 ft. Prohibited." At mile 40.8 there's a good view of the James River, and at mile 42.7 there's the interesting sight of the Appalachian Trail Bridge over the James.*

Mile 48.2—Turn left at the fork in the road to remain on VA 130. *You'll begin to see dinosaurs towering over the town of Glasgow at mile 48.7 and continuing until you leave town about a mile later.*

Mile 54.5—Turn left onto US 11. *This intersection is where you'll find the Natural Bridge Park, Hotel, Wax Museum, Monster Museum, Haunted House, and Toy Museum. Down the road (right on US 11) is the Natural Bridge Cavern. You'll actually cross the Natural Bridge at mile 54.6 (marked by a high wooden privacy fence on the side of the road).*

Mile 56.4—The ride ends at the intersection of US 11 and I-81. *Turn south on I-81 to reach Roanoke, or head north toward I-64 and Skyline Drive.*

Peaking at Dinosaurs...

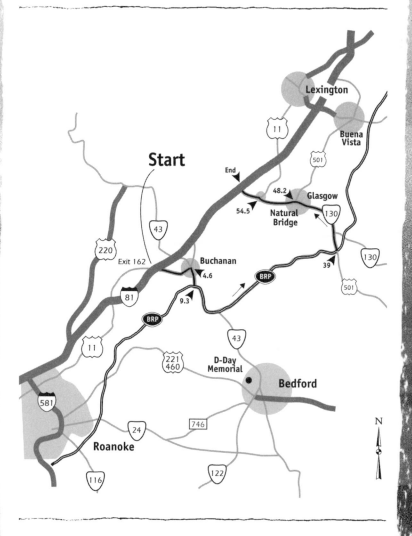

Start

End

Lexington

Buena Vista

11

501

48.2

Glasgow

54.5

Natural Bridge

130

43

220

Exit 162

Buchanan

4.6

39

130

81

9.3

BRP

501

BRP

11

43

221
460

D-Day Memorial

Bedford

581

24

746

N

Roanoke

116

122

	Interstate Highway	640	State Highway	▬▬▬ Route
27 US Highway		606 County Road	5▶ Milepost	═══ Blue Ridge Parkway
				─── Other Road

Patriot's Run

On this ride, you'll cruise through the town of Eagle Rock, pass several unique restaurants that add a bit of spice to the great American melting pot, and see some pre-Civil War iron smelters. The ride won't end until you've passed an American Flag mounted on a bluff high above the James River. This quick run makes optimum use of sweetly-paved ribbons of asphalt through the Jefferson National Forest, leading to Clifton Forge and I-64.

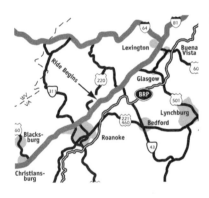

GETTING TO THE START

This ride starts on Lee Hwy. (US 11) near Buchanan. To get there, take I-81 to exit 162, and turn onto north US 11. Reset your trip meter as you turn north onto US 11.

RIDE OVERVIEW

Most motorcyclists hate the interstate, and you're probably in the large group of super-slab haters. This ride will take you from I-81 to I-64, and is particularly good if your travel plans happen to include riding north on I-81 to I-64 West, because this run cuts the corner between these two interstates.

After leaving I-81, you'll ride for about a mile on a four-lane section of US 11. If you have ever ridden for any amount of time on I-81, you've probably noticed US 11 seems to parallel the interstate. In fact it does, and it was the closest thing to an interstate the region had until I-81 was paved. Several interstates have smaller routes following them. For example, US 41 parallels I-75—for the same reason US 11 parallels I-81.

US 11 follows the James River downstream in the shadow of Purgatory Mountain into the town of Buchanan. Buchanan is small-town America personified, complete with flags hanging from the telephone poles and friendly folks greeting each other on its neat sidewalks. You'll find a couple of gas stations and two restaurants here. Both restaurants are near the intersection of US 11 and VA 43 South, which leads to the Peaks of Otter (check out the *Peaking at Dinosaurs and*

GAS
Gas is available at the start and at miles 2.2, 3.7, 4.6, 17, 23.5, 31.9, and 33.7. It's also plentiful at the ride's end in Clifton Forge.

the Natural Bridge ride on p. 98). At this intersection a pedestrian bridge swings over the James River where US 11 once crossed on stone pillars. Fanzarelli's Pizzeria Ristorante on the left in a white, single-story building is home to the best pizza pies for about a thousand miles in any direction. Across the street from Fanzarelli's is the Sunflower Grill, offering tasty meals for low prices.

After crossing the James, you'll turn left onto VA 43 North. VA 43 is a Virginia Byway, meaning it has been recognized by the State of Virginia as having scenic and historic value. Ride along the bank of the James River upstream and under I-81. After passing under I-81, you'll see a narrow rock outcropping from the mountain on the right side of the road. There is one other rock formation like this farther along in this run. To see similarly odd geological features, take the *Seneca Rocks!* ride, which starts on p. 180.

Entering the town of Eagle Rock on VA 43, you'll have to negotiate a sharp right turn to ride down Main St. On the left side of Main St. is Ma &

TOTAL DISTANCE
34 miles

TIME FRAME
1 hour from start to finish. Add time to eat in one of the three great restaurants mentioned in this chapter.

Pa's Diner, where Ma cooks up breakfast, lunch, and dinner, and Pa charges a surprisingly low price for her home cooking. Beyond the diner are three tall stone structures on the left side of the road. These unusual pillars of rock stand nearly 20 ft. tall and are nearly obscured by trees growing nearby. One might assume they have something to do with the rail yard below. In fact, these three stone towers were used to smelt iron before and during the Civil War. Today, the openings where the fires once burned are sealed with stone, but they are still interesting to see.

Buchanan is a nice little town where you can take a break and get a bite to eat.

Choose a route that includes a Virginia Byway, and you're guaranteed a scenic ride.

VA 43 ends at US 220 where this run makes a right turn and begins to follow the banks of the James River upstream again. Looking at the whitewater rapids on this part of the James, it's difficult to imagine that in the Chesapeake Bay, where the James River empties, this river is wide enough to support seagoing vessels. In fact, Jamestown, one of the first European settlements in North America, was built on the shores of the James, hundreds of miles from where you are now. On this narrow section, someone has scaled a sharp rock spine on the far side of the river, installed a flagpole, and hoisted the Stars and Stripes. From the tip of the outcropping, the flag is an impressive contrast to the natural beauty around it, a reminder that so much of this country is full of rich, natural beauty.

When crossing the next bridge over the river, keep an eye peeled for the open joints. Who would intentionally leave open joints in a bridge? The Virginia Department of Transportation would, to prevent damage to the roadway by allowing the bridge to heave under the pressures of wide seasonal temperature differences.

Cross these open joints by riding over them at as close to a 90-degree angle as traffic will allow. If you happen to cross the joints at a shallow angle, one or both of your tires might enter the joint and cause a catastrophic end to this scenic ride.

This route passes through the town of Iron Gate on the way to its end at Clifton Forge and I-64. Once reaching I-64, you can continue on US 220 by heading west on I-64 for a couple of exits and following US 220 North into the town of Warm Springs. Here you can join in the *Great Big Thing Tour* where it cuts through Warm Springs.

RIDE ALTERNATIVES

There are no alternatives to this ride, but it ends on US 220 in Clifton Forge, where you can continue on US 220 North to reach the town of Warm Springs and the *Great Big Thing Tour* (p. 28) already in progress.

ROAD CONDITIONS

The roads of this run are all two-lane with the exception of the first mile of US 11 toward Buchanan. After that, expect some sweeping curves along the James River. As a matter of fact, you'll be negotiating sweeping curves throughout the ride, interspersed with a couple of tight twists. The asphalt is generally in good condition, but patchy. One hazard sticks out like a sore thumb: the exposed joints on the US 220 bridge over the James River near the end of the ride. The Virginia Department of Transportation has posted a sign illustrating a motorcycle traversing the joints correctly. Cross as the sign shows (as close to 90 degrees as you can), and you should have no problems.

POINTS OF INTEREST

Swinging Bridge of Buchanan, rock outcroppings, stone Civil War-era iron smelters in Eagle Rock, American Flag atop the rock, James River.

RESTAURANTS

Buchanan is home to two great restaurants, and a third great dining establishment makes its home in Eagle Rock. In Buchanan, the Sunflower Grill is open for breakfast, lunch, and dinner, while Fanzarelli's Pizzeria Ristorante is open just for lunch and dinner. In Eagle Rock, Ma & Pa's Diner serves up breakfast, lunch, and dinner.

In Buchanan, both restaurants are in the heart of town at the intersection of US 11 and VA 43 South. The **Sunflower Grill** (540-254-1515) is closed on Tuesdays, but is open from 7 am to 8 pm on the other days of the week, except for Sunday when it is open from 11 am to 3 pm. Inside, omelets are just $3, and a cheeseburger for lunch is just $4. Breakfast items include handmade Southern biscuits, eggs, and waffles. Lunch items at the Sunflower Grill include burgers, sandwiches, and salads. For dinner, expect large portions, but the price still won't exceed $10.

Fanzarelli's Pizzeria Ristorante (540-254-3070) stands next to the swinging footbridge at the intersection of US 11 and VA 43. Closed on Mondays, Fanzarelli's is open for dinner Tuesdays and Wednesdays 4 to 9:30 pm and open for lunch and dinner Thursday through Sunday from 11 am to 9:30 pm (until 10 pm on Friday and Saturday). Fanzarelli's is in a whitewashed single-story building surrounded by a white picket fence and has ample outside seating on a huge wooden deck. Simple but delicious pizzas can be custom-ordered as mild or wild as you like. Expect to spend $8 to $22 per pie.

In Eagle Rock you're invited to **Ma & Pa's Diner** (540-884-3240). This classic roadhouse diner is open Tuesday through Saturday 6 am to 8 pm and Sundays 7 am to 3 pm but is closed on Mondays. If you want Ma's delicious biscuits and gravy, get there early on Saturday—that's the only day of the week she makes gravy, and it's a popular dish. The breakfast menu includes items that range from a Western omelet served with grits and potatoes for $6 to a single biscuit with an egg for $1.50. Lunch isn't expensive, either, with their priciest burger (the bacon cheeseburger cooked to order) for just $3. You'll get a sandwich, fries, and a soft drink all for less than $6. Dinner gets a bit more costly with Ma cooking up steak for $14 and chicken dishes for less than $10.

DETAILED DIRECTIONS

Mile 0—Take exit 162 and ride north on US 11 (Lee Hwy.) toward Buchanan. *You'll see Purgatory Mountain on the left side of the road across the James River. You'll enter Buchanan at mile 3.8 and find the Sunflower Grill on the right at mile 4.4 and Fanzarelli's Pizzeria Ristorante on the left at mile 4.6.*

Next to Fanzarelli's is the swinging pedestrian bridge, hung where the old section of US 11 once crossed the James River. Use US 11 to cross the James River at mile 4.7.

Mile 4.8—Turn left onto VA 43 North. *You'll ride next to the James River back toward I-81 and ride under the interstate at mile 6.5. Around mile 11 keep your eye peeled for a chunk of rock jutting out from the mountainside. At mile 13.9 CR 688 turns off to the left and continues to follow the James River upstream. Keep going straight to enjoy the better asphalt offered by VA 43. Enter the town of Eagle Rock at mile 19, and follow VA 43 as it makes a sharp right turn at mile 19.2 through the center of town. Ma & Pa's Diner is on the left at mile 19.4, and the Civil War-era stone smelters tower over the left side of the road at mile 19.7.*

Mile 21.5—VA 43 North ends into US 220; turn right. *You'll see some rapids on the James River at mile 30.1. At mile 31.4 the town of Iron Gate swings open for you. You'll ride several more miles before reaching its downtown section. There's an overlook at mile 32.8 that offers views of the James River and the rock on which the American Flag is displayed. Get a closer look at the rock with the flag atop at mile 33.1 as you cross over the James River; there's a sign warning you of "exposed joints on bridge."*

Mile 33.5—Fork to the right to remain on US 220 North.

Mile 34—The ride ends at the intersection of US 220 and I-64 in Clifton Forge, VA. *You can head west on I-64 to see the humpback covered bridge in Covington or keep heading north on US 220 into Warm Springs to intersect the* Great Big Thing Tour (p. 28). *Go east on I-64 to return*

Patriot's Run

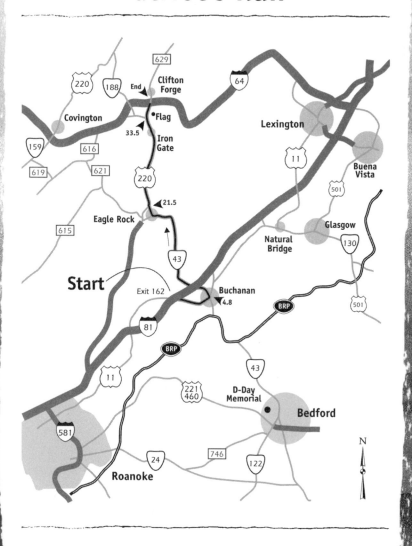

Clifton Forge · End · Flag · 33.5 · Iron Gate · 629 · 220 · 188 · Covington · 159 · 616 · 619 · 621 · 220 · 21.5 · Eagle Rock · 615 · 43 · Start · Exit 162 · 81 · 11 · BRP · BRP · Buchanan · 4.8 · 221 460 · D-Day Memorial · 43 · Bedford · 581 · 24 · 746 · 122 · Roanoke · 64 · Lexington · 11 · Buena Vista · 501 · Glasgow · 130 · Natural Bridge · 501 · N

75 Interstate Highway	640 State Highway	Route	
27 US Highway	606 County Road	Other Road	
	5 Milepost	Blue Ridge Parkway	

Southwest Virginia

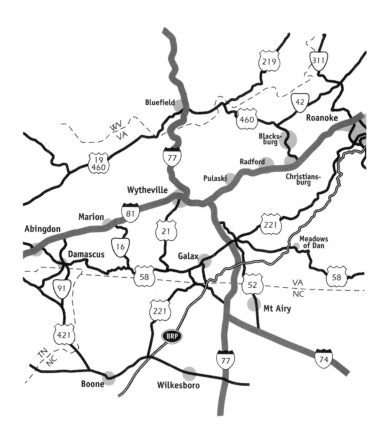

From vintage gristmills to rail trails, southwest Virginia offers a full measure of fascinating history, all wrapped up in classic Southern mountain style, with great music, good food, and more.

Area Covered

Mabry Mill

*T*his adventure is easy to find, fun to ride, and offers the most photographed scenery on the Blue Ridge Parkway. You and your bike will be transported back in time as you near Mabry Mill. At the Mill, you can tour a homestead from the 1860s, and stop for breakfast, lunch, or coffee. Once you turn off the Blue Ridge Parkway, the road becomes twistier and the scenery more diverse. You'll ride through Tuggle's Gap, over Lover's Leap, and into Meadows of Dan, home to the motorcycle-only campground known as Willville.

GAS

Gas is available at the start and at miles 1.6, 7.6, 37.5, 43.8, 53.6, and mile 61.6 at the ride's end.

GETTING TO THE START

This ride starts in Virginia on I-77 at exit 8 (VA 148). Upon reaching the bottom of the exit ramp, turn north on VA 148 toward US 52. Reset your trip meter at the bottom of the ramp.

RIDE OVERVIEW

Leaving the ultra-efficient (and ultra-boring) I-77 behind, VA 148 and US 52 work together to get you back to the motorcycle roads you long for. In under two miles, these two will deliver you onto the welcoming pavement of the Blue Ridge Parkway.

Once on the Parkway, you'll turn north and begin to see why it's one of the most famous motorcycle destinations in the world. The asphalt is in excellent condition, there's no commercial vehicle traffic, and the mountainous scenery is awe-inspiring. On the side of the Parkway, there are several interesting pullouts and overlooks, but a few really stand out. The first of these interesting sights is the Puckett Cabin, just over 11 miles into this run. You'll find the Puckett Cabin on the left as you're northbound on the Parkway. Built in the late 1800s, it's too fragile to go inside, but you can peer through the windows. This residence, surrounded by a fence row, was once the home of Orlena Hawks Puckett, who worked her entire life as a midwife. She attended her last delivery at the tender age of 102. Ironically, while Mrs. Puckett performed her midwife duties at over a thousand births, none of Mrs. Puckett's own children survived infancy. Don't linger too long, there are more sights up the road.

One mile north of the Puckett Cabin is Groundhog Mountain Overlook. You'll find this lookout on the right side of the road with a large paved parking area, including restrooms. The lookout tower is well worth the 50-yd. walk from the parking area. Unlike the locked Puckett Cabin, this overlook is unlocked, but like the Puckett Cabin, it is a primitive log structure. Climb a few steps to the second floor to get a bird's-eye view of the surrounding area. Examples of different kinds of fencing used by the settlers of the area encircle the lookout tower. To learn all about the differences and advantages of picket, snake rail, buck rail, and post-and-rail fencing, spend a few minutes reading the informative signs.

Back on the Parkway, ride north toward the town of Meadows of Dan. Along the way, you'll pass the Mayberry Trading Post, open daily from 9 to 5, offering country crafts and refreshments, but no fuel. You'll cross Round Meadow Creek and may

TOTAL DISTANCE
65.7 miles

TIME FRAME
2 hours from start to finish. Include some time to explore Mabry Mill or dine in one of the many restaurants vying for your travel dollar.

want to take the 20-minute loop hike that begins from the parking area on the left side of the road just after crossing the creek.

You'll ride over US 58 past Meadows of Dan. Don't worry—you'll be back there in a little while. This route continues north on the Parkway and back in time to 1910. You might notice the reduced speed limit before you notice the signs for Mabry Mill. On the right side of the road is the Mabry Mill Visitor Center, gift shop, restrooms, and of course, the mill itself. The restaurant is open from 7:30 am to 6 pm, with reasonable prices for breakfast and lunch items. The lunch special is usually barbecue. The gift shop next

Mabry Mill is one of the most photographed sights on the Blue Ridge Parkway.

Hay harvest on Groundhog Mountain.

door offers t-shirts, postcards, and nearly any other trinket you might need to prove that you visited Mabry Mill—oh yeah, the mill! Leave the restaurant/gift shop/information center and walk toward the mill. Built in 1910 by Ed Mabry, it was used to mill corn and lumber. After building it, Mr. Mabry realized he didn't have sufficient water flow to turn the millstone fast enough to grind the corn or saw the lumber, so he built two additional flumes. By capturing three streams, he had plenty of power. Today, the flumes still stand as a testament to Mr. Mabry's perseverance in bringing a mill to this remote area. Waterpower was used until the 1930s, when it was replaced by a gasoline engine. The National Park Service has beautifully and painstakingly preserved this mill, and it still grinds corn on Fridays, Saturdays, and Sundays.

The park also includes a blacksmith shop, a cabin, and even a moonshine still. Park employees and volunteers wear period clothing and do necessary work as it would have been done in the late 1800s. A cabin, built in 1860, stands in the place of the Mabry's home, which was destroyed by fire. It is open for visitors, and its furnishings include a small loom on which a blanket is being made. Outside, along the short path that leads you from the mill to the cabin and past the blacksmith shop, you might find a young man recaning a chair or performing some other task of the period. The moonshine still is not open for tours (or samples!), but you can see its many pots and wild twists of tubing. Moonshine had an undeniable influence on the area's economy during the 1890s. Before turning back northbound on the Parkway, take a photo of the Mabry Mill from the parking area's exit driveway (it's one of the vantage points for a picture).

Rolling north, take in some great sights as you enjoy the smooth and sweeping curves of this section of the Parkway. Two of these great sights are the Rocky Nob and Rock Castle Gorge overlooks. Both offer spectacular views from the ridge crest before the road begins to descend sharply toward Tuggles Gap.

As you near Tuggles Gap, you'll come to an opening in the trees and turn left off the Parkway, then turn left again onto VA 8. Tuggles Gap is little more than a restaurant/motel/gas station combination located within a geographic gap between two mountains. But don't let the small size of Tuggles Gap Restaurant fool you—the food offered inside is delicious, and the choices are wide ranging. It's open from 7 am to 9 pm daily (until 10 pm on weekends), serving up breakfast, lunch, and dinner. Expect to spend just $3 for breakfast (coffee and a biscuit) and up to $12 for a steak dinner. The menu can best be described as "down-home Southwestern." For example, at lunch the menu lists handmade burgers, as well as burritos with homemade salsa. Beer and wine are on the list, too. Most of the wine is from a local vineyard, and you can sample one of many micro-brew beers (they also have the national brands). If you're on a diet, skip to the beginning of the next paragraph, because you won't want to hear about Tuggles Gap pie. This delectable, devilishly indulgent creation is sure to send you into dessert nirvana, layering cream cheese, chocolate, whipped cream, walnuts, and other "secret ingredients" in a piecrust to create the best dessert you'll ever add to your gut! Well, you're on vacation—enjoy. If you have too much pie, beer, wine, or a combination of them all, stay in the cheap Tuggles Gap Motel right next door, which has simple rooms for just $36 a night. Give them a ring at 540-745-3402. Just don't expect room service or a mint on your pillow.

Leaving Tuggles Gap, VA 8 gets twisty and steep—so much so that it warns truckers of the steep winding road ahead. Often, what truckers hate is what motorcyclists love. VA 8 is well marked and free of debris, with asphalt in excellent condition. As the elevation changes (you'll be descending here) you'll feel your ears pop. The scenery is so pretty, your eyes might pop, too!

The twisties run out into the Smith River Valley, making the road a scenic but more tame stretch of asphalt. Enjoy a few sweeping curves as you ride past an apple orchard and through small farming communities.

The Blue Ridge Parkway rolls past the rustic Puckett Cabin, home of legendary midwife Olena Puckett.

Willville Motorcycle Campground makes a good home base while motorcycling in the area.

You'll see signs directing you to the Bob White and the Jacks Creek Covered Bridges. The Jacks Creek Bridge is to the right down CR 615. This 48-ft. covered bridge was built in 1914 and is visible from VA 8. To see the 80-ft. Bob White Bridge, built in 1921, you'll have to turn left onto CR 618 and ride 1.5 miles down to CR 869 where you'll turn right and travel another tenth of a mile. To see more covered bridges, take the *Covered Bridge Run* that begins on p. 92.

VA 8 will take you to US 58 where you'll turn right to head toward Meadows of Dan. Hills Store is at this intersection. After refueling your motorcycle's tank, refuel yourself with a $1 biscuit or a $3 sandwich. Take it to go so you can dine on Lover's Leap, just up the road a piece.

Just as VA 8 descended in a wild set of twists and turns, US 58 climbs with the same enthusiasm. After reaching nearly the top of Spoon Mountain, you'll come to Lover's Leap pullout on the right side of the road. This well-marked but poorly maintained overlook gives a narrow view into the Smith River Valley and of the mountains to the north. A quick check of the area shows that lovers

don't actually leap here, but they do express their love with spray paint. The beauty of the scenery subdues any distraction created by the paint.

After Lover's Leap, US 58 takes you through a series of twists and turns before you arrive at the top of Naked Ridge. You'll know you're on Naked Ridge when you don't see trees covering the top of the mountain (it's *naked*). Just past the summit, US 58 takes you past a Texaco station that still has the old-style glass cylinder fuel pump. The store is closed and the pump ran dry years ago, but it's an interesting sight. You'll see Meadows of Dan just round the bend. If you keep your eyes peeled, you'll see the spot where US 58 crosses Dan Creek, which becomes the Dan River. The meadows in this section of the Blue Ridge were named for the creek that flows through them. Stated more simply, these are the Meadows of Dan. Today, Meadows of Dan is a thriving small town with several gas stations, restaurants, and accommodations. Don't miss the Poor Farmers Market and Gas Station near the center of town. Inside, you can purchase a gallon of gas, a liter of locally made wine, a sandwich, a tourist trinket, and even a rocking chair, if you can tie it to your motorcycle.

Lodging in Meadows of Dan is available for $37 a night at the Blue Ridge Motel (540-952-2244). You'll find the motel on US 58 just north of the Blue Ridge Parkway. Also in Meadows of Dan, just half a mile north of the Blue Ridge Parkway, is the brainchild of a man named Will Beers. Will loved to ride motorcycles and loved the Blue Ridge Parkway but had a hard time finding motorcycle-friendly campgrounds close to it. In April of 2001, Will opened the Willville Motorcycle Campground. I wonder how many more visitors he would be getting if he named his campground "Beerville." Anyway, since then motorcycles have been filling the flat campsites with trailers, tents, and the sounds of purring engines. Built on 26 grassy acres, the campground charges $12 to camp solo or just $20 two-up, and that gets riders access to a comfortable bath house, restrooms, breakfast (biscuits catered from the Poor Farmers Market), and a covered picnic area that has the elusive "honor system coffee pot." Didn't pack a tent? That's okay—you can rent a tent and a sleeping pad from Will. If you find yourself in need of motorcycle parts, you'll even find motorcycle parts and accessories here. Will is a friendly man who enjoys company, so expect a warm reception, regardless of whether or not there's a chill in the air. Even if you aren't camping, stop in and spend a buck or two to help ensure that Willville will remain open for the season when you do want to stay here. Check out Willville on the web at www.willvillebikecamp.com, or by phone at 276-952-CAMP.

This adventure ends at the intersection of US 58 and the Blue Ridge Parkway. *Squirrel Gap* Loop (p. 122) begins in Meadows of Dan, the *Pipers Gap* ride (p. 123) starts a few miles south on the Blue Ridge Parkway, and *Roanoke Valley Run* (p. 78) runs nearby, cutting through Tuggle's Gap as it snakes its way back to Roanoke.

RIDE ALTERNATIVES

There are no ride alternatives, but carry this book with you, because several rides begin where this route ends in the town of Meadows of Dan, VA.

ROAD CONDITIONS

The twists and turns of this ride range from gently sweeping curves on the Blue Ridge Parkway to wildly twisty sections of VA 8 and US 58. The Blue Ridge Parkway is excellently paved and adequately banked with fresh, clean asphalt. The roads off the Parkway are twistier than the Parkway itself, and with the exception of an occasional patch of asphalt, are in good condition. No commercial traffic is allowed on the Blue Ridge Parkway, and signs warn truckers to avoid most of the other roads you'll ride on this adventure.

Expect some heavy traffic around Mabry Mill on summer weekend days; after all, it's the most photographed site on the Blue Ridge Parkway.

POINTS OF INTEREST

The Blue Ridge Parkway, Puckett Cabin, Groundhog Mountain Lookout, Mabry Mill and the Mabry Homestead (moonshine still, etc.), Lover's Leap roadside overlook, and Willville Motorcycle-Only Campground.

RESTAURANTS

You won't starve on this adventure! There are many places to dine, but a few really stand out.

At **Mabry Mill** (mile 25.3), you'll find a small restaurant open from 7:30 am to 6 pm, offering breakfast and lunch items from $3 to $10, with Southern barbecue a specialty. Tuggles Gap (mile 37.5) is home to the **Tuggles Gap Restaurant**/Gas Station/ Motel (540-745-3402). The restaurant is open from 7 am to 9 pm (10 pm on weekends) offering breakfast, lunch, and dinner with a hard-to-find Southwestern flare. The tacos are just $1.85 and burgers just $2.25. You can expect to drop between $6 and $12 for dinner, depending on whether you're in the mood for chicken strips or a grilled steak. There's beer and wine offered as well. If you have too much to drink, the motel rooms are a paltry $36 a night.

Down the hill from Tuggles Gap is **Hills Grocery** (mile 53.6). Don't let the fact that this little gem is in a gas station/grocery store fool you; it's quite a good restaurant. A homemade egg biscuit for breakfast will set you back only $1, and the lunch sandwiches are as cheap as $3.

At the end of the ride, in the town of Meadows of Dan is the **Poor Farmers Market**. It too is in a gas station/grocery store combo, but don't let that turn you off. It's a perfect place to hit if you're staying in Meadows of Dan (at the Willville Motorcycle Campground), because it opens at 6 am and closes at 10 pm. You can fuel your bike, fuel your need for souvenirs, and fuel your body with breakfast and lunch items available for $3. For added energy, ice cream is available as well.

DETAILED DIRECTIONS

Mile 0—At the bottom of the exit 8 ramp from I-77, turn north onto VA 148.

Mile 0.7—At the T intersection, turn right onto US 52.

Mile 1.6—Turn right onto the ramp to the Blue Ridge Parkway. At the top of that ramp, turn left onto the northbound lane of the Blue Ridge Parkway. *At mile 11.2 is the Puckett Cabin. The Groundhog Mountain lookout is on the right at 12.5. Restrooms there, too. The Mabry Mill and the Mabry Homestead are at mile 25.3. Expect reduced speed limits and heavy traffic in this area on weekends.*

Mile 36.7—Turn left onto the exit ramp from the Parkway to VA 8 in Tuggles Gap. At the bottom of the ramp, turn left. *At mile 37.5 is the Tuggles Gap Restaurant/Gas Station/ Motel.*

Mile 53.6—Turn right onto US 58. At the intersection, you'll find Hills Grocery (food and fuel). *You'll ride over Lover's Leap at mile 59. At mile 63.3 an old glass-topped gas pump is no longer working, but still cool to see. The Poor Farmers Market is on the left at mile 65.5 in the heart of Meadows of Dan.*

Mile 65.7—The ride ends at the intersection of US 58 and the Blue Ridge Parkway. *Continue west on US 58 to reach the Willville Motorcycle-Only Campground, or flip over a few pages and choose another adventure that starts in this small town.*

Mabry Mill

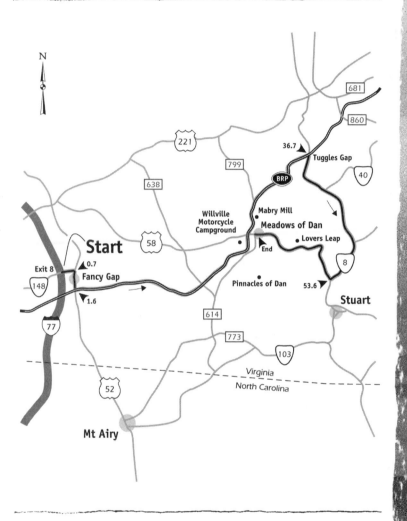

681
860
36.7
Tuggles Gap
221
799
40
BRP
638
Mabry Mill
Willville
Motorcycle
Campground
Meadows of Dan
58
Lovers Leap
Start
End
Exit 8
8
148
Fancy Gap
1.6
Pinnacles of Dan
53.6
Stuart
77
614
773
103
Virginia
North Carolina
52
Mt Airy

N

75 Interstate Highway	640 State Highway	▬ Route
27 US Highway	606 County Road	▬ Other Road
	5 ▶ Milepost	▭ Blue Ridge Parkway

Squirrel Gap Loop

This loop ride has the following posted near its beginning: "Tractor Trailers Not Recommended." Signs like that read as an invitation to motorcyclists! Get your adrenal glands ready for maximum output as this wild ride takes you through some of the least known, twistiest, and narrowest country lanes of southern Virginia. Along the way, you'll not see much other traffic, but you will see some small farms, a great coffee house, Lover's Leap, and Willville, a motorcycle-only campground.

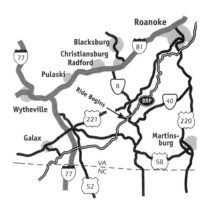

GETTING TO THE START

This ride starts and ends in Meadows of Dan, VA. To get there from I-77, take exit 8 to VA 148 North to US 52, which will lead you to the Blue Ridge Parkway. Follow the Parkway north for 22 miles to US 58. Turn left to head south on US 58 toward the center of town.

From Roanoke, follow the Blue Ridge Parkway south about 45 miles to US 58. At US 58, exit the Parkway and turn left onto US 58 toward the center of town. The beginning of this ride is the first right turn on US 58 from the Blue Ridge Parkway. Zero your trip meter as you turn onto Squirrel Gap Rd.

RIDE OVERVIEW

After getting your fill of the "uptown" section of the Meadows of Dan, turn south onto narrow and winding Squirrel Gap Rd. (CR 614). Squirrel Gap Rd. undulates away from town, paralleling the Blue Ridge Parkway for the first several miles. This section follows the crest of the Blue Ridge, making the scenery spectacular and the presence of farmsteads a little surprising. Yet at this high elevation, meadows have formed along the banks of the Dan River, creating a level area on which to farm. That's the story about how the town got its name—besides, "Meadows of Dan" is much easier to write on an envelope than "Town-built-in-the-flood plain-of-the-Dan-River-near-the-Crest-of-the-Blue-Ridge-Mountain-Range."

Just over six miles out of town, the road makes a hard left turn and begins to descend into Squirrel Gap. The road will narrow, the centerline will disappear (remember that despite the absence of centerline markings, it's a two-way road) and a warning to truckers will appear. The warning reads, "Tractor Trailers Not Recommended." As you proceed down through Squirrel Gap, you'll understand the reason for the warning. The road is so narrow and has so many cutbacks it would be impossible to navigate a big rig on the road without doing some serious trailblazing. While you and your bike will certainly enjoy the curves, watch out for a couple of patched spots in the asphalt. Just when you're getting used to the rhythm of left, right, left, right, you'll emerge from the gap into pastureland.

After leaving Squirrel Gap, you'll come to a stop sign in the tiny hamlet of Carters Mill. This ride makes a left turn onto the Ararat Hwy. (CR 773). If you were to turn right and ride just a couple of miles, you'd come to the town of Ararat (it's as small and void of amenities as Carters Mill). Turning left from Squirrel Gap Rd. on Ararat Hwy., you'll ride through farm country and past an old cemetery. The ride makes another left onto VA 103. You'll only be on VA 103 for a few hundred yards, crossing the bridge over Hookers Creek (named for the Confederate General, not the oldest profession) before making another left onto Little Dan River Rd. (CR 738). Little Dan River Rd. changes names and CR numbers about as often as you'll change gears on this section of the ride. Don't let the frequent road name and number changes confuse you; keep heading straight. While not steep and windy like the mountainous part of Squirrel Gap Rd., Little Dan River Rd. has curves galore on excellent asphalt. Watch for the sharp

TOTAL DISTANCE
47.9 miles

TIME FRAME
1 hour from start to finish. Add half an hour to explore Stuart.

left turn at mile 20 near the blink-of-an-eye town called Dobyns. From Dobyns to Stuart the road is named Dobyns Rd. (CR 631). Near Stuart, you'll see a bank (as in savings and loan) on the right side of the road. This bank is your landmark for the turn ahead. Dobyns Rd. will meet North Main St. near "downtown" Stuart. Stuart is divided into two sections—"uptown" is higher in elevation than "downtown." This ride makes a right onto North Main St. to meet Patrick Ave. The turn from North Main St. to Patrick Ave. is a very hard left (140 degrees) just a block away from Dobyns Rd. Patrick Ave. then takes you on a few fun curves as it climbs from downtown to uptown. If you care nothing about seeing the curves and hills of Patrick Ave. but love freshly roasted coffee, turn left onto North Main St. to reach the Honduras Coffee House.

Regardless of how you reach "uptown," once there you'll see the Patrick County Courthouse in the town square. You'll find the Honduras Coffee House by parking on the square, walking to North Main St., and walking to the left just a block. Once there, you're sure to enjoy the flavors of this family-run business which takes the term "family business" to the extreme. Not only are most of the company's employees from the same family, even the coffee grower in Honduras is the son-in-law of the store owner! The beans are shipped from his fields to Stuart, VA, to be

Meadows of Dan is a sleepy little town just off the Blue Ridge Parkway.

enjoyed by you. You can enjoy a bagel or a tasty dessert here, too.

The ride continues along North Main St. until you get to US 58 North, where you'll turn left. This section of US 58 was widened in the summer of 2003 and is freshly paved. It has a few sweeping curves before beginning the climb up to Naked Ridge. Just before this steep climb is the intersection of US 58 and VA 8. To reach Tuggles Gap and a couple of cool covered bridges, turn right onto VA 8 and follow it to the Blue Ridge Parkway (learn more by reading *Mabry Mill* on p. 114). If you're hungry or need fuel, stop in at Hills Store. It's open seven days a week, with the restaurant serving up good grub for just a few dollars. An egg biscuit costs only $1.50, and a sandwich will set you back $3. Once you're filled up, continue uphill on US 58 North. This is where US 58 begins to climb steeply up to Naked Ridge. Along the way, you'll come to Lover's Leap overlook on the right side of the road. The views to the north are spectacular, if you don't mind the spray paint. Apparently, lovers don't leap from this overlook. Instead they express their emotions with spray

paint. Perhaps someone should rename the overlook Lover's Canvas Overlook? Beyond Lover's Leap the road becomes wildly twisty on the way to Naked Ridge.

Naked Ridge is not a clothing-optional commune. It's a geographical feature so-named for its lack of trees. The Poor Farmer's Farm on Naked Ridge claims to have the world's best cabbage, so if cabbage is your expertise or your passion, stop in. Just past Naked Ridge, you'll gently descend toward Meadows of Dan. An old gas station on the right side of the road (from the era when such places were referred to as "service stations") still has its glass cylinder gas pump. What it lacks in fuel, it makes up for in nostalgia.

Cross the Dan River and enter the town of Meadows of Dan. The Poor Farmers Market will be on the left side of the road in the center of town, offering fuel, groceries, souvenirs, and tasty food. You'll ride past the Poor

Farmers Market and reach the Blue Ridge Parkway where the ride ends. Travel just another half a mile north on US 58 to reach the Willville Motorcycle Campground. There you'll find 26 acres of level campsites under a canopy of trees. Willville was the brainchild of Will Beers, who opened the campground in 2001 to accommodate the thousands of motorcyclists who travel the Blue Ridge Parkway each year. If camping isn't in your plans and you need some cheap accommodations, try the Blue Ridge Motel on US 58 next to the Blue Ridge Parkway. For just $37 a night, enjoy a warm shower, a comfortable bed, and a TV with five channels!

RIDE ALTERNATIVES

At mile 31.4, this ride turns right onto North Main St. to take advantage of a few fun curves and hills offered by Patrick Ave. For a more direct route to uptown Stuart, turn left onto North Main St., and you'll find the Honduras Coffee House a few blocks away. Beyond the coffee house, you'll come to the town square; turn right to hit West Blue Ridge St. Once at West Blue Ridge St., turn left to rejoin this ride.

At mile 36 of this ride, US 58 intersects VA 8. You can take VA 8 up to Tuggle's Gap and then ride south on the Parkway, passing Mabry Mill.

ROAD CONDITIONS

The county roads at the beginning of this adventure are twisty, narrow, absent of signage, and have some rough sections, but they're well worth the trip. Asphalt on US 58 is in good condition, and signs warn you of the smooth sweeping curves and tight twists. Don't let the frequent and seemingly illogical changes in county road numbers in the middle of this ride get to you. And don't turn off; keep going until you see a small bank (that is, a financial institution) at mile 31.4.

POINTS OF INTEREST

Narrow and twisty country lanes, downtown and uptown Stuart, Lover's Leap, Meadows of Dan.

RESTAURANTS

In Stuart you'll find the **Honduras Coffee House** at 121 N. Main St. The Coffee House is open weekdays from 7 am to 4 pm and Saturdays 8 am to 3 pm. This small, family-owned business gets its coffee from the owner's son-in-law, a grower in Honduras. The beans are shipped to Stuart where they are roasted, filling uptown Stuart with a wonderful aroma. They're then packaged or brewed for your enjoyment. You'll spend $1.50 for a cup o' joe. Bagels are $1.25, and decadent cheesecake desserts are $2.50.

Hills Gas/Grocery/General Store is at the intersection of US 58 and VA 8 at mile 35.9. Hills offers inexpensive grub, served in hearty proportions—$1.50 for a biscuit, $3 for a sandwich. You won't find steak on the menu, but you will get full for a few bucks.

At the end of the ride in Meadows of Dan is the **Poor Farmers Market**. The Poor Farmers Market has a sandwich shop in the back room so you can place your order at the counter and sit a spell in one of the porch rocking chairs while they get your meal ready. It's open from 6 am to 10 pm and serves breakfast and lunch items. With a wide assortment of sandwiches and homemade biscuit combinations, you're sure to get your money's worth. Expect to spend about $5 for a sandwich and drink. Add $1.50 if you order a piece of pie for dessert.

DETAILED DIRECTIONS

Mile 0—Turn off of US 58 in Meadows of Dan, VA, onto Squirrel Gap Rd. (CR 614). *This section of Squirrel Gap Rd. runs parallel to the Blue Ridge Parkway. Watch out for the 90-degree left turn at mile 6.4. At mile 7.2 is the sign warning truckers to avoid the road ahead; get ready to enjoy the curves. You'll be in farm country at mile 12.*

Mile 12.6—Turn left at the intersection onto the Ararat Hwy. (CR 773). *You'll ride past an old cemetery at mile 14.2.*

Mile 17.2—Turn left onto VA 103 North. Cross the bridge and get ready to turn left again.

Mile 17.8—Turn left onto Little Dan River Rd. (CR 738, which becomes CR 646, 645, and 631). *You'll have to negotiate a hard left turn at mile 20. If you miss this turn, you'll end up getting wet—going down an embankment and into a creek! Along the way, the road name changes to Dobyns Rd. You'll pass a small bank with an ATM before having to turn right.*

Mile 31.4—Turn right onto North Main St. toward downtown Stuart. *If you turn left here, you'll head directly into uptown (without the fun hills of Patrick Ave.) toward the Honduras Coffee House. Once at the courthouse, make your way across the square to W. Blue Ridge St. to rejoin this adventure.*

Mile 31.7—Turn left onto Patrick Ave. (this will feel more like a U-turn than a left turn since the two roads meet in a V where this ride turns left). *You'll ride up some hills as you get close to "uptown."*

Mile 32.3—Turn left onto US 58 Business North (West Blue Ridge St.). *You'll ride past the sandwich shop, a laundromat, and the Patrick County Courthouse.*

Mile 33.8—Turn left onto US 58 North. *At mile 35.9, you'll pass Hills Store (Food/Fuel/Groceries) and VA 8, which is the ride alternative that will take you on a twisty ride up to Tuggles Gap. There's a good view from Lover's Leap at mile 40.3. There's an old-style, glass-cylinder gas pump at mile 45.4 on the right side of the road. The road begins to straighten and climb toward Meadows of Dan. You'll find the Poor Farmers Market on the left side of the road at mile 47.6.*

Mile 47.9—This ride ends where US 58 crosses under the Blue Ridge Parkway. *Keep heading north on US 58 just half a mile to visit the Willville Motorcycle Campground on the left.*

Squirrel Gap Loop

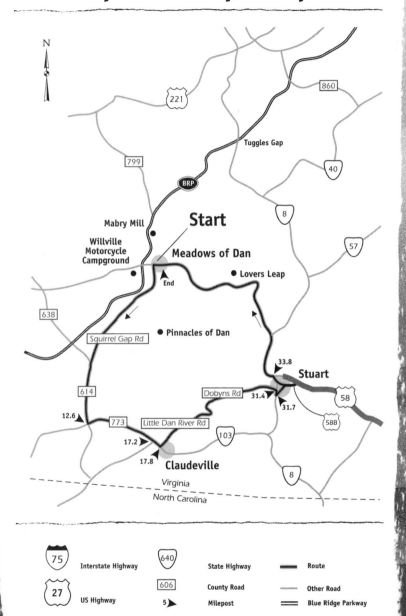

N

221

860

Tuggles Gap

799

40

BRP

8

Mabry Mill

Start

Willville
Motorcycle
Campground

Meadows of Dan

57

• Lovers Leap

End

638

• Pinnacles of Dan

Squirrel Gap Rd

33.8

Stuart

614

Dobyns Rd

31.4

58

31.7

12.6

773

Little Dan River Rd

58B

17.2

103

17.8

Claudeville

8

Virginia

North Carolina

75 Interstate Highway	**640** State Highway	▬▬ Route
27 US Highway	606 County Road	── Other Road
	5 ▶ Milepost	═══ Blue Ridge Parkway

Pipers Gap

*I*f you happen to be traveling on I-77 near the border of North Carolina and Virginia, give yourself a break from the monotony of the super-slab, and sample the fun curves and seldom-used roads that run through Pipers Gap. This ride begins and ends on I-77, so it's a great introduction or fond farewell to the roads of Virginia. Along the way, you'll ride a single-lane road, take in a couple miles of the Blue Ridge Parkway, and return through some farming communities. This ride is a quick fix for those needing to get off I-77.

GAS

Gas is available near the end of this ride at mile 27.7.

GETTING TO THE START

This ride starts on CR 620 off I-77 (exit 1) in Virginia. Zero your trip meter under I-77, and begin to ride north toward the town of Lambsburg on CR 620.

RIDE OVERVIEW

With I-77 behind you, CR 620 makes a breathtaking contrast. I-77 is a wide superhighway carrying all types of motorcycles, cars, trucks, vans, and big rigs. CR 620 is one of those roads where large vehicles are warned to turn back to avoid the steep, narrow asphalt ahead. One man's trash is another man's treasure!

As you ride north on this well-paved stretch of road, you'll pass through the small town of Lambsburg and onto the narrow section of CR 620. This section was too narrow to paint a center line, but do remember it's a two-way road. To avoid becoming a hood ornament, keep your bike over on the right half of the road. You'll enjoy the shady, tree-lined hairpin turns of CR 620 as you climb up to Pipers Gap. Once there, ride under the Blue Ridge Parkway and turn left onto CR 608, which will lead you up to the Parkway itself. At the Parkway, this ride turns right to enjoy the road and views to the south of Pipers Gap. If the word "piper" gets you thinking of bagpipes or pipe organs, you might be musically inclined; in which case, the next stop on the Blue Ridge Parkway is for you. It's the Blue Ridge Music Center.

Blue Ridge Music Center (276-236-5309) is on the left side of the road, and its paved driveway is well marked, guiding you to the activities there. The Music Center opened in October, 2001, with the purpose of offering visitors a chance to hear the traditional music of the Blue Ridge. Impromptu sessions of pickin' are featured, along with a luthier's (instrument builder's) shop, a museum, restrooms, and a few hiking trails to stretch your legs after all that dancing you're sure to do. Bluegrass bands like The Seldom Scene and the New Ballards Branch Bogtrotters fill the air of the amphitheater with their knee-slapping, toe-tapping music on Saturday nights beginning at 7 pm. Most of the programs are free, but occasionally there's a charge for nationally recognized performers. Check out the schedule of concerts at www.blueridgemusiccenter.net. The Center is open every day from the first weekend in June to the last weekend in September—that is, until the fall of 2004, when they expect to have all construction completed and will remain open year-round.

Back on the Blue Ridge Parkway, you'll take in a few more curves and pretty scenery until reaching VA 89. As you near VA 89, you'll notice the bridge that stretches over the Blue Ridge Parkway. This handsome stone structure was built with a double arch. One arch allows the traffic of the Blue Ridge Parkway to pass beneath, and the other allows the cool water of the West Fork Creek to flow unabated. The construction for the Blue Ridge Parkway began just south of VA 89. Consequently, the VA 89 bridge was one of the first to be built for the Parkway, and it became a standard by which many other bridges were built.

This route crosses the VA 89 bridge as you ride south toward North Carolina. You'll enter North Carolina and be greeted by several well-paved

TOTAL DISTANCE
28.1 miles

TIME FRAME
1 hour from start to finish. Add time to visit the Blue Ridge Music Center or to take a break on the Blue Ridge Parkway.

twists and turns along this rhododendron-lined roadway. From the back of Cumberland Knob, NC, 89 descends down into the Fisher River Valley. Once in the valley, twists and turns are replaced by gently sweeping curves through rolling farmland.

You'll continue to follow NC 89 all the way back to the ride's end at I-77. If your thirst for riding is not yet quenched and you have the time, take I-77 North back into Virginia to exit 8, where the *Mabry Mill* ride begins (see p. 114).

County Road 620 is just too narrow for a center line.

RIDE ALTERNATIVES

Just south of where you'll get off the Blue Ridge Parkway is the Cumberland Knob Recreation Area. To get there, stay on the Parkway for about two more miles, into North Carolina, where you'll find the Recreation Area on the left, with restrooms, information, and picnic tables.

ROAD CONDITIONS

VA 620 is a narrow, winding country road, well-banked and free of debris, but don't expect any signage. The Blue Ridge Parkway is in excellent condition and is famous for its sweeping curves. VA 89, which becomes NC 89, is a well-maintained ribbon of asphalt that's twisty for the first few miles off the Parkway, but becomes more tame as you ride through the Fisher River Valley.

POINTS OF INTEREST

Hairpin turns on CR 620, the Blue Ridge Parkway, and the Blue Ridge Music Center.

RESTAURANTS

This short route has no restaurants to mention. You might find a biscuit or burger in the gas station near the end of the ride.

DETAILED DIRECTIONS

Mile 0—From exit 1 off of I-77 in Virginia, ride toward Lambsburg (north) on CR 620. *You'll be through Lambsburg at mile 1.8 where the road becomes too narrow for centerline paint. Remember it's still a two-lane road, so watch for the rare oncoming vehicle.*

Mile 4.7—After passing under the Blue Ridge Parkway, turn left onto CR 608, which will lead you to the Parkway.

Mile 5.0—Turn right (south) onto the Blue Ridge Parkway. *The Blue Ridge Music Center is on the left at mile 11.6.*

Mile 14.5—Exit the Parkway to the right toward VA 89 (you'll see the double-arched VA 89 stone bridge).

Mile 14.7—Turn left onto VA 89 South. *You'll enter North Carolina at mile 15.4 where VA 89 becomes NC 89. At mile 17.8, you're done with the twisties as NC 89 takes you through the Fisher River Valley in a series of sweeping curves and rolling hills.*

Mile 28.1—This adventure ends at I-77. *To take in the Mabry Mill ride, head north on I-77 back into Virginia to exit 8 where that ride begins.*

Pipers Gap

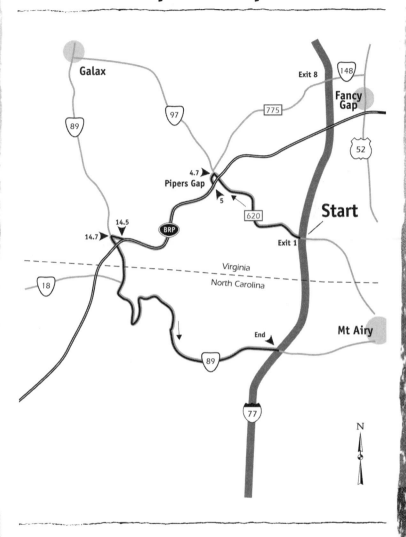

Galax

89

97

775

Exit 8 148

Fancy Gap

52

4.7
Pipers Gap

5

620

Start

14.5

14.7 BRP

Exit 1

Virginia

North Carolina

18

End

Mt Airy

89

77

N

75 Interstate Highway	640 State Highway	▬▬▬ Route
27 US Highway	606 County Road	▬▬▬ Other Road
	5 ▶ Milepost	▬▬▬ Blue Ridge Parkway

Highlands Loop

To get from Abingdon to Marion, VA, you have two choices. The first choice is to ride the super-slab I-81 26 miles north. The scenery is dull, and the absence of fun curves will give your rear tire a flat spot. The second choice is this ride. You'll get to Marion, but along the 86 miles you'll ride the best twisty and curvy roads in southern Virginia. Included with the second choice is a tour through the Mt. Rogers National Recreation Area, several restaurants, the Virginia Creeper Trail, Grayson-Highlands State Park, and a chance to boast that you've traversed Hurricane Ridge on your bike!

GAS
Gas is available at the start in Abingdon and at miles 1.7, 5.2, 10.9, 11, 28.4, 32.8, 40.4, 44.7, 47.8, 59.7, and 60.3, and in Marion at the end of the ride.

GETTING TO THE START

This ride starts from I-81, taking exit 19 onto US 58 East in Abingdon, VA. The mileage is measured from under the I-81 bridge. Reset your trip meter as you turn east on US 58.

RIDE OVERVIEW

For the first several miles of this ride, US 58 undulates through the southern Virginia countryside like a ribbon of asphalt paved over ocean waves. Virginia's rich soil attracts nearly every kind of agriculture. You'll see cattle, vegetable farms, Christmas tree nurseries, and even a vineyard or two. To reach the Abingdon Vineyard and Winery, turn right from US 58 onto CR 722 and follow the signs 2.5 miles down the road to enjoy a tasting and tour. Just don't taste too much!

Continuing east on US 58, you'll see a narrow gravel trail on the left side of the road. This was the railroad bed of the Virginia Creeper, a train that, until 1974, linked several remote mountain towns. Today the tracks are gone, and in their place is a well-packed gravel hiking and bicycling trail. It stretches from Whitetop all the way to Abingdon, but the most popular section, because it is nearly all downhill, is from Whitetop to Damascus. Damascus bicycle outfitters offer bicycles for rent and shuttles to Whitetop as well, so you can ride 17 relaxing miles down to Damascus.

Approaching Damascus, US 58 makes a sharp (well-marked) turn to the left. Next to this turn is a caboose, locomotive, and restrooms. The caboose serves as an information center for the city of Damascus and the Virginia Creeper Trail. Bicycle outfitters are just ahead along the main drag through town.

Also in downtown Damascus, you'll find two great restaurants. The first is the Damascus Old Mill Restaurant, Inn, and Conference Center. To get there, turn left onto Reynolds St., and follow Reynolds St. to its end, where the mammoth structure is impossible to miss. The Old Mill stands on the site of the original Damascus Mill. The original mill was closed after World War II and stood vacant until 2001 when it was reopened, producing delicious dinners overlooking Laurel Creek. Serving only dinner, the mill is open Wednesday through Saturday 5 to 9 pm, and Sundays 11 am to 4 pm. Plan to spend between $10 and $20, depending on your chosen entree and beverage.

In the heart of Damascus, consider a quick, two-mile trip to Backbone Rock in Tennessee. Backbone Rock is a half-mile-long, 80-ft.-tall, 20-ft.-wide slab of rock that once stood in the way of the railroad. Engineers cut through the rock, creating "the world's shortest tunnel." Today, the sounds of train whistles are replaced

TOTAL DISTANCE
68.7 miles

TIME FRAME
3 hours from start to finish. Add time to dine, hike, explore and enjoy.

by the thunder of motorcycle engines. To get there from Damascus, turn right onto Shady Ave. (VA 133).

Following US 58, you'll come to the In the Country Bakery and Eatery on the far side of town. This little sandwich/ice cream shop is open seven days a week, 6:30 am to 8 pm, and offers up delicious breakfast and lunch items for little money. While it caters mostly to the bicycle crowd, motorcyclists are warmly received.

Leaving Damascus, bear left to remain on US 58 East. You'll see the Virginia Creeper Trail crossing the road. While it is true that most motorcycles would fit onto the Virginia Creeper Trail, only nonpowered vehicles are allowed. You may see a few people on horseback, which is nearly as popular as bicycling.

The Old Mill Restaurant in Damascus is a great place for dinner.

The most popular section of the Virginia Creeper Trail starts at Whitetop and goes to Damascus.

US 58 got a fresh coat of asphalt in 2003, so you're sure to enjoy the tight twists and turns ahead as the road enters the Mt. Rogers National Recreation Area (part of the Jefferson National Forest). As the name implies, the Mt. Rogers National Recreation Area is home to Mt. Rogers, the highest peak in Virginia. Stretching 5,729 ft. into the sky, the summit is accessible only to hikers. However, you can enjoy the views of this peak, which will be on your left as you ride east. Other glimpses you'll steal are through the trees to your right. You'll see two old railroad bridges that traverse Whitetop and Laurel Creeks. These two bridges are now part of the Virginia Creeper Trail.

If you're in a mood for other activities, stop in at the Beartree Recreation Area. There you'll find opportunities for fishing, camping, picnicking, and swimming.

US 58 becomes known as the Highlands Parkway as you near Whitetop. In the burg of Whitetop there's a sign directing you to the Virginia Creeper Trailhead. From this point east you won't suffer any more bicycle outfitter vans slowing your progress, but don't get going so fast you miss the great views of the Blue Ridge on the right side of the road. The mountains off to the right are in North Carolina. To see more great views, turn into the Grayson-Highlands State Park.

Grayson-Highlands State Park is on VA 362, and it costs just $1 to enter on weekdays and $2 on weekends. Inside, you'll see what your entrance fee pays for—well-maintained overlooks, campsites, and hiking and horseback riding trails with views of distant vistas. Five miles up the winding VA 362, the road ends at a parking area near the top of Haw Orchard Mountain. You'll find restrooms, a gift shop, and a museum chronicling the history of the area from 1800 to 1900. There's even an old moonshine still on display. From the museum, hike the Twin Pinnacles Trail half a mile up to the craggy summit for some beautiful 360-degree views.

Continuing along US 58 you'll enter the town of Volney, where this ride turns left onto VA 16 toward Marion. At this turn you'll find fuel, groceries, and Ona's Country Kitchen. Ona's cooks up tasty, traditional, Southern-style food for breakfast, lunch, and dinner, seven days a week. Prices are reasonable, too.

Once you turn onto VA 16, you might wonder why you have to ride on such a straight road. Fear not, biker buddy, curves lie ahead. You must first roll through Christmas tree farm country before climbing the twisty section of VA 16 on Hurricane Ridge.

Hurricane Ridge is a narrow pass separating the "settled" part of Virginia from the woodsy and wild section. After passing through the ridge, you'll enjoy thick woods along a twisty portion of well-paved asphalt. Gone are the farms and homesteads that dotted the landscape; in their place are towering trees and babbling brooks. You'll descend into a speck of a town known as Sugar Grove and again be lifted away into the wilderness. Atop Brushy Mountain on the far side of Sugar Grove is an Appalachian Trail crossing and the W. Pat Jennings, Sr., Visitor Center for the Mt. Rogers National Recreation Area. Open weekdays from 8 am to 4:30 pm, Saturdays 9 am to 5 pm, and Sundays 1 pm to 5 pm, this visitor center is informative and interesting. Inside is a small museum about hiking the Appalachian Trail, information about the area, a small bookstore, and clean restrooms.

As you descend Brushy Mountain, you'll enjoy a few more curves before entering the city of Marion. On the outskirts of town is the Marion Fish Cultural Station on the right. This fish hatchery supplies area streams with native fish.

The ride ends at the intersection of VA 16 and I-81. Get on the interstate, and ride north about a hundred miles to reach Roanoke, or head south to get to Tennessee.

RIDE ALTERNATIVES

In Damascus, VA, consider a two-mile side trip to Backbone Rock. To get there, turn right at mile 10.5 onto Shady Ave. (VA 133 South). Standing 80 ft. tall, nearly 20 ft. thick and about half a mile long, this unique geological feature is home to the

"world's shortest tunnel." A small park ($2 admission) has been built near the hole cut in the rock to allow the train to pass through. Today, the satisfying rumble of motorcycle engines has replaced the high-pitched whistles of trains.

ROAD CONDITIONS

All the roads for this ride are two-lane blacktop and generally in excellent condition. There are ample signs to warn of approaching curves, and those curves are usually well banked. Watch for gravel in the curves on US 58, and slow bicycle shop vans between Abingdon and Whitetop. These vans are picking up and dropping off bicyclists riding the Virginia Creeper Trail from Whitetop to Abingdon.

POINTS OF INTEREST

The Virginia Creeper Trail, town of Damascus, view of Mt. Rogers (at 5,729 ft., the highest mountain in Virginia), Grayson-Highlands State Park, Hurricane Ridge.

RESTAURANTS

Damascus has several great eateries, but two stand out, and they are wildly different from each other. **The Damascus Old Mill Restaurant, Inn and Conference Center** (540-475-5121) opened in 2001 to accommodate the huge influx of bicyclists. It can be found by turning left onto Reynolds St. at mile 10.4; Reynolds St. ends in the restaurant parking area on the banks of Laurel Creek. The restaurant is open Wednesday through Saturday 5 pm to 9 pm and Sundays 11 am to 4 pm. Menu items range in price from $9 to $19. A full wine and beer list is available, and views of the spill dam on Laurel Creek are equally pleasing. Damascus Old Mill Restaurant does not take reservations.

If your time or budget won't accommodate the Old Mill, try the **In the Country Bakery and Eatery** on US 58 on the east side of Damascus. Open seven days a week from 6:30 am to 8 pm, you can get a hearty breakfast or a delicious sandwich for under $5. If you're dieting, be forewarned—there's also ice cream.

In the last half of this ride at the intersection of US 58 and VA 16 (mile 44.7), **Ona's Country Kitchen** offers breakfast, lunch, and dinner 7:30 am to 8 pm, seven days a week (until 9 pm on Sundays). You'll spend just $4 for a breakfast of eggs, biscuit, and coffee. For lunch, the Double Ona Burger is $3; fries and other sides are a buck extra. The dinner menu includes Southern meals like the barbecue platter and country ham steak, both for about $6.50. Seafood and steak dinners are a little more. If you aren't from the South, Ona's is a good place to try the Southern delicacy fried okra.

DETAILED DIRECTIONS

Mile 0—Head east on US 58 from I-81. *At mile 4.9 a sign directs you toward the Abingdon Vineyard and Winery. You'll see the gravel-paved Virginia Creeper Trail that parallels US 58 beginning at mile 7.4. At mile 9.4 you'll enter the town of Damascus.*

Mile 10.3—Turn left to remain on US 58 East. *You'll see a caboose and a small locomotive (restrooms, too) on the right side of the road in this left turn. The caboose serves as the information center for Damascus and the Virginia Creeper Trail. To reach the Damascus Old Mill Restaurant, Inn, and Conference Center, turn left onto Reynolds St. at mile 10.4. Wanna ride through a rock? Make a right turn at mile 10.5 onto Shady Ave. (VA 133) to ride to Backbone Rock. It's less than 2 miles away.*

Mile 10.8—Turn right to remain on US 58 East. *Pass the In the Country Bakery and Eatery at mile 11.1.*

Mile 11.8—Turn left at the fork to remain on US 58 East. *You'll spy a couple of old railroad bridges through the trees after making this left. At mile 18.5, the Beartree Recreation Area offers swimming, fishing, camping, and picnic spots.*

Mile 21.5—Turn right to remain on US 58 East. *Pass through the town of Whitetop at mile 27.3, where signs direct you to the Virginia Creeper Trailhead. At mile 36.9 is the left turn into the Grayson-Highlands State Park (VA 362). To visit this park, turn left, pay the small entrance fee, and ride 5 miles up to the museum near the summit of Haw Orchard Mountain.*

Mile 44.7—Turn left onto VA 16 North. *Ona's Country Kitchen is at this intersection. Riding north on VA 16, you'll pass a few Christmas tree farms on your way to Hurricane Ridge. At mile 53.5, you'll ride through Hurricane Ridge and be able to boast about it later! The W. Pat Jennings, Sr., Visitor Center for the Mt. Rogers National Recreation Area is on the left at mile 62.9, with restrooms and information about the area. There's a state fish hatchery at mile 67.*

Mile 68.7—The ride ends at the intersection of VA 16 and I-81 (exit 45). *Head north on I-81 to reach Roanoke (about 100 miles) or turn south toward Tennessee (45 miles away).*

Highlands Loop

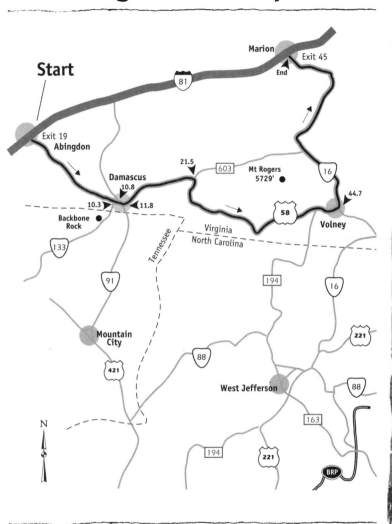

Start

Marion
Exit 45
End

81

Exit 19
Abingdon

Damascus
10.8
10.3
11.8
21.5
603
Mt Rogers
5729'
16
44.7
58
Volney

Backbone
Rock

133

Tennessee

Virginia
North Carolina

91

194
16

Mountain
City

221

88

421

West Jefferson

88

163

N

194
221

BRP

75	Interstate Highway	640	State Highway	▬▬	Route
27	US Highway	606	County Road		Other Road
		5▶	Milepost	═══	Blue Ridge Parkway

West Virginia's Southern Highlands

Area Covered

Natural wonders or amazing structures built by humans—who can say what's most impressive? From the New River Gorge to the New River Bridge, sights in this region are a testament to the awesome character of the mountain state.

The Bridge

If you're headed to West Virginia, chances are you've heard of the New River Gorge Bridge. If you haven't, surely you've seen it in commercials, stunt shows, or an "amazing video" show. This quick tour will take you from the bridge overlooks to its "underlooks," crisscrossing beneath the bridge along the old route taken by travelers prior to its completion in 1977. As impressive as this bridge is, the real treasure is what it spans. The natural beauty of the New River Gorge and the awe-inspiring human accomplishment of the giant bridge make an interesting contrast. Don't expect to speed through the sharp curves; they are too steep and too poorly maintained to ride quickly. This ride is all about looking at the bridge and the beauty that surrounds it.

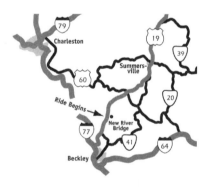

GAS

Gas is abundant in Fayetteville near the start and end of this ride, but along its 6.8-mile length, there is none.

GETTING TO THE START

This ride starts at the National Park Service's Canyon Rim Visitor Center on US 19 just north of the New River Bridge in Fayetteville, WV. To get there, take I-77 to Beckley, where you'll find US 19 North. Follow US 19 North through Fayetteville. The Visitor Center is on the far side of the bridge. Reset your trip meter as you turn out of the Visitor Center on the road to Fayette Station.

RIDE OVERVIEW

Before you go for your ride 800 ft. down into the gorge, under the bridge, over the river, and back out of the gorge, there are a few things you should know about the river, the history, and the bridge.

About the New River: It's only new compared to the Nile. Many speculate that the New River got its name from early cartographers who, when they discovered this body of water, wrote "a new river" on the chart. The name stuck. In fact, the New River is the second oldest river in the world, second in age only to the Nile. How old is that? Since it began flowing (between 65 and 100 million years ago), the single continent of Pangaea has broken apart to create the seven continents we know today, the Appalachian Mountain chain has pushed up from the earth, dinosaurs have come and gone, ditto ice ages, and more recently motorcycles have begun filling the area with satisfying engine noise. The New River begins near Blowing Rock, NC, and flows northwest, which is highly unusual for rivers in North America; most flow south. And because the New River Gorge is so remote, it is home to rare birds and plant life.

The history: There's so much history in this area that much of it remains undiscovered. In recent (recorded) history, say, the last few hundred years, the human population of the New River Gorge has undergone a metamorphosis. When Europeans first came to the region, life was pretty hard. The scenery was beautiful, but attracting other people to the area was next to impossible. Rough agriculture, trapping, and hunting were the only early industries. Then, in the mid-1800s, the railroad came to town to transport coal to market—coal easily mined from the gorge walls. The area boomed. Towns sprang up and coal mines opened left and right. Mines honeycombed the sides of the gorge. Those honeycombs later became an engineering obstacle for the bridge designers. How could they anchor a huge bridge into such an unstable land mass?

The Bridge: The New River Gorge Bridge was anchored over the abandoned honeycombs of coal mines. Engineers bored down to the void

TOTAL DISTANCE
6.8 miles

TIME FRAME
45 minutes from start to finish. Add time for sight-seeing.

spaces and pumped gravel into them, creating a firm foundation for the bridge. On that foundation they began building in June of 1973. The bridge was completed in October of 1977, with a price tag of $37 million. The entire bridge spans 3,030 ft., and the arch spans 1,200 ft. From the center of the bridge down to the water is 876 ft. It takes less than a minute to cross the bridge today, but before 1977, motorcyclists spent more than 45 minutes negotiating the hairpin curves from Fayetteville down to Fayette Station, across the New River, and back out of the Gorge on the north side. At the time of its completion, the New River Gorge Bridge was the longest steel arch bridge in the world. It held that record until February of 2003, when the Lupu Bridge in Shanghai, China, 105 ft. longer, was completed.

The New River Bridge is the second longest single-span, steel arch bridge in the world.

West Virginia's Southern Highlands **141**

Overlooks provide spectacular views of the New River Gorge.

The National Park Service showcases the New River Gorge, the Bridge, and the river itself at the Canyon Rim Visitor Center. There's ample paved parking for motorcycles in the large parking area. The Visitor Center offers several great spots for viewing. One view is an easy, flat walk of 100 yd. from the parking area; another leads you down 200 ft. into the gorge via a wooden staircase. The walk up is what takes most of your energy, so plan accordingly. Inside the Visitor Center a small theater shows movies about the region, its history, and the bridge construction. The Center is also home to a small museum showcasing the life and times of the early settlers. Admission is free, and hours are 9 am to 5 pm. The restrooms are refreshingly clean.

This route starts at the Canyon Rim Visitor Center sign at the entrance to the parking area. Turn right (away from US 19) and follow the signs down CR 82 toward Fayette Station. The first turn will give you a feel for the overall road conditions on this ride. Just 100 yd. from the Visitor Center, the road makes a wicked right-hand, steeply descending hairpin turn. You'll have no problem making this turn, but

be prepared for more like it farther along the ride. As CR 82 dives into the gorge, it makes a series of zigzags below the skeleton of the New River Gorge Bridge. While the bridge is amazing, you're sure to enjoy the natural wonders of the gorge as well.

As you descend toward the river, you might wonder about the source of the unusual but pleasant odor. That is what the outdoors is supposed to smell like! The weather, water, and geography work together to keep the Gorge relatively free of pollutants, so breathe deep!

Approaching the bottom of the Gorge, the road will lead you into what used to be the town of Fayette Station, one of many coal mining towns that thrived in the Gorge from the mid-1800s to the mid-1960s. Today, all that's left of the boom are railroad tracks, a few bridges, and some rusting buildings. Once the coal mining industry discovered that strip-mining coal was cheaper than digging and blasting, the gorge was abandoned by the industry. The outdoor recreation industry has replaced it.

As you cross the wild New River on the wooden-decked Tunney/Hunsacker Bridge, you'll probably see some paddlers a few feet below, taking on the whitewater. Rafters and kayakers come from far and wide to boat two rivers in the area—the New and the Gauley (pronounced "Golly"). For a great place to watch the paddlers, cross the bridge and follow CR 82 to a parking lot on the right, where there's a pretty wicked-looking set of rapids. This area is also the landing zone for people jumping off the bridge.

Before you go off thinking it's so popular to jump off the bridge that a special splat zone was created, think again. You see, there are these types of adventurers known as B.A.S.E. jumpers and bungee jumpers. Because the New River Gorge Bridge is 876 ft. above the water, the B.A.S.E. jumpers have time to leap, open their parachutes, and land safely. Bungee jumpers like to play a game called "kissing the water." In this game, they leap from the bridge with bungee cords calibrated so precisely that they barely touch or "kiss" the river before being shot back upwards by the elasticity of the cords. Sound crazy? Many people agree. The U.S. Park Service agrees so much that instead of arresting people for being unable to avoid the temptation of leaping from the bridge, they allow it on only one day each year—the third Saturday of October. So, if you want to witness people jumping from a big bridge, you now know where and when to go.

As CR 82 climbs out of the gorge on the southern wall, you'll pass the Kaymoor Trailhead, where there's a small parking area. This two-mile trail will lead you to the former mining town—now a ghost town—of Kaymoor. Abandoned in 1962, the only residents today are wild animals. Many of the structures still stand, and you'll be able to imagine how life was

during the coal boom. Aren't you glad biker boots are a good substitute for hiking boots?

Continuing your ride out of the gorge, you'll pass under the bridge a couple more times as you near the Rivers Whitewater Resort. The road will turn away from the Gorge along a small creek as you approach the resort. You'll know you've arrived when you see all types of people standing near the road wearing wet clothes and neoprene wet suits. You don't have to be a paddler to enjoy the amenities of this resort; it offers everything—a flat campsite, a cold drink, a hot meal, live music, and even trips down the river! Summers are busy here, so if you're considering mixing your motorcycle adventure with a whitewater adventure, call ahead (800-879-7483), or dial them up on the web at www.riversresort.com.

This ride ends when CR 82 meets US 19. To get better acquainted with the New River Gorge, turn left to get to the start of the *Hawks Nest* ride (p. 146). It begins where this one did at the Canyon Rim Visitor Center. To get a taste for Fayetteville, turn right onto US 19, then left onto WV 16, and ride through downtown. Cathedral Café is a great coffee shop on the square, and farther down the road is the Canyon Grill.

RIDE ALTERNATIVES

None. Because parts of CR 82 are one way, DO NOT ride this route in reverse.

ROAD CONDITIONS

Paved with ancient asphalt, twisty, narrow, and poorly maintained. Very little traffic, and plenty of places to stop and check things out. Potholes and gravel strewn across the road will demand your attention.

POINTS OF INTEREST

New River Gorge Bridge, Canyon Rim Visitor Center, Tunney/Hunsacker Bridge, New River, hiking trails to old mining towns.

RESTAURANTS

Near the end of the ride is the Rivers Whitewater Resort, home to the **Red Dog Saloon**, with a few menu items and plenty of frosty beverages. At this writing, another restaurant is undergoing remodeling at the resort.

In Fayetteville, don't miss the **Sedona Grill** (304-574-3411), on WV 16 off US 19 about a mile and a half past the town square. The grill offers gourmet entrees like crab cakes and stuffed steak filets for $10 to $18, and is open Thursday through Tuesday until 9 pm. Weekdays require no reservation, but on weekends it's best to call ahead. Try the fire sticks. They defy description, but sure are tasty.

The **Cathedral Café** on WV 16 near the courthouse in downtown Fayetteville was so named because it was opened in a former church. At the intersection of US 19/WV 16 sits **Tudor's Biscuits**, a good spot for breakfast and lunch. Several other fast food restaurant chains also have a foothold in Fayetteville.

DETAILED DIRECTIONS

Mile 0—Turn right out of the Canyon Rim Visitor Center parking area onto CR 82 toward Fayette Station.

Mile 0.2—You'll have to make a hard right turn to continue on CR 82. *Continue following the signs for CR 82. Along the way, 82 switches from one-way to two-way and back again. Following the directions in this chapter will keep you from going the wrong way on the one-way sections. Gravel pullouts abound on this adventure. If you miss one, don't worry. These pullouts are like buses in the big city; another one will be along shortly.*

At mile 2.7 you'll cross some railroad tracks and the wooden-planked Tunney/ Hunsacker Bridge. Originally built in 1899, until 1977 this bridge was the only span across the river for miles around. The bridge has been refurbished and rebuilt. At mile 3.2 you'll find a small parking area on the left side of the road in a hard right-turning hairpin curve. That small parking area serves as the trailhead to the Kaymoor Hiking Trail, which will lead you on a two-mile hike to the abandoned mining town of Kaymoor.

Rivers Whitewater Resort is on the right side of the road at mile 5.9. During weekend summers, expect to see busloads of rafters and outdoor adventurers wandering around this large area.

Mile 6.8—The ride ends when CR 82 meets US 19. *Turn left to go back across the bridge to the Visitor Center. Turn right onto US 19 South to reach WV 16, and turn left there, too.*

The Bridge

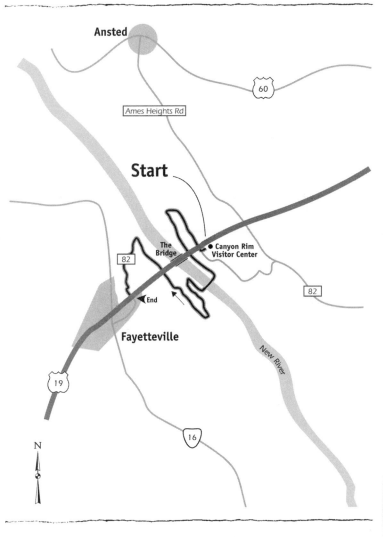

Ansted

60

Ames Heights Rd

Start

The Bridge

● Canyon Rim Visitor Center

82

82

◄ End

Fayetteville

New River

19

16

N

Interstate Highway

State Highway

Route

US Highway

County Road

Other Road

Milepost

Blue Ridge Parkway

75

640

606

5 ►

27

Hawks Nest

You don't have to be named Hawk to enjoy this ride, but I sure did! To know the New River Gorge, you have to see more than the New River Gorge Bridge. Sure, the bridge is spectacular, but the gorge offers so much more. With its great scenery and curvy roads, the area around the gorge deserves some foot-peg-scraping attention. For some off-road excitement, try a jet boat tour of the New River Gorge. Much of this ride skirts along the rim of the New River Gorge. The locals say the road is so twisty you'll see your own taillight in your rearview mirror.

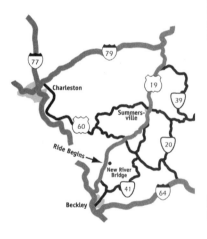

GAS

Gas is available at miles 5.8, 7.7, 11.1, 11.7, 21.2, 28.8, 31.2, 31.9, 42.7, 49.7, and 55, and at the end of the ride in Oak Hill, WV.

GETTING TO THE START

This ride starts from the Canyon Rim Visitor Center at the famous New River Gorge Bridge. To find the bridge from Beckley, WV (I-77), take US 19 North through Fayetteville, WV. The Canyon Rim Visitor Center is on the north side of the bridge. Zero your trip meter at the Canyon Rim Visitor Center sign near the park's exit as you turn north on US 19.

RIDE OVERVIEW

You'll begin this adventure from the sign in front of the Canyon Rim Visitor Center and ride the super-slab US 19 North for about 5 miles. After exiting onto US 60, you'll discover a more fun road to travel. US 60 is also known as Midland Trail. It's a National Scenic Byway stretching from the West Virginia State Capitol in Charleston, WV, to White Sulphur Springs, right through the middle of the state or "midland" area. The Midland Trail showcases interesting sites along the way.

After exiting the super-slab section of US 19 onto the two-lane blacktop of US 60, this adventure leads you into the town of Ansted. One sight that might be easy to miss in Ansted is the home of Blue Smoke Salsa. On Main St. in the center of town, Robin Hildebrand, Cecilia Backus, and Ellie Martel create their nationally known Blue Smoke Salsa, jellies, and sauces.

Just past the Main St. section of Ansted is a small but handsome home known as Contentment. Once the home of Colonel George W. Imboden, a member of the staff of General Robert E. Lee, it now serves as a museum of Civil War artifacts. Built in 1830, the home is also home to the Fayette County Historical Society. Behind it sits a restored one-room schoolhouse. Nearby, the African-American Heritage Family Tree Museum, offers African Americans a chance to trace their roots and find lost relatives.

Just around the bend from Contentment is the entrance to Hawks Nest State Park. Take a minute or take a couple of days, but stop here. The Hawks Nest State Park Lodge offers 31 rooms, most with views of the New River Gorge, from $55 to $75 nightly (less in the winter months). You can go for the deluxe suite at $83 to $104. It boasts a gorge view, a fireplace, fridge, microwave, and other amenities. You'll also find a restaurant offering delicious views of the Gorge, and tasty food to boot. Open from 7 am to 9 pm, it's a full-service family restaurant. For reservations and information, check the web at

TOTAL DISTANCE
57.2 miles

TIME FRAME
2 hours from start to finish.
Add time to check out
Hawks Nest State Park.

www.hawksnestsp.com, or call 304-658-5212 or 1-800-CALLWVA.

Venturing outside the Lodge, you'll see the Tramway, which transports you 500 ft. down into the gorge. Once there, consider a jetboat ride for just $6 for children (ages 5-16), $16 for adults, and $14 for seniors (60 and up). Jetboat captain Rick Larson will take you on an adrenaline-pumping, 30-minute ride from Hawks Nest Dam to the New River Gorge Bridge. The very competent Captain Larson holds a Master's License from the U.S. Coast Guard. That's not to say that he's not without a sense of humor; he named his boat *Miss M Rocks*. Check her out at www.newriverjetboats.com or call 304-469-2525.

Restrooms at Hawks Nest State Park are housed in this stone building dating from 1937.

As you pull back out onto US 60 West from Hawks Nest State Park, you'll learn that it's actually two parks in one. The original Hawks Nest State Park is just half a mile down the road. Completed in 1937, this section of the state park offers a museum, covered picnic areas, a castle-like restroom, and a great view of the Hawks Nest Dam—an engineering feat and also a tragedy for its builders. Looking at the dam, you'll see a metal plate to the right. This plate serves as the valve for a tunnel that redirects the New River from the riverbed and through Gauley Mountain to a power plant in the town of Gauley Bridge. The 3.5-mile, 40-ft. in diameter tunnel was constructed in the 1930s, mostly by hand. Workers were proud to be engaged in such an ambitious project and glad to have a job during the Great Depression. But after it was finished, thousands became ill, and nearly 500 workers died of "white lung" from breathing dust of the silica sandstone they had dug through. The first Workers' Compensation laws were written as a result of this tragedy.

Beyond Hawks Nest State Park, US 60 becomes a wild set of twists and turns as it follows the rim of the New River Gorge and heads over Gauley Mountain. On the way is a Quonset hut with a VW Beetle stuck in the side—a tourist trap known as Mystery Hole. According to the literature, at Mystery Hole gravity is upset, balls roll uphill, and other strange phenomenan occur. Signs at the ticket counter warn that viewing Mystery Hole can make you dizzy, so consider keeping your $4; you'll need your sense of balance for the rest of the ride.

In the tiny hamlet of Chimney Corner, US 60 turns right. If you want to skip the rest of this ride, turn left here onto WV 16, which will lead you back to Fayetteville. Your reward for continuing will be some clean asphalt and fun twists. Chimney Corner is little more than a curve with a general store. Follow the twists out of Chimney Corner and away from the New River Gorge area toward the town of Gauley Bridge.

On the way to the town of Gauley Bridge, you'll pass the Hawks Nest State Park Golf Course. This course is an executive nine-hole course offering different tees on the same nine holes that serve as the "back nine." Golf is cheap here—$19 for nine holes with a

Hawks Nest Dam on the New River. The tunnel entrance is on the far right shore, just above the water line.

cart, and just $2 more on weekends. No clubs on your scooter? They'll rent you some.

Entering the town of Gauley Bridge, stop at the small paved parking area on the right side of the road at Cathedral Falls. The falls cascade 60 ft. down over dark mossy rocks, making a perfect spot for picnicking or resting. The town has constructed a covered picnic area. Further into town is a bridge over the Gauley River. Riding over that bridge, look to your right. Just upstream, you'll see a few stone bridge piers—all that remains of the bridge from which the town got its name. The Confederate Army destroyed it in 1861 to prevent its use by the Union Army. On the left the confluence of the New River and the Gauley River creates the Great Kanawha River. Follow the Great Kanawha as it flows northwest.

The road passes through the town of Glen Ferris. In the heart of this small town is the Glen Ferris Inn, opened in 1839 and offering deluxe accommodations and delicious meals. Choose breakfast, lunch, or dinner served in a gazebo by the river, on a deck overlooking the river, or in the dining room. Menu prices range from $10 to $19 per plate for dinner, and a paltry sum for a delicious breakfast and lunch. The inn serves beer and wine, too. Rooms are priced from $60 for a single bed on the mountain side of the inn to $130 for the honeymoon suite overlooking the river. For reservations, call 304-632-1111.

One of the most impressive business sites along the Great Kanawha River is the Elkem-Alloy plant in Alloy. The Elkem Plant boasts the largest silicon furnace in the world and produces manganese, chrome, and silicon for the aerospace, chemical, and electronics industries. The Elkem Company is based in Oslo,

Norway, and purchased the plant from Union Carbide in 1981.

This ride crosses the river at Montgomery and turns north on WV 61 toward the town of Deep Water. Montgomery is home to West Virginia University Institute of Technology. Once in Deep Water, watch for the sharp right turn signaling the end of the sweeping curves along the riverside and get ready for a few more miles of tight twists and turns.

At Oak Hill, there's food and fuel aplenty. In Oak Hill's downtown district, this ride makes a left onto WV 16 North, which leads to US 19. At US 19, you can go north back toward the beginning of this ride in Fayetteville, or head south toward Beckley and I-77.

RIDE ALTERNATIVES

You can cut this ride in half by turning left onto WV 16 at mile 16.7 to return to Fayetteville.

ROAD CONDITIONS

Two-lane roads in good condition and many sweeping curves, with a few tight twists in the first half of the ride. The asphalt has a few potholes and an occasional piece of gravel in the roadway. Many of the overlooks and other stopping places are not paved, and the gravel migrates onto the road. Watch for a few railroad grades as well. Cross them at 90 degrees and you'll have no problem.

POINTS OF INTEREST

Blue Smoke Salsa, Hawks Nest State Park, New River Jetboats, New River Gorge, Mystery Hole, Gauley River, Cathedral Falls, Glen Ferris Inn.

RESTAURANTS

At **Hawks Nest State Park** (304-658-5212), there is a good restaurant overlooking the New River Gorge. This restaurant is open from 7 am until 9 pm, offering reasonably priced menu items for breakfast ($4-6), lunch ($5-8) and dinner ($10-18). While the food is tasty, the view of the gorge creates the perfect atmosphere. The lodge also has hotel rooms. For more info, log onto hawksnestsp.com.

Glen Ferris Inn (304-632-1111) in Glen Ferris, WV, offers breakfast, lunch, and dinner with prices mirroring those at Hawks Nest State Park. Like Hawks Nest, Glen Ferris Inn offers rooms, with prices ranging from $60 to $130 nightly, depending on just how fancy you want your sleeping accommodations.

DETAILED DIRECTIONS

Mile 0—Zero your trip meter as you turn left out of the parking lot of the Canyon Rim Visitor Center. Turn right onto US 19 North.

Mile 5.0—Exit onto the ramp from US 19 onto US 60.

Mile 5.4—At the top of the ramp, turn right onto US 60 West, also known as Midland Trail. *At mile 11.8 in the town of Ansted is the headquarters for Blue Smoke Salsa. Tudor's Biscuits at 12.3 invites you to dine on handmade biscuits. The residence of Confederate Colonel George W. Imboden is on the right at mile 12.5. Mile 13.5 is the entrance to Hawks Nest State Park, lodge, restaurant, jetboats, paddle boats, aerial tramway, golf, and hiking trails.*

Hawks Nest Park has an overlook at mile 14.1, as well as a museum, picnic tables, and castle-like restrooms. Mystery Hole invites you to lighten your wallet by $4 at mile 15.2 to discover what this tacky tourist trap has to offer.

Mile 16.7—Turn right to stay on US 60 West. *To skip the remainder of this run, turn left here onto WV 16 and ride back to Fayetteville. There are a couple of gravel overlooks at miles 17.9 and 18.3. The 9-hole Hawks Nest Golf Course is at mile 19. The beautiful Cathedral Falls and covered picnic area are on the right at mile 20.3. At mile 20.4, watch out for the rough railroad crossing. You'll cross the Gauley River at mile 21.3. This is the confluence of the New and Gauley Rivers. Combined, they form the Great Kanawha River. Since 1839 people have been enjoying the hospitality of the Glen Ferris Inn at mile 23.2. Watch out for the rough railroad crossing at mile 23.8. The large industrial plant on the left side of the road at mile 28.2 is the Elkem Metals Company.*

Mile 32.4—Exit right onto VA 61 and cross the Great Kanawha River.

Mile 32.9—Turn right onto VA 61 South. *There's another railroad crossing at mile 38.3. At mile 38.4 , VA 61 makes a hairpin turn to the right up and away from the Great Kanawha River. The road becomes fun again! You'll enter the city of Oak Hill at mile 55 where you'll find fast food and fuel.*

Mile 56.7—Turn left onto WV 16 North.

Mile 57.2—The ride ends at the intersection of WV 16 and US 19. *Go north on US 19 to return to Fayetteville and the New River Gorge Bridge. Turn south onto US 19 to head back to Beckley and I-77.*

Hawks Nest

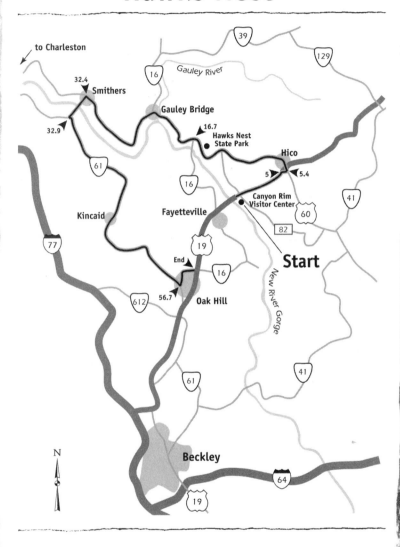

to Charleston

39

Gauley River

129

16

32.4 Smithers

Gauley Bridge

32.9

16.7
Hawks Nest
State Park

Hico

61

5 ◄ ►5.4

16

Canyon Rim
Visitor Center

41

Kincaid

Fayetteville

60

82

77

19

Start

End ►

16

New River Gorge

612 56.7

Oak Hill

41

61

N

Beckley

64

19

Interstate Highway | State Highway | Route
US Highway | County Road | Other Road
Milepost | Blue Ridge Parkway

75 — Interstate Highway
27 — US Highway
640 — State Highway
606 — County Road
5 ► — Milepost
— Route
— Other Road
═ Blue Ridge Parkway

Gristmill Escape

Beginning near Fayetteville and leading you to Beckley, this adventure will have you thundering down some of the most remote and lightly used roads in the U.S. The beautiful scenery and good road conditions are reason enough to embark. Along the way, you'll visit a working gristmill. This ride's sweeping curves invite you to get your tires white-hot!

GAS

Gas is available at miles 7.7, 8, 11.1, 14.8, 24.1, 44.9, and at the end of the ride throughout the town of Beckley.

GETTING TO THE START

This ride starts at the sign to the Canyon Rim Visitor Center at the New River Gorge Bridge on US 19 just north of the city of Fayetteville. To get there, take I-77 to Beckley, WV, and follow US 19 North through Fayetteville, across the famous bridge, and turn right into the Visitor Center. Zero your trip meter while parked in front of the big sign for the Visitor Center.

RIDE OVERVIEW

This adventure was named Gristmill Escape for a couple of reasons. First, there's an actual working gristmill on this route. Second, it will take you "the long way home" from Fayetteville to Beckley—an escape from the monotony of US 19.

You'll begin on the dull super-slab portion of US 19 from Fayetteville, but you won't be on it long. Along the way you'll spot a few outfitters offering rafting on the New and Gauley Rivers—a favorite activity for tourists. Just five miles north of the New River Bridge, take the exit for US 60. At the top of the ramp, turn left (east) onto US 60. This part of US 60 is also known as the Midlands Trail. As its name suggests, this "trail" slices through the middle of West Virginia.

Follow US 60 through its sweeping curves on your way to WV 41.

At the intersection of US 60/WV 41, turn right toward Babcock State Park. Most of the traffic stays on US 60, making WV 41 a pleasure to ride. The entrance to Babcock State Park is on the right side of the road about 3.5 miles down WV 41. Turn in and ride the half-mile entrance road to the Visitor Center and the Glade Creek Grist Mill.

At the Visitor Center, you can get information about the many activities offered in Babcock State Park. The campground has many campsites, plus cabins for those of us for whom "roughing it" means something a little different. Cabins range in price from $62 to $147 depending on size, season, and day of week. Camping is just $15 to $19 per night depending on whether you want electricity at your campsite. For complete rate information, call 304-438-3004 or 800-CALLWVA, or log onto the web at www.babcocksp.com. The park also has a swimming pool, tennis courts, basketball courts, paddle and row boats for rent on Boley Lake, and of course a gristmill.

Completed in 1976, the Glade Creek Grist Mill isn't really new. As fire, natural disasters, and development threatened mills across West Virginia, several mills were cannibalized to build it. Today, this mill grinds cornmeal and buckwheat flour as did the 500-odd mills like it that once dotted the streams and rivers of West Virginia. Buy a pound of stoneground flour to keep this treasure alive.

Just south of the park entrance on WV 41 is another unique treasure. In the O'Possum General Store you'll find items ranging from hot grits to hunting rifles. They'll cook you breakfast, lunch, and dinner and sell you a rare coin while you wait. If it's not for sale at the O'Possum, you probably don't need it.

Leaving Babcock State Park, WV 41 has many sweeping curves, rolling over hill and dale, passing through

TOTAL DISTANCE
46.2 miles

TIME FRAME
2 hours from start to finish. Add time for a tour of the gristmill at Babcock State Park and chow time at the O'Possum General Store.

several small towns on the way to the New River Gorge National River Area. It boasts beautiful scenery and a good road surface, but there's little else— no park amenities or visitor centers. On the far side of the River Area is the Amtrack Passenger Train Station in Prince. The train stops in Prince only two days a week, but the station itself is interesting to peek into. Just past the train station, WV 41 crosses the New River. As you cross, look to your left. After seeing the condition of the rusting railroad bridge, you may be glad to have missed the train!

From Prince, WV 41 climbs out of the New River Gorge in a series of well-paved twisties, heading to the intersection of WV 41 and WV 61. Turn right onto WV 61 and follow it into Oak Hill, picking up US 19 North to return to the greater Fayetteville area, or continue along this adventure by turning left, remaining on WV 41 south into the city of Beckley. All too soon, the twisties give way to city streets, and the ride ends at the intersection of US 19 (Business) in Beckley. Turn left to reach I-77, or turn right to head back to Fayetteville.

RIDE ALTERNATIVES

Near the end of this ride at mile 42.4, you can turn right onto WV 61 to go to the town of Mt. Hope, WV, where you'll find US 19. Go north on US 19 to return to the New River Gorge Bridge.

ROAD CONDITIONS

Other than the first five miles, this ride is entirely two-lane asphalt. Most of the traffic will disappear after the first 15 miles of this ride. After turning from US 60 onto WV 41, the road becomes sparsely populated as you rumble through several small towns along well-banked, and well-maintained asphalt. Expect to find a few patches in the asphalt, but potholes are nonexistent. As with most rides in West Virginia, you can expect a few railroad crossings as well.

POINTS OF INTEREST

Babcock State Park, Glade Creek Grist Mill, O'Possum General Store

RESTAURANTS

There are a few, but one stands out; the **O'Possum General Store** on the left side of the road on WV 41 just south of the entrance to Babcock State Park. At the General Store, you can buy a hunting rifle or a few rare coins, then dine on biscuits and gravy. Open from 7 am to 9 pm, the friendly folks at the O'Possum General Store make hearty meals at moderate prices, serving breakfast, lunch, and dinner. The dinner menu has an item called "O'Getti," which is the O'Possum General Store's version of spaghetti. Don't expect fancy food, but do expect tasty food, and nearly too much of it.

While it no longer has a restaurant, Babcock State Park does have camping, cabins, and many other amenities and attractions. The cabin rental rates range from $62 to $147 depending on size and season. Their highest prices are in the summer months, but even then, the cabins are still a steal.

DETAILED DIRECTIONS

Mile 0—Zero your trip meter in front of the big sign that reads "Canyon Rim Visitor Center" near the New River Gorge Bridge in Fayetteville, WV. Leave the parking area and turn right onto US 19 North.

Mile 5.0—Exit from US 19 onto US 60. At the top of the ramp (mile 5.4), turn left onto US 60 East.

Mile 14.9—Turn right onto WV 41 South. *The entrance to Babcock State Park is on the right at mile 18.8. Just half a mile into the Park, you'll find the Park's Visitor Center and the Glade Creek Grist Mill. Past the entrance to the Park at mile 19.7 is the O'Possum General Store.*

Mile 24.1—Fork right to stay on WV 41. *At mile 33, you'll enter the New River Gorge National River Area. You'll be crossing the New River at mile 37.3. There's a nice spot on the side of the road to check out the rapids at mile 39.6.*

Mile 42.4—Turn left to stay on WV 41 and head toward Beckley. *This is where the ride alternative begins. If you want to return to the Fayetteville area, turn right here onto WV 61 and head into the town of Mt. Hope, where you'll pick up US 19 North back toward the New River Gorge Bridge. Back on the ride, you'll enter the busy part of Beckley, WV, around mile 45.*

Mile 46.2—The ride ends here at the junction of WV 41 and US 19B; turn left to reach I-77.

Gristmill Escape

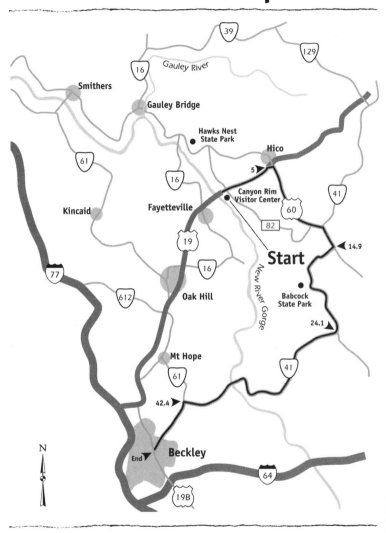

West Virginia's Southern Highlands **155**

Highland Scenic Highway

The 22-mile section of this ride stretching over Black Mountain on the Highland National Scenic Highway compares best with the Cherohala Skyway, featured in my first book, Motorcycle Adventures in the Southern Appalachians: North Georgia, East Tennessee, Western North Carolina. *Little traffic, beautiful scenery, superb road conditions, and a top elevation of 4,545 ft. make this ribbon of asphalt what motorcycle crowds crave. Getting to and from the Highway, you'll ride through several nice towns and into the Monongahela National Forest. On the Scenic Highway commercial traffic is prohibited as you climb along the spine of Black Mountain. The views and fresh air are worth the trip!*

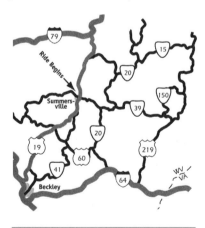

GAS

Gas is available at the start and at miles 3.2, 11.4, 21, 23.1, 23.7, 72.2, 75.7, 77.3, and 79.8.

GETTING TO THE START

This ride starts at the intersection of US 19 and WV 39 East. To get there from the south, take I-77 into Beckley and ride north on the interstate-like US 19 into the town of Summersville, about an hour and a half north of Beckley. From the north, follow I-79 South to exit 57, which is US 19 near the town of Sutton. Follow US 19 South for about 45 minutes to the town of Summersville, where you'll turn east on WV 39. Zero your trip meter as you turn east onto WV 39 from US 19.

RIDE OVERVIEW

Turning from US 19 near Summersville onto WV 39 East, you might be interested to learn about the lake of the same name. Summersville Lake is the result of a dam which allows the use of the Gauley River both to generate hydroelectric power and to create a recreation area. Planners tentatively named the dam after the river. But when they heard how "Gauley Dam" sounded, they quickly changed it to Summersville Dam.

Between Summersville and Richwood, WV 39 is not in great shape, but the scenery is beautiful. The road passes through several small towns and rural farms, following the banks of the Cherry River. Once in Richwood, you'll see its downtown business section built of stone blocks. The town fathers probably never considered that the stone buildings would still be in service

100 years after they were constructed, but you'll be glad they are. These handsome structures are home to the local bank, feed store, hardware store, and more.

After passing through Richwood, you'll enter the Monongahela National Forest and the section of road designated as the Highlands National Scenic Highway. The road begins to twist like mad as it climbs and descends along the side of Fork Mountain. The homes become more sparse, and the chance to see wildlife increases. Follow FS 223 to the right if you want to take in the view of the Falls of Hills Creek Scenic Area on foot. If you're not in a hiking mood, check out the Cranberry Glades Botanical Area by turning left onto FR 102 and riding about 1.5 mi. to the boardwalk. The boardwalk will lead you along a half-mile self-guided walking tour of a kind of bog more common in Canada than in the United States. The remoteness of the West Virginia forests have left this remnant of the ice age unchanged for thousands of years. The boardwalk is a smooth, raised, walking surface, with several bench seats where you can rest your bones. More bogs like the one at Cranberry Glades are listed in the *Seneca Rocks!* ride on p. 180. To learn more about Cranberry Glades and the area, stop in at the Cranberry Mountain Visitor Center at the intersection of WV 39 and WV 150. This visitor center offers information and restrooms seven days a week from 8 am to 5 pm.

The ride makes a left at the Visitor Center onto WV 150. You'll notice WV 150 is nearly straight. That's because the road was paved on the spine of Black Mountain. You'll reach the summit of the mountain at an elevation of 4,545 ft. Several scenic overlooks dot the side of the road. Riding along, it's hard to imagine this mountain was the

TOTAL DISTANCE
90.6 miles

TIME FRAME
3 hours from start to finish. Add time to explore the half-mile boardwalk through the bogs at the Cranberry Glades, explore the overlooks on Black Mountain, and dine in Marlinton.

location of one of the worst ecological disasters of the 20th century.

In 1930, just after the Great Depression struck, work was plentiful in the area. The woods of West Virginia were being logged with painful efficiency. Narrow-gauge railroads carried the timbers into town where they could be processed and then shipped to destinations across the United States. The small steam locomotives burned coal and wood to fire their boilers. Fires tend to spark, and that's what happened on Black Mountain. A spark from the exhaust of one of the steam locomotives ignited a forest fire that burned for months, fed by the very same trees that were to be harvested for lumber. There was no firefighting equipment in place. The fire burned so hot for so long that even some of the soil burned. Finally, after a heavy rain, the blaze was extinguished, but the erosion that followed was horrific. The forest that had once promised thousands of jobs was gone, and bare boulders stood where trees had once competed for sunlight. The area has slowly regrown to what you see today, but evidence of the 1930 fire is still present. Take the 200-yd. walk at the Big Spruce Overlook to learn more about the fire and the logging industry in the area.

Finding the route is easy!

Descending Black Mountain, WV 150 offers more sweeping curves as you ride through a black bear sanctuary. Consider yourself lucky if you see a black bear. Chances are, the bear will have more fear of you on your chrome machine than you will have of its large fuzzy stature. Regardless of how you feel about bears, don't feed them. It might make them dependent on human visitors, increasing the contact between the bears and humans. Every time there is extended contact with humans, bears lose.

When WV 150 Ts into US 219, turn right onto US 219 South to continue this ride. If you were to turn left onto US 219 North, you'd reach WV 66 in a few miles. WV 66 East would lead you to the Snowshoe Ski Resort Area and the Cass Scenic Railroad State Park. However, this ride continues to descend Black Mountain into the Greenbrier River Valley. You'll be near the valley floor when you reach the

farming community of Edray. Edray is just one of several towns you'll pass as you near Marlinton.

Marlinton is where you should satisfy your hunger pangs. Don't let the size of Marlinton mislead you, the town offers several fast food outlets and great restaurants. To reach most of them, turn left onto WV 39 east (also known as Eighth St.) and ride into the downtown section of Marlinton. On the right after crossing the bridge is River Place. This restaurant overlooking the Greenbrier River offers tasty food seven days a week. You can stay the night at River Place as well; it offers rooms and a cottage. About a block past River Place is French's Diner. While certainly not fast food, the meals at this small-town diner are prepared quickly and artfully, and you can order breakfast any time they are open. So, if a breakfast dinner is what you're in the mood for, stop in here. To get an ice-cold beer or a glass of wine with dinner, you'll have to drive to the Roadhouse Bar. Open for dinner only, it offers steak and fish dishes prepared to order.

The ride continues south on US 219, through Marlinton along the western bank of the Greenbrier River as you near WV 39 West. Along the way, you'll pass the Chick Inn, which offers fast food-ish fried chicken dishes. There's a small Harley accessories dealer on the right side of the road that advertises "hats and more." Then turn right onto WV 39 West, ride away from the Greenbrier Valley, and head back up into the Monongahela National Forest.

RIDE ALTERNATIVES

This ride ends at the intersection of WV 39 and WV 150. From there you have two choices. The first is to follow WV 39 back into Summersville where you can ride back down US 19 toward the New River Gorge Bridge. Or, go north on WV 150, riding over Black Mountain again and turning left onto US 219 North. The second choice will lead you toward the Snowshoe Ski Resort and the Cass Scenic Railway State Park.

ROAD CONDITIONS

With the exception of the cracked and poorly patched 25 miles of pavement at the beginning of this ride, road conditions are excellent. Within Monongahela National Forest, the road is a pleasure to ride. With clean asphalt well-banked and well-marked, the twists and turns of WV 39 are a blast. WV 150 climbs the back of Black Mountain in a series of well-paved, sweeping curves, with no commercial traffic allowed. US 219 South makes a couple of tight turns shortly after you leave WV 150, but then sweeps through the countryside.

POINTS OF INTEREST

Monongahela National Forest, Cranberry Glades boardwalk, Scenic overlooks on Black Mountain, Black Bear Sanctuary.

RESTAURANTS

There are several great restaurants in Marlinton. To get to them, you'll turn left from US 219 South onto WV 39 (a.k.a. Eighth St.) and cross the bridge into downtown Marlinton.

The **River Place** (304-799-7238) is on the right after crossing the bridge on WV 39. It's open from 7 am to 9 pm seven days a week, serving breakfast, lunch, and dinner at tables overlooking the Greenbrier River. Breakfast starts at $1.50 for a breakfast biscuit and goes to $4 for eggs and the trimmings. For lunch, sandwiches range from a $2.50 burger to sub sandwiches for $3 to $6, depending on the size and features. Dinner starts at $7 for a hamburger steak and stretches up to $13 for steak. Five rooms are for rent from $39.95 for a single to $49 for two double beds. Rates rise $10 on weekends. There's also a three-bedroom cottage for $99 nightly. Check out River Place on the web at www.riverplacewv.com.

For quick but delicious food, try **French's Diner** (304-799-9910), located a block past the River Place. French's Diner is open from Monday

Marlinton is a scenic little town where the Greenbrier River Trail crosses.

through Saturday 7 am to 8 pm and on Sundays from 7 until noon. French's serves breakfast all day, which is not to say their other meals aren't delicious. Country ham and burger items for $3 are a staple on the lunch menu. Dinner gets a bit more costly at $7 for a piece of fish and $12 for a steak.

The Roadhouse Bar (304-799-4383) sits across the street from the River Place and offers beer, wine, mixed drinks, and pool tables along with tasty meals. Expect to spend $9 to $19 for dinner, depending on what you order. Visit on Friday for the $10 dinner buffet. The Roadhouse Bar is closed on Sundays, but open all other days from 3 pm to 11 pm. The kitchen closes at 11, but on Friday and Saturday nights the bar proper serves until 3 am.

DETAILED DIRECTIONS

Mile 0—Follow the two-lane WV 39 East away from the four-lane, divided US 19. *Cross the Gauley River at mile 1.5.*

Mile 20.1—Turn right to stay on WV 39 (well marked). *You'll follow the Cherry River upstream for several miles into Downtown Richwood with its businesses made of handsome stone.*

Mile 23.7—Turn left to remain on WV 39 East. *You'll enter the Monongahela National Forest and the Highlands National Scenic Highway at mile 24.9, with a picnic area at mile 30.9 and the entrance to the National Park Campground at mile 31. On the right at mile 40.5 is the paved driveway to the Falls of Hills Creek Scenic Area. To reach the Cranberry Glades Botanical Area, turn left at mile 45.1, and follow FR 102 North for 1.5 miles. Cranberry Mountain Visitor Center (restrooms and info) is on the right at mile 46.*

Mile 46—Turn left onto WV 150. *At mile 52.4 is the Williams River Valley Overlook (with restrooms). At an elevation of 4,520 ft., the Big Spruce Overlook offers a 200-yd. hike to an overlook deck. Along the way you'll be able to read about the catastrophic fire that charred the side of the mountain in the 1930s. Watch for black bear at mile 56.1 as you enter their sanctuary on the far side of Black Mountain. There's a bridge and campground at the Williams River, mile 59.5. At mile 62.9, Little Laurel Overlook offers nice views of the Williams River Valley. The Red Lick Overlook is at mile 66, with views of a small creek. The Shearers Run Trailhead at mile 68 posts signs prohibiting snowmobiles from using the trail.*

Mile 68.6—Turn right onto US 219 South, and enter the town of Edray at mile 72. *At mile 74.5 is the Rustic Inn and Café in Marlinton, WV. There's fast food galore at mile 74.8.*

Mile 75.7—US 219 South merges with WV 39 West. Keep going straight. *Check out the store at mile 77.3, offering "Harley Hats and More." You'll pass the Pocahontas Hospital at mile 77.3 and the County Golf Club at mile 77.7.*

Mile 84—Fork to the right to stay on WV 39 West (away from US 219). *You'll reenter the Monongahela National Forest at mile 89.*

Mile 90.6—This ride ends at the Cranberry Mountain Visitor Center at the intersection of WV 39 and WV 150. *Turn right onto WV 150 to head toward Snowshoe Ski Resort Area and the Cass Scenic Railroad State Park, or keep following WV 39 West back into Summersville and US 19 South to the New River Gorge Area.*

Highland Scenic Highway

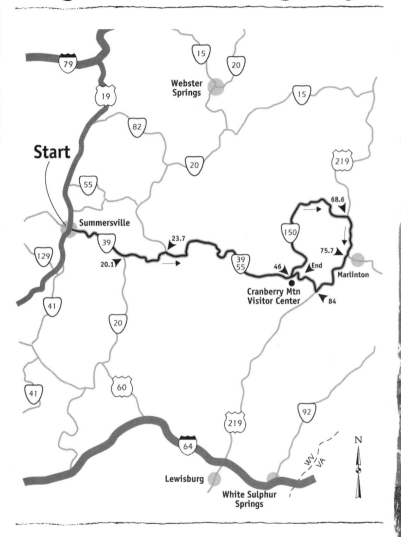

Start

Webster Springs

Summersville

Cranberry Mtn Visitor Center

Marlinton

Lewisburg

White Sulphur Springs

79 · 19 · 15 · 20 · 15 · 82 · 20 · 55 · 219 · 39 · 129 · 23.7 · 20.1 · 150 · 68.6 · 75.7 · 39 55 · 46 · End · 84 · 41 · 20 · 41 · 60 · 92 · 219 · 64

WV/VA

N

75 Interstate Highway	640 State Highway	Route
27 US Highway	606 County Road	Other Road
	5 ▶ Milepost	Blue Ridge Parkway

West Virginia's Northern Highlands

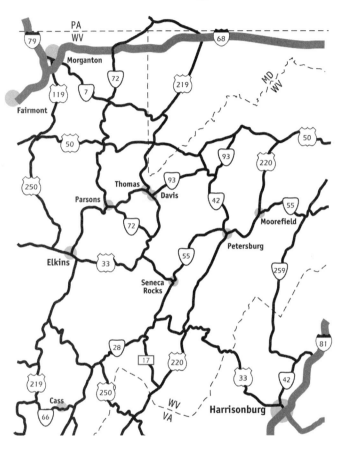

Area Covered

Here you'll find vintage steam locomotives, remote country roads, and a history of old-fashioned feuds. Then, when you least expect it, you'll see state-of-the-art, wind-powered electric turbines. Welcome to West Virginia, land of the time warp.

Snowshoe South Loop

With road conditions ranging from long sweeping curves to wild twisties, this ride has asphalt to satisfy all types of motorcyclists. Adding some fun and delicious local flavor and history, the towns of Marlinton and Cass provide a taste of down home West Virginia. You'll have the chance to ride an old steam train or tour part of the Highland Scenic Highway. Finally, with streams on the roadsides for most of the route and shade overhead, this is a cool ride for a warm summer day.

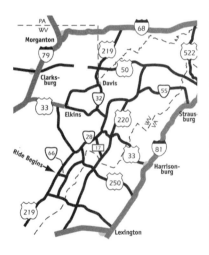

GAS

Gas is available at the start where US 219 and WV 66 intersect. You'll also find it at miles 4.0, 17.7, 20.6, 21.1, 21.7, 27, 27.7, and 51.1, and at the end of the ride.

GETTING TO THE START

This ride begins at the intersection of US 219 and WV 66. From the East and South, follow I-64 West from Virginia and take exit 169 onto US 219 North. Follow US 219 North to WV 66. From the West and North, follow I-79 to Weston, WV, take exit 99 onto US 33, and go east to Elkins, WV. In Elkins, follow US 219 South to the intersection of US 219 and WV 66. Reset your trip meter as you turn east on WV 66 from US 219.

RIDE OVERVIEW

This ride starts at the intersection of US 219 South and WV 66, in the shadow of Snowshoe Mountain Resort. Snowshoe attracts thousands of skiers each winter, which explains the ski and snowboard outfitters you'll see as you negotiate the smooth curves of US 219. You'll ride near the Elk River as it flows north over the rocks, creating a cooling effect on hot summer days.

From the tiny town of Slatyfork, US 219 South hugs the side of Gauley Mountain before climbing up Elk Mountain. At the road's apex, you'll see WV 150, the Highland Scenic Highway, turning off to the right. There's no commercial traffic along its 20-mile length. What you'll see along the way are beautiful forests, distant vistas, some wildlife, and improved overlooks with information on the history of the area. If you ride the Highland Scenic Highway, turn left at the other end to return to this ride in Marlinton.

Riding down from Elk Mountain, there's a gravel overlook on the left side of the road offering good views of the Greenbrier River Valley. US 219 descends into the valley in a series of sweeping curves. Once in the valley, you'll pass the Marlinton Motor Inn. You're still several miles north of Marlinton. As a matter of fact, the Marlinton Motor Inn is in the town of Edray. Regardless, they offer cheap rooms and can be reached at 304-799-4711.

US 219 enters Marlinton, the county seat of Pocahontas County, WV. Pocahontas County has plenty of attractions to offer motorcyclists. So many, actually, the Convention and Visitors Bureau advertises in national motorcycle magazines. The ride makes a left turn onto WV 39 (Eighth St.), crossing the bridge over the Greenbrier River and entering the downtown section of Marlinton.

Downtown Marlinton has three main attractions: restaurants, the Greenbrier River Trail, and the Pocahontas County Convention and Visitors Bureau. Restaurants in Marlinton appeal to every taste. Stop in at French's Diner for a plate of eggs and a cup of coffee (lunch and dinner items, too), or hit the Roadhouse Bar, a local biker hangout. Inside you'll find hot food, cold beer, and level pool tables. For more elegant dining, try the patio overlooking the Greenbrier River at the River Place Restaurant. The Greenbrier River Trail stretches from Caldwell to Cass, and is open to hikers, bicyclists, and horses. No powered vehicles are allowed on the trail, which was once the old C & O Railroad bed. Along its 77-mile length, the trail passes over 35 bridges and through two tunnels. In Marlinton, you'll see bicycle outfitters offering bicycles for rent. This trail is similar to the Virginia Creeper Trail mentioned in the *Highlands Loop* ride

TOTAL DISTANCE
67.5 miles

TIME FRAME
2 hours from start to finish. Add time to eat in Marlinton, rent a bicycle to ride on the Greenbrier River Trail, and explore Cass and the Cass Scenic Railroad State Park.

(p. 132) that starts in Abingdon, VA. The Pocahontas County Convention and Visitors Bureau is in the old train depot on WV 39 at the Greenbrier River Trail. Inside the bureau, you'll find tons of useful information, including the pamphlet on motorcycle touring in the county.

As you ride out of Marlinton, you'll climb a bit as you ride around Marlin

The Snowshoe hare welcomes you.

Mountain. On the right side of the road is Knapp Creek. The powdery green color of this water might appear to be the by-product of some ecological disaster. There's no reason to call the EPA about the water, though—the color is caused by light rock dust naturally eroded from the banks of the creek and carried downstream. It's an unusual sight in West Virginia; the phenomenon is more often associated with active glaciers.

In Huntersville, you can take the other ride alternative by turning left onto WV 28 and riding north through the narrow Brown's Creek Valley. However, this ride continues to Minnehaha Springs before turning north onto WV 92. With long, sweeping curves, WV 92 continues to follow Knapp Creek upstream through farm country and into the town of Frost. In Frost, you'll have to make a well-marked left turn to stay on WV 92 North. WV 28 rejoins the ride a few miles before you turn left toward Cass on WV 66.

Love curves? West Virginia's got 'em!

After turning onto WV 66, ride about 0.75 mile and take a look to the right side of the road, over the cattle farm, and feast your eyes on that giant white satellite dish! It looks like the farmers here are serious about their TV reception. Actually, what you are seeing there is the GBT, the Great Big Thing. The letters GBT also stand for Green Bank Telescope, but at 485 ft. tall, 16,000,000 lbs., and a price tag of $79 million, it really *is* a Great Big Thing. As a matter of fact it's the biggest movable, man-made Great Big Thing on land. The GBT is part of the National Astronomy Radio Observatory (NARO), where scientists come from all over the world to listen to transmissions made in outer space. The GBT is truly out of this world. You can get a closer look at the NARO and the GBT by stopping in the visitor center a couple of miles north on WV 28 between 8 am and 7:30 pm.

From the strange sight of the GBT, the road makes a couple of nice bends before reaching Cass. On the left after entering town is CC's Café. This small café offers coffee, muffins and sandwiches. Past CC's, the road curves sharply left, crossing the Greenbrier River and the railroad tracks of the Cass Scenic Railroad State Park. The large white building standing next to the tracks is the park headquarters. Inside you can get information and schedules about the three different train excursions offered in the park. You can ride up to Bald Knob (4,842 ft.) and see two states, take in the Spruce Ride which takes you to the abandoned logging town of Spruce, or ride to Whittaker Camp No.1 to learn about the logging life in the early 1900s. These excursions cost between $13 and $19 and are cheaper on weekdays; there are dinner tours as well. If you're planning for a train

While in Cass, be sure to stop in at the 1902 country store for information or most anything else.

excursion, it's best to call ahead. You can reach the Cass Scenic Railroad State Park by phone at 800-CALL-WVA or 304-456-4300, or on the web at www.cassrailroad.com.

So, why a railroad in such a remote location? The town of Cass was once a booming lumber town. There were two types of railroads that used Cass. One railroad was the standard gauge railroad owned by the C & O Railway (now the Greenbrier River Trail). The C & O transported lumber out of Cass to market. The Cass Railway was a smaller gauge, using small but powerful locomotives known as Shays to climb up and down the steep mountains, transporting trees from the mountainsides to the lumber mill in Cass. Standard gauge rail trains were designed to handle a 2% grade, while the Shays could handle a steep 11% grade. Today the state park runs the same trains used by the West Virginia Spruce Lumber Company in the early 1900s. The locomotives, several miles of track, and the flatbed lumber cars were bought by the State of West Virginia in 1961. The flatbed cars were refurbished and became passenger cars. The tracks were refurbished and expanded back to

their original length. When West Virginia bought the property in 1961, some thought it would be a losing bet—after all, who would ride for hours off the interstate to visit Cass? The gamble has paid off. Today Cass is a destination and a jumping-off point for visitors wanting to see the interesting sights all around.

Just past the State Park headquarters, WV 66 makes two 90-degree turns, first to the right, then immediately to the left. As you make the second turn, you'll notice all the houses in this part of Cass are exactly the same. Each two-story, white frame structure is the same size, design, and color. Houses in Cass were built by the lumber company to accommodate the hard-working West Virginians who worked here. When the lumber industry dried up due to deforestation, the town was abandoned. Fearing Cass would go the way of the town of Spruce (now only a series of concrete foundations), the State of West Virginia offered the buildings rent-free to individuals who were willing to live in Cass. Hundreds flocked to the area, and Cass became an artist's colony in the 1960s. Residents had to pay for

Pretty white frame houses lining a boardwalk give Cass's main street its charm, and serve as a reminder of days gone by.

the upkeep of the house in which they were residing. Realizing there was no return for their money spent on upkeep, the occupants began to move out, and today only a few permanent residents remain. Many of the vacant houses serve as rental cottages managed by the state park. It has proven to be an inexpensive way for West Virginia to maintain the charm of this tiny town.

Leaving Cass, WV 66 climbs the back of the Alleghenies toward Snowshoe Mountain Resort. If it's curves you crave, this is the part of the ride for you! Well-banked twisties take you up, up, and away. About two miles outside of town, there's one last good view of Cass to the left before turning completely away into the woods and curves.

You'll pass the rear entrance to Snowshoe Mountain Resort and begin descending down into the valley at the base of Snowshoe Mountain. Just before entering the valley, the road makes a couple of wild twists, so watch your speed. Once in the valley, sweeping curves lead you to the entrance of Snowshoe Mountain Resort. Impossible to miss, a tall sign with a stylized bunny and the words "Snowshoe Mountain" marks the road

to the resort. If you want to take in some great views, turn right and ride the seven miles up to an elevation of 4,484 ft. at the summit. The resort is open year-round and really booms in the winter when they get an average of 180 in. of snowfall, not to mention the man-made snow they can make. Aware that there are vacationers 12 months a year, the staff at Snowshoe has summertime events (HOG and BMW owner rallies) and activities. Among the amenities of Snowshoe, there are 21 restaurants, 16 pubs, and one comedy club. There are 1,800 rooms available; finding something for any budget is possible. Contact Snowshoe Mountain Resort at 877-441-4FUN, or check them out on the web at www.snowshoemtn.com.

Back on WV 66, you'll take in two more sweeping curves before ending this ride where it began at the intersection of US 219 and WV 66. Turn left onto US 219 South to return to Marlinton, or turn right onto US 219 North to head toward Elkins and the rides in and around the Canaan Valley.

RIDE ALTERNATIVES

At mile 14, you can turn right onto the Highland Scenic Highway and ride the 20 miles over the Yew Mountains and then left onto WV 39 to return to Marlinton and this ride. On the Scenic Highway, there are plenty of overlooks (and no commercial traffic allowed) as you ride on some of the highest elevations of West Virginia.

At mile 26, you can turn left onto WV 28 North and shave about five miles off this adventure. In doing so you'll have a more mountainous ride, without the distant vistas offered by WV 92. WV 28 and WV 92 parallel each other and rejoin in Dunmore before you'll turn left onto WV 66 to ride through Cass.

ROAD CONDITIONS

All the roads on this ride are two-lane asphalt. US 219 offers many tight twists on the side of Gauley Mountain and then becomes a tame country road in the Greenbrier River Valley. WV 39 will lead you through the heart of Marlinton, WV, and through some curves near Marlin Mountain. The ride then turns left onto WV 92, which is a calm road with only sweeping curves. Turning onto WV 66 and riding through Cass you'll ride a few curves, but after Cass the road gets wildly twisty for several miles back into the Snowshoe Valley.

POINTS OF INTEREST

Elk River Valley, Highland Scenic Highway, Town of Marlinton, Greenbrier River Trail, powdery green color of Knapp Creek, view of the Green Bank Telescope, Cass Scenic Railroad State Park, historic town of Cass, Snowshoe Mountain Resort.

RESTAURANTS

In Marlinton there are several places to eat, but three stand out.

River Place (304-799-7233) overlooks the Greenbrier River and is on the right side of WV 39 at the intersection of First Ave. After turning from US 219 and crossing the Greenbrier River, River Place is on the right and is open seven days a week from 7 am to 9 pm, offering breakfast, lunch and dinner. Breakfasts start at $1.50 for a muffin and go up to about $7 for an omelet and hash browns. Lunch has the $2.50 burger, served a la carte (fries are extra), or you can get a 12-in. sub for $6. Dinner starts at $6.95 for pasta and goes up to $16 for steak. Also on the menu are burgers, soups, salads, and appetizers. Lodging is available at River Place, in the form of rooms and a cottage. Rooms start at $40 single and $49 double, while the cottage rents for around $100. Check River Place out on the web at www.riverplacewv.com.

The biker bar in town is the **Roadhouse Bar** across the street from River Place on First Ave. Inside there are pool tables, cold beer, good eats, and plenty of music to party to. The Roadhouse is open every day from 3 to 11 pm and until 3 am on Friday nights (closed on Sundays). You can order steak for $19 or shrimp for $10, with plenty of other bar food on the menu. On Friday nights, there's usually a buffet for $10 and live music. The Roadhouse isn't fancy, but it's as comfortable as a worn shirt.

At **French's Diner** (304-799-9910) you can enjoy a cup of coffee or a full meal. You'll find it at the intersection of WV 39 and Second Ave. in the heart of Marlinton. Open Monday through Saturday from 7 am to 8 pm and Sunday until noon, French's offers breakfast, lunch, and dinner in a cozy atmosphere. It's a local favorite where you'll rub elbows with the bigwigs of Pocahontas County. The meals there are inexpensive, with a bacon and egg breakfast setting you back just $2 (add 80 cents for a bottomless cup of coffee). For lunch, sandwiches and burgers dominate the menu. Dinner is not that different from lunch, but dinner entrees are larger. You can call ahead if you want, but they don't take reservations.

In Cass, **CC's Café** (304-456-4288) is on the left side of the road just before you cross the Greenbrier River. Inside there's good coffee, muffins, and sandwiches. CC's is open from 8 am to 4 pm daily.

At the end of the ride at **Snowshoe Mountain Resort** (877-441-4FUN), there are dozens of places to eat, drink, and be merry—a pizza parlor, a comedy club, a steakhouse, a pub, and everything in between. Even if you aren't hungry, drive the seven miles up to Snowshoe Mountain Resort and check out the views. You can learn more about Snowshoe's dining and lodging choices on the web at www.snowshoemtn.com.

DETAILED DIRECTIONS

Mile 0—Head south on US 219 from WV 66 near Snowshoe Resort. *The road curves along the banks of the Elk River for the first several miles. At mile 132 you'll climb out of the Elk River Valley and reach the north end of the Highland Scenic Highway on the right at mile 14. There's a gravel overlook of the Greenbrier River Valley on the left side of the road at mile 15.2. You'll enter the town of Marlinton at mile 20.6.*

Mile 21.1—Turn left onto WV 39 (cross the bridge over the Greenbrier River and enter the heart of Marlinton). *You'll cross the Greenbrier River Trail at mile 21.5; the Pocahontas County Visitor's Center is on the left in the old train depot. WV 39 follows the margarita-green Knapp River for several miles out of*

town. This adventure continues straight on, but the ride alternative makes a left onto WV 28 at mile 26.8.

Mile 30.2—Turn left onto WV 92 in Minnehaha Springs.

Mile 40.4—Turn left to remain on WV 92. *At mile 48, WV 28 rejoins this adventure already in progress.*

Mile 51.3—Turn left onto WV 66. *There's a quiet farm on the right side of the road at mile 52.1. Beyond that farm is the gargantuan Green Bank Telescope. You'll enter the town of Cass at mile 55.5. CC's Café is on the left at mile 55.9. You'll cross the Greenbrier River and some railroad tracks at mile 56. The Cass Scenic Railroad State Park is on the right at mile 56.1.*
The road curves left, right, then left again into the historic district of the town of Cass. There's a view off to the left at mile 58.7. At mile 62.5 you'll pass the rear entrance to Snowshoe Resort. Watch your speed for a sharp right turn at mile 65.1. The front entrance to Snowshoe Resort is on the right at mile 66.8.

Mile 67.5—This ride ends where it began at the intersection of WV 66 and US 219.

Snowshoe South Loop

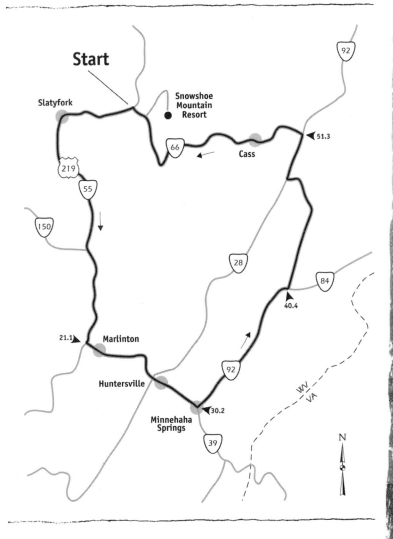

Start

Slatyfork

Snowshoe Mountain Resort

92

51.3

66

Cass

219

55

150

28

84

40.4

21.1

Marlinton

92

Huntersville

30.2

Minnehaha Springs

39

WV
VA

N

75 Interstate Highway

640 State Highway

Route

27 US Highway

606 County Road

Other Road

5▶ Milepost

Blue Ridge Parkway

Time Travel

On this ride, your motorcycle is your time machine. You'll begin your journey in the present at Snowshoe Mountain Resort, then ride into the past at the Cass Scenic Railroad State Park, getting a glimpse of the future as you pass the Green Bank Telescope. You'll ride back in time again at the Durbin & Greenbrier Mountain Railroad. Even if you don't stop for any of the sights along the way, you'll enjoy smooth roads, mountain scenery, and twisty mountain passes. It's all hours away from the interstates and bustle of the big city.

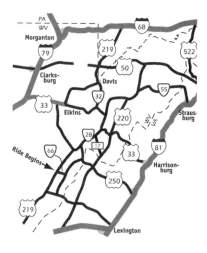

GETTING TO THE START

This ride begins at the intersection of US 219 and WV 66. From the East and South, follow I-64 West from Virginia and take exit 169 onto US 219 North. Follow US 219 North to WV 66. From the West and North, follow I-79 to Weston, WV, take exit 99 onto US 33, and go east to Elkins, WV. In Elkins, follow US 219 South to the intersection of US 219 and WV 66. Reset your trip meter as you turn east on WV 66 from US 219.

RIDE OVERVIEW

Turning onto WV 66 from US 219 in Linwood, WV, the road begins a series of sweeping curves through the narrow valley at the foot of Snowshoe Mountain. In this valley there's fuel, a bank (the kind with an ATM), and several ski rental shops and ski outfitter shops. The ski shops cater to visitors at the Snowshoe Mountain Resort.

Less than a mile from where this ride begins is the entrance to the Snowshoe Mountain Resort. If you're interested in taking in some distant vistas, enjoying a good meal or checking into a room, turn left and ride about seven miles up the mountain to reach the Top of Snowshoe Lodge. You don't have to be a skier to enjoy the 11,000 acres of Snowshoe, although in the winter months skiing is clearly the attraction. Snowshoe offers skiers a 1500-ft. drop on 57 ski trails, 14 ski lifts, snow tubing, snowboarding, and even guided snowmobile tours of the nearby mountaintops. In the summer months, when the snow has melted,

Snowshoe Mountain Resort offers adventurous outdoor activities like canoeing, horseback riding, mountain biking, rock climbing, golf, swimming, and even motorcycle touring! In recent years, the management of Snowshoe Mountain Resort has discovered motorcyclists love the mountains and attractions of the Monongahela National Forest. It now offers special rates and incentives for motorcycling clubs and groups. The resort is home to a dozen different restaurants ranging in price and sophistication from a pizza parlor to a steak house. With over 1,800 lodging options from three bedroom condos to single-bed hotel rooms, you'll find the cheapest lodging rates to be found in midweek of the summer months. You can call Snowshoe Mountain Resort at 877-441-4FUN, or check them out on the web at www.snowshoemtn.com.

Back on WV 66 you'll begin to climb out of the valley at the base of Snowshoe Mountain. The first of several sharp twists starts before your third mile into the ride. The road gets mighty twisty before getting you through the mountain pass. To the right after crossing the pass there's a nice view overlooking the Greenbrier River Valley and town of Cass, and then you'll begin your descent.

Once in Cass, you'll notice that all the homes in the downtown area are exactly the same. They are the same shape, color, size, design, same everything! The town of Cass was built by the West Virginia Spruce Lumber Company around 1901 and named for the Chairman of the Board, Joseph K. Cass. A company town if there ever was one, Cass boomed as all of its residents worked for the railroad, the lumber mill, or the company store. The lucrative lumber mill and shipping

TOTAL DISTANCE
75.1 miles

TIME FRAME
2 hours from start to finish. Add time to enjoy the amenities of Snowshoe Mountain Resort, look into the past at the Cass Scenic Railroad, and glimpse the future at the Green Bank Telescope.

center changed hands several times. Its last owner was the Mower Lumber Company, which operated it until 1960, when they had to abandon the area due to deforestation. The residents of Cass followed the money out of town, leaving it nearly vacant. In an attempt to attract new residents, the state offered the houses in Cass rent-free to anyone who would settle in them, providing they agreed to keep them in their original

The rails at Cass once carried West Virginia lumber to market.

condition. The offer attracted hundreds of residents, and for a few years, Cass was known as an artist's colony. The cost of maintenance for homes they didn't own proved to be too much for the occupants, and the town was once again left vacant. There are a few locals living in the white frame structures lining the main street, but most of the houses in Cass now serve as rental cottages for the Cass Scenic Railroad State Park.

To be a successful town, the goods of that town must be portable; you have to get the goods to market. In Cass, those goods were the trees from the surrounding mountains. Harvesting the lumber and moving it to the mill in Cass was made possible by the small but powerful Shay locomotives. Powered by steam, the small Shays could climb an 11% grade, while standard trains could only handle a 2% grade. These mighty trains pulled both lumber and workers up and down these mountains to the town of Cass, where the timber was milled and shipped out on larger, more conventional trains.

Once the timber was gone, the rail lines were abandoned. The locomotives remained unused until 1961 when the State of West Virginia bought the locomotives and the seven miles of track for $125,000. The idea of a tourist attraction in the remote reaches of West Virginia seemed like a gamble at the time, but it has paid off. More money was spent to create the park, refurbish the locomotives, change the flatbed cars into passenger cars, and have additional track restored. Today the Shays pull passenger cars up through the old logging country on scenic train rides.

There are three destinations to choose from: Whittaker Station, Spruce, and Bald Knob. On the Whittaker Station ride you'll see what life was like as a "wood hick" when

Miles away, the Green Bank Telescope is still one Great Big Thing!

you pay a visit to Whittaker Camp 1. The Spruce ride will take you to explore the remnants of the town of Spruce. Once a thriving town, Spruce is now just a collection of concrete foundations, as nature reclaims the land that man once thought he owned. The Bald Knob ride is the highlight, as the train climbs to the dizzying elevation of 4,842 ft. above sea level onto Bald Knob. From Bald Knob you can see two states on a clear day. Some train rides include dinners and entertainment. The cost is just $13 to $19 per adult, depending on which train ride you take and what day of the week it is (weekdays are cheapest).

The park offers accommodations in several of the mill house cottages in the downtown area. The summer rates for the cottages start at $70 nightly, and and each cottage sleeps four. Expect to spend a few extra dollars for weekend nights. Learn more by calling 800-CALL-WVA or 304-456-4300, or check them out on the web at www.cassrailroad.com.

Leaving the past behind, WV 66 crosses the Greenbrier River and makes a sharp right turn. You'll enjoy a few good curves as you climb out of the Greenbrier River Valley into some farmland. On the left side of the road, you'll have to look over a farm for the first glimpse of the Green Bank Telescope (GBT). You'll have a closer look at the GBT in just a few minutes after turning onto WV 28.

WV 66 meets WV 28 in a T intersection. This ride makes a left turn and rides into the town of Green Bank. If you are a dedicated cell phone addict, be ready for some downtime. The GBTelescope is a radio telescope, which requires radio silence in the area to prevent interference.

To get a closer look at the GBT and tour the National Radio Astronomy Observatory (NRAO), turn left into the driveway and stop in at the Visitor Center. Open from 8 am to 7:30 pm, the Visitor Center is the place to start tours, visit the museum, watch a movie about the GBT, have a hot dog at the snack bar, or buy some souvenirs at the gift shop. To get a close-up view of the GBT and the other six radio telescopes at the NRAO, you have to take a tour. No gasoline combustion engines are allowed within a certain distance of the GBT, because spark plugs cause interference. The NRAO uses diesel-powered tour buses to shuttle visitors through the NRAO.

So, what's the GBT? Some refer to it as the Great Big Thing. And a great big thing it is. Standing 485 ft. tall, it weighs in at 16,000,000 lb. and has 2,004 metal panels covering an area larger than two acres. These panels capture the radio waves transmitted by stars and molecules millions of miles away. The whole thing moves, too—making it the largest man-made, movable object on land. It cost a whopping $79,000,000 to build and receives but does not transmit radio signals. Radio telescopes detect radio waves, not light waves, so they do not have lenses. They can produce an image in all weather, but the image shows up on a computer screen, not in the ocular of a telescope. The NRAO was first opened in Green Bank in 1956 and is one of a group of observatories found from the Virgin Islands to Hawaii. It costs nothing to tour the NRAO.

Leaving the GBT behind you, turn back north on WV 28 and ride up to US 250 North. At the intersection of WV 28 and US 250, turn left. This will lead you through the towns of Bartow and Durbin. In Bartow, the Hermitage Restaurant and Motel are on the left side of the road. The motel welcomes motorcyclists, and the restaurant is open until 8 pm nightly except from December to March, when it is closed. The motel does not accept reservations for the winter months, but advertises that walk-ins are welcome. You'd better call ahead if you're planning to stay at the Hermitage. You can reach them by phone at 304-456-4808 or on the web at www.hermitagemotel.com.

You'll continue on US 250 toward the town of Durbin. If you're a rail nut and the train rides in the Cass Scenic Railroad State Park didn't fully satisfy you, stop in at the Durbin & Greenbrier Valley Railroad in Durbin for more experiences with locomotives. You can take a seven-hour trip on the *Tygart Flyer* with a buffet included for $42, or opt for the two-hour trip on a steam locomotive, the *Durbin Rocket*, for $12. Or there's the three-hour trip on the *Cheat Mountain Salamander*, a "rail bus," for $18. Learn more about the Durbin & Greenbrier Valley Railroad by calling

877-MTN-RAIL (877-686-7245), or try the web at www.mountainrail.com.

From Durbin the road twists upward onto Shavers Mountain and then over Cheat Mountain. As you descend toward the Tygart Valley from the back of Cheat Mountain, you'll enjoy some great curves on well-maintained asphalt as you ride through the Huttonsville Wildlife Management Area.

Once in the valley, keep an eye peeled for hitchhikers, particularly hitchhikers wearing bright orange jumpsuits (the old black-and-white striped prison suits went out of vogue years ago). Tygart Valley is home to several thousand individuals who are serving time in the Huttonsville Correctional Center. The Correctional Center is the large prison on the left side of the road, with a high, razor-wire-topped fence and guard towers. Just past the prison, this adventure makes a left turn onto US 219 South.

Don't let the fact that US 219 is a US route give you nightmarish visions of a super-slab interstate highway. Thankfully, this section of US 219 is a quiet two-lane stretch that meanders through the western side of the Tygart Valley. The Tygart Valley is a deep valley in the Alleghenies, with dozens of cattle farms taking advantage of its relatively level floor. The road follows the curves of the foothills that make up the western side of the valley. You'll cross the Tygart Valley River on a steel superstructure bridge. After crossing the bridge, the valley begins to narrow, forcing the road to follow tighter curves of the seemingly encroaching mountains. You'll leave the valley by passing through the town of Valley Head.

From Valley Head, US 219 twists southward to Mingo, as the road winds through the shade of trees and along several small streams, making rides cooler on hot summer days. In Mingo, you can really cool off in the BrazenHead Inn & Pub. A traditional Irish Inn, The BrazenHead offers rooms, food, and plenty of ale for visitors. In the winter months, only overnight guests can take advantage of these delicious meals, and from St. Patrick's Day to early June, you won't find the restaurant open during the week. Call ahead if you want to stay there. You can reach the BrazenHead Inn & Pub at 304-339-6917, toll free at 866-339-6917, or on the web at www.brazenheadinn.com.

From Mingo, US 219 South gets even more twisty and steep than before. The road climbs up between Mace Knob and Valley Mountain (Mace Knob will be on your left, and Valley Mountain will be on your right). From the apex of this climb, the road descends steeply with sweeping curves and great views. One particularly good view opens up to the left as you descend. Once reaching the bottom of the mountain, you'll again be in the valley at the base of Snowshoe

Barns are everywhere in West Virginia.

Mountain. The ride ends where it began at the intersection of US 219 and WV 66. You can add more great riding to this adventure by taking the Snowshoe South Loop Ride which begins on US 219 South at WV 66 (p. 164).

RIDE ALTERNATIVES

This ride ends at the beginning of the Snowshoe South Loop Ride. If you take that ride, you'll add another 67 miles to your ride by visiting the town of Marlinton, WV.

ROAD CONDITIONS

Two-lane asphalt abounds, most of which is in excellent shape. WV 66 is very well maintained, as is US 219; however, US 220 has a few patches of asphalt that creates a bit of a bumpy ride. WV 28 is the only road on this ride that has no tight twisties, only sweeping curves. The other roads begin docilely enough with gentle sweeping curves then get wild as you climb in elevation.

POINTS OF INTEREST

Snowshoe Resort, town of Cass, Cass Scenic Railroad State Park, Green Bank Telescope, Greenbrier Ridge, Huttonsville Correctional Facility, BrazenHead Inn & Pub.

RESTAURANTS

There are dozens of places to eat in the **Snowshoe Mountain Resort**. If you are in need of a meal and are nearby, ride the seven miles up from WV 66 to the main lodge and inquire about the steak house, comedy bar, pizza parlor, or sandwich shop.

In Cass, just after you cross the Greenbrier River, you'll find **CC's Café** (304-456-4288) on the right side of the road, with good coffee, muffins, and sandwiches. CC's is open from 8

am to 4 pm daily. There is a snack bar at the **National Radio Astronomy Observatory**. The snack bar is open from 8 am to 7:30 pm (matching the hours of the visitor center). From the snack bar you can get a sandwich or a hot dog, but think "snack" when ordering—it won't be a real meal. In Bartow, on US 250 just west of WV 28, is the **Hermitage Restaurant and Motel** (304-456-4808). The restaurant serves a continental breakfast from 7 am to 10 am, and it reopens at 11:30 am to offer lunch and dinner until 8 pm, seven days a week. The Hermitage Restaurant and Motel is closed from December to March, but offers motel rooms for walk-ins in the off-season. Check them out on the web at www.hermitagemotel.com.

In the last leg of this adventure in the small town of Mingo is the **BrazenHead Restaurant & Pub** (304-339-6917, or 866-339-6917). Open year-round for overnight guests, this traditional Irish inn and pub offers 20 rooms and delicious meals (most with an Irish flavor). The restaurant is open on weekends only during the spring. In the summer and fall the restaurant is open seven days a week from 8 am to 11 am for breakfast, lunch from 11 am to 5 pm, and dinner from 5 pm to 10 pm. The pub is open from Wednesday through Sunday from 4 pm throughout the evening. The room rate at the BrazenHead is highest during ski season at $149 nightly and lowest during the summer at $99 to $119 nightly, depending on which floor you want (upstairs is more expensive). The menu at the BrazenHead includes ham and cabbage for $8.95, fish and chips for $7.95, and corned beef and cabbage for $8.95. Riders who aren't interested in Irish cuisine can choose from lasagna at $7.95, grilled salmon at $12, and a variety of sandwiches on the lunch menu—$4.95 for grilled cheese to $6.95 for a grilled chicken sub, with nearly every kind of sandwich in between. Breakfasts include items like a Western omelet for $6.95 or a plain bagel for $1.00. Call ahead to check if they are open, or to make room reservations. The web address is www.brazenheadinn.com.

DETAILED DIRECTIONS

Mile 0—Turn onto WV 66 East from US 219. *You'll pass the entrance to Snowshoe Mountain Resort on the left at mile 0.7. Watch your speed at mile 2.4 as the road makes a sharp left turn. The curves begin in earnest at mile 3.4, and you'll pass the alternate entrance to the resort at mile 5. There's a good view to the east from the saddle of your bike at mile 8.8 . You'll enter the historic town of Cass at mile 11. The Cass Scenic Railroad State Park is on the left at mile 11.4. You'll cross the railroad tracks and the Greenbrier River at mile 11.5. CC's Café is on the right at mile 11.6. You'll leave the town of Cass at mile 12. The unusual sight of the Green Bank Telescope behind a quiet farm is on the left at mile 15.4.*

Mile 16.2—Turn left onto WV 28. *The entrance to the Green Bank Telescope (National Radio Astronomy Observatory) is on the left at mile 19.4.*

Mile 27.8—Turn left onto US 250/WV 92 North. *The Hermitage Restaurant and Motel is on the left at mile 27.9. At mile 32, you'll be in the town of Durbin, home of the Durbin & Greenbrier Valley Railroad. You'll ride across the Cheat Bridge at mile 37.3. Wild, twisting turns await you as you climb Shavers and Cheat Mountains beginning at mile 34.4. At mile 36.3 you'll enter Tygart Valley. Don't pick up any hitchhikers near mile 49.3 as you pass the Huttonsville Correctional Center.*

Mile 50.3—Turn left onto US 219 South (also WV 55). *The Victorian-style Cardinal Inn is on the right at mile 51. You'll cross the Tygart Valley Bridge at mile 59.3. In Mingo, WV, at mile 63.1, you'll find the BrazenHead Inn & Pub on the right.*

Mile 75.1—The ride ends where it began at the intersection of US 219 and WV 66. *Continue south on US 219 to reach the town of Marlinton, WV, or turn left onto WV 66 to head back to Snowshoe and Cass.*

Time Travel

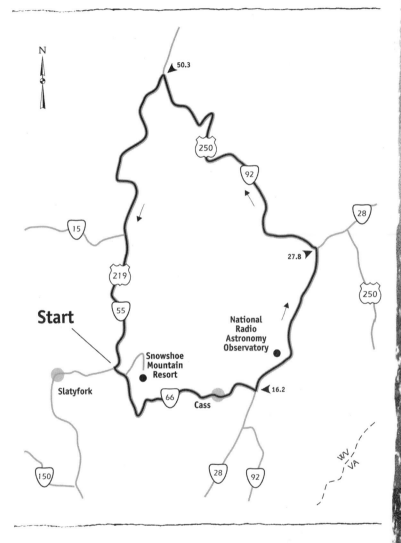

N

▲ 50.3

250

92

28

15

219

250

55

Start

National
Radio
Astronomy
Observatory

27.8 ►

Snowshoe
Mountain
Resort

16.2 ◄

Slatyfork

66

Cass

WV
VA

150

28   92

75   Interstate Highway

640   State Highway

━━━ Route

27   US Highway

606   County Road

Other Road

5 ►   Milepost

═══ Blue Ridge Parkway

Seneca Rocks!

*J*ust getting to the start of this ride is a pleasure. You'll enjoy well-paved roads, which deliver smooth sweeping curves and a couple of tight twisties. The scenery is unique and beautiful. Along the way, you'll pass sphagnum bogs, rock outcroppings, and a cavern; ride through several mountain passes; and end only after riding the crests of several mountains.

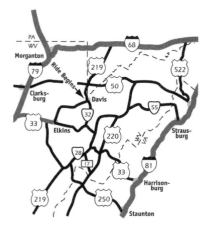

GAS
Gas is available at the start in Davis, WV; at miles 0.3, 0.6, 7.9, 12.5, 15.3, 28.7, 31.7, 44.4, 53, 64.1, 74.3, and 91.8; and at the ride's end.

GETTING TO THE START

This ride starts in the town of Davis, WV, on WV 32 at CR 29, which is the entrance road to Blackwater Falls State Park.

From the west and I-79: Take exit 119 onto US 50 East between Bridgeport and Clarksburg. Follow US 50 East into Maryland where you'll turn south onto US 219, leading you back into West Virginia and to the town of Thomas. Once in Thomas, take WV 32 east into Davis. The ride begins at the intersection of WV 32 and CR 29. Zero your trip meter as you ride east through that intersection.

From the east: I-81: Follow US 250 from Staunton, VA, to Monterey, VA. In Monterey, pick up US 220 North into West Virginia. Once in West Virginia, turn left onto CR 17 (Snowy Mountain Rd.). It ends at WV 28; turn right and ride up to Judy Gap where you'll take WV 33 North to Seneca Rocks, then turn left to stay on US 33 North into Harman. In Harman, turn right onto WV 32 and follow that up through the Canaan Valley to Davis. You'll find the beginning of the ride at the intersection of WV 32 and CR 29. Zero your trip meter as you turn back south on WV 32 where it intersects with CR 29.

RIDE OVERVIEW

At the ride's beginning, you'll motor through the small town of Davis, WV. Davis was built by the timber industry in 1889, on the banks of the Blackwater River. It was one of the first towns in the Nation to have electricity.

Today Davis thrives because of the outdoor adventure tourism industry. In the summer mountain biking is king, and in winter skiing (alpine and nordic both) drive the economy. Davis is home to Granny Gear Productions, whose founder, Laird Knight, is the madman responsible for the insane sport of 24-hour mountain bike racing. Laird's original race has spawned 24-hour competitions all over the world, but one of the best is still right here in West Virginia.

Back to motorcycles—to head out of town and into the Canaan Valley, ride over the Blackwater River on the bridge with the iron superstructure. On the way there, you'll enjoy a few sweeping turns before reaching the ultra-straight section of WV 32 that lies atop undulating hills among the ski resorts. The locals teach that here, "Canaan rhymes with insane." Considering the 24-hour mountain bike racing and the wild winter sports

TOTAL DISTANCE
91.8 miles

TIME FRAME
3 hours from start to finish. Add time to explore Seneca Rocks, dine at Harper's Country Store, or visit Smoke Hole Caverns.

in the area, that seems like poetic justice. The Canaan Valley Resort State Park entrance is on the right side of the road just before the first gentle bend out of the valley. In the state park you'll discover a good restaurant offering beautiful mountain views, lodging, trails, and other amenities.

Leaving the Canaan Valley, descend and climb back up through some fun curves of the Allegheny Mountains,

The visitor center below Seneca Rocks has good interpretive exhibits, and it's a great place to watch the rock climbers on the cliffs above.

West Virginia's Northern Highlands **181**

then cross the Eastern Continental Divide in a mountain pass. Rainfall on one side of this pass flows downhill to the Atlantic Ocean. On the other side, rainfall flows to the Gulf of Mexico. You, too, will seem to flow down toward the Seneca River. As you near the river, Seneca Rocks comes into view.

At the intersection of WV 32 and WV 28/55, the narrow, quartzite spine of Seneca Rocks extends out from the mountainside and stretches over 900 feet into the sky. This unusual formation is common in the area, due to an ancient upheaval of the Appalachian Mountains. The Seneca Rocks Discovery Center is a museum and gift shop, offering restrooms and information about the formation, the area, and the Sites Homestead. The homestead was built by Jacob Sites and has been welcoming guests since 1839. Today, the Sites Homestead gives riders a glimpse of what life was like in Seneca Valley over 150 years ago.

This area is rich with history. In fact, during the construction of the Discovery Center there were archeological artifacts unearthed in what was to become the parking area, so the parking area was moved, and the site was preserved for future archeological digs. Now when you visit, you'll know why the parking area is so far from the Discovery Center's entrance.

Across the street at the intersection of WV 32 and WV 28/55 is Harper's Old Country Store. The store bills itself as one of the oldest continuously operated businesses in West Virginia. Opened in 1902, it has changed little. The wooden floor of the business is made of different sized boards, indicating it was built before the lumber mills of the 1920s gave construction material a standard size.

Harper's still offers nearly everything a person might need or want. The family business has passed from generation to generation of Harpers, but the store has remained largely unchanged, except for the Front Porch Restaurant. Harper's added the restaurant to give passersby an option for dining in the Seneca Valley. The Front Porch serves lunch and dinner items (pizza, pita pockets, and sandwiches) with excellent views of the natural wonder across the street.

This ride turns left onto WV 28/55 and follows the North Fork of the South Branch of the Potomac River toward Smoke Hole Caverns and the town of Petersburg, WV. Along the way, you'll pass Champe Rocks. Much like Seneca Rocks, Champe Rocks are an exposed spine of quartzite jutting out from the side of the mountain. You'll see more exposed quartzite as you ride toward Petersburg. Shortly after passing Champe Rocks is a shortcut opportunity. To take the shortcut, turn left onto CR 28-7, also known as Jordan Run Road. You'll miss Smoke Hole Caverns and some pretty farmland, but you'll shave about 20 minutes from this ride and cover some excellent asphalt with nice mountain views.

If you continue on the ride, you'll pass Smoke Hole Caverns. These privately owned, active caverns continue to slowly build their interesting formations inside. Considering the temperature inside is a constant 56° F, it's a great place to stop on a hot summer day or a bitter cold winter day. Either way, they're interesting to visit. Inside, there aren't any concrete elves painted to look like movie stars, but you will see stalactites, stalagmites, ribbon stalactites, and other naturally formed features under one of the highest

Don't miss West Virginia's largest souvenir shop at Smoke Hole Caverns.

ceilings in the eastern United States. Admission is $8 for the 45-minute walking tour of the Cavern. It costs nothing to tour what the proprietors boast is the largest souvenir and gift shop in West Virginia, complete with plastic tomahawks. There's also a "wildlife museum" which displays several handsome hunting trophies of animals killed years ago. Smoke Hole Caverns also has a rustic log motel and offers log cabins for rent. Motel rooms go for $59 to $99 nightly, and cabins rent for $159 per weekend night and $129 per night during the week. The cabins sleep six. Reach them on the web at www.smokehole.com or by phone at 800-828-8478.

With your saddlebags stuffed with plastic tomahawks and faux leather moccasins, ride north again toward the town of Petersburg. You'll pass between two pieces of exposed quartzite that seem to extend toward the roadway like knife edges. Before you reach the busy traffic of Petersburg, the ride makes a left turn onto WV 53 at a fork in the road. You'll discover you've been riding on one of the fork tines and must negotiate two left turns to get on the other fork tine, leaving the handle of the fork heading for the busy traffic

of Petersburg. Once you've made those turns, you'll roll comfortably along the banks of Lunice Creek on the shoulder of a farm valley, high enough to see over the crops and low enough to enjoy the fragrant odor associated with modern agriculture. Soon the valley narrows, and the road begins to twist through the woods and foothills. After passing Jordan Run Road (the shortcut road) you'll negotiate a fun set of switchbacks as you begin to climb what some call Mt. Storm. Actually, Mt. Storm is a small community about three miles north of the intersection of WV 42 and WV 93. The mountain you're climbing is Fore Knobs. Once atop Fore Knobs, you'll turn left onto WV 93 and ride toward the Mt. Storm power plant. This huge structure was built in close proximity to the coal mines that supply it with fuel. The burning coal creates steam that spins large turbines, which create electricity. The water used to make the steam comes from Mt. Storm Lake, next to the power plant. This route crosses the Mt. Storm Lake Dam.

After crossing the dam, you'll pass a coal strip-mining operation. These mines are not dug into the ground by black-faced men with picks. A strip

Harper's Old Country Store is one of the oldest continuously operated businesses in West Virginia. You can buy anything there, from lumber to rock-climbing equipment.

mine is the type of mine where the topsoil is pushed aside to expose black coal, and that coal is simply shaved, or stripped, from the surface. While this method is effective in excavating large amounts of coal, the impact on the environment can be devastating. Still, there is one natural feature that has survived for years alongside the strip mines—sphagnum bogs.

Sphagnum bogs line the sides of WV 93 as you near the end of this ride in Davis, WV. These treeless wetlands are where sphagnum moss grows in abundance. Sphagnum moss is highly absorbent—so absorbent that Native American Indians used dried sphagnum moss as a kind of diaper material for their infants. Sphagnum bogs can be seen in Canada, in the Canaan Valley of West Virginia, and rarely elsewhere. These bogs are not very hospitable for people, but wildlife abounds in them.

All too soon, WV 93 ends at WV 32. Turn left to reach the end of the ride in Davis near the Blackwater Falls State Park. Once in Davis, take a load off in one of the great restaurants in town and relax—you just finished one heck of a ride!

RIDE ALTERNATIVES

You can shave about 20 minutes off this ride by turning onto Jordan Run Rd. (CR 28) at mile 43.8. It will lead you along the eastern slopes of the Allegheny Mountains to WV 42, where you'll pick up the rest of the ride. Taking this shortcut will cause you to miss Smoke Hole Caverns.

ROAD CONDITIONS

If you don't like the road conditions in West Virginia, ride a mile farther and they'll change. This ride has every kind of road condition known to bikers—a long straightaway near the start of the ride through the Canaan Valley, a series of tight twists and turns through the Allegheny Mountains, sweeping turns along scenic rivers, and finally, switchbacks climbing up the back of mountains. While not all of the asphalt is fresh, it's all well-paved and generally free of cracks and dips. Watch for a few chunks of gravel in the tightest turns.

POINTS OF INTEREST

Blackwater Falls State Park, town of Davis, Canaan Valley, Seneca Rocks, Harper's Old Country Store, Smoke Hole Caverns, the sphagnum bogs of Canaan Valley.

RESTAURANTS

At the beginning of the ride in Davis, your choices for restaurants abound. While a complete chapter could be written about each one, here's the rundown. There's Italian fare at Sirianni's Pizza Café, and micro-brewed beer served with bar food at the Blackwater Brewing Company. The Bright Mountain Inn offers momma's cookin' seven days a week, and the Saw Mill Restaurant is famous for its buckwheat pancakes. All of these establishments are on WV 32 in Davis.

The Bright Morning Inn and Restaurant (866-537-5731) is more than a bed and breakfast inn. It serves breakfast, lunch, and dinner seven days a week, with breakfasts named for the town regulars. For example, you can order a Danwich, which is a bagel with cheese and bacon. Try the Mr. Chazz Platter for a taste of eggs, bacon, and three pancakes, and order a blue Chazz for blueberry pancakes. The Granny's Gear-Up is a Tex-Mex breakfast featuring an open biscuit with eggs, salsa, and sour cream. It's named for Granny Gear Productions (inventors of insane 24-hour long mountain bike races) whose corporate office is just around the corner from the Inn. You'll spend less than $6 for most breakfast items. For lunch, the Inn offers $6 sandwiches (like a Reuben or a club); if you are so inclined, try the hummus pita. The rest of the lunch menu has a Tex-Mex flavor. You'll find dinner at the Inn only on Fridays and Saturdays. As the name implies, it is an inn, offering rooms from $65 to $105 per night with prices based on room size and season.

Sirianni's Pizza Café (304-259-5454) isn't shy about the use of garlic. Open from 11 to 11 every day, they offer great pizzas and other Italian favorites. Leave room for one of their desserts! You can expect to spend between $10 and $18 for dinner at Sirianni's.

For details about the other restaurants in Davis, flip to p. 193 in the *County Feud Loop* chapter.

Just down the road in Canaan Valley Resort State Park, you'll find a good restaurant with great views of the Canaan Valley. **The Aspen Room** is open for breakfast, lunch, and dinner until 9 pm. Breakfast fare will run you from $4.50 for two eggs to $6 for a bagel with salmon and cream cheese. Lunch is a few dollars more, with a burger setting you back $5.75, and dinner gets really costly at $20 for filet mignon and chicken dishes for $16. Feeling adventuresome? Try the Bourbon Buffalo Meatloaf for $16. At Seneca Rocks, **The Front Porch Restaurant**, which sits atop Harper's Old Country Store, is open seven days a week from 11 am to 9 pm (until 10 pm on Saturdays). It offers pizza for about $12, salads for $8, and pita pocket sandwiches for just $6. Nothing fancy, but the views of Seneca Rocks from the porch are awe-inspiring.

DETAILED DIRECTIONS

Mile 0—Head south on WV 32 from CR 29, which is the road to the Blackwater Falls State Park.

Mile 0.6—Turn right to remain on WV 32 and cross the Blackwater River. *You'll ride along a straight section of road through the Canaan Valley beginning at mile 7.*

Mile 19.3—Fork to the left onto US 33 South. *You'll cross the Eastern Continental Divide over the Allegheny Mountains at mile 23.2.*

Mile 31.7—Turn left onto WV 28/55. *At this intersection, the Seneca Rocks Discovery Center sits across the street, and Harper's Old Country Store is on the right side of the road. Riding north on WV 28/55 you'll pass several other rock outcroppings that resemble Seneca Rocks, like Champe Rocks at mile 37.7. To take the shortcut mentioned in the ride alternative section, turn left at mile 43.8 onto Jordan Run Rd. (CR 28-7), which will lead you to WV 42 North. Smoke Hole Caverns, Gift Shop, and Motel are on the left at mile 45.2. You'll pass more exposed rock at mile 46.3.*

Mile 53—Near Petersburg, turn left onto WV 42 North. This requires a left and another immediate left (this turn is in a fork in the road; you'll be approaching on one of the tines of the fork and heading out on the other tine, never riding the handle of the fork). *Mile 64 is where the shortcut meets back up with the ride. Great views from the road at mile 73.8 as you twist through some switchback turns.*

Mile 74.3—Turn left onto WV 93 and head toward the Mt. Storm power plant. *You'll ride over the Mt. Storm Lake Dam at mile 77.3 and pass some coal strip mines at mile 81.5. The sphagnum bogs are the wetlands on both sides of the road near mile 87.5.*

Mile 91.5—Turn left onto WV 32 and end the ride where it began at mile 91.8—the intersection of WV 32 and CR 29 (entrance to Blackwater Falls State Park).

Seneca Rocks!

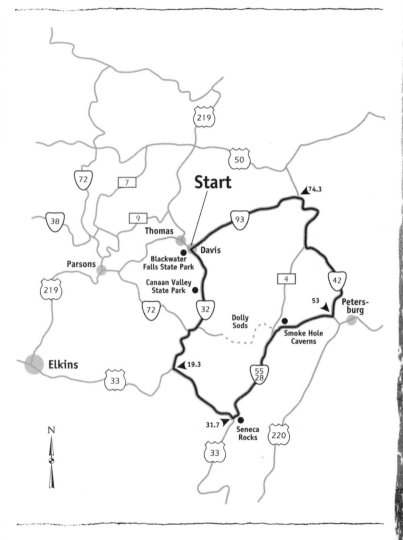

Start

219

50

72

7

38

9

Thomas

93

74.3

Davis

Blackwater
Falls State Park

4

42

Parsons

Canaan Valley
State Park

53

Petersburg

219

72

32

Dolly
Sods

Smoke Hole
Caverns

19.3

55
28

Elkins

33

31.7

Seneca
Rocks

220

N

33

Interstate Highway — 75

State Highway — 640

Route ▬▬▬

US Highway — 27

County Road — 606

Other Road

Milepost — 5▶

Blue Ridge Parkway ═══

County Feud Loop

This loop was named for the feud between the small towns of St. George and Parsons. The feud began in 1893 when the people of Parsons took the records of Tucker County from the town of St. George and installed them in Parsons, unceremoniously moving the county seat in the middle of the night. You'll ride through some of the most remote locales of West Virginia—of North America, for that matter. This ride also features the wave of the future in electricity production. You'll see 44 wind turbine generators spinning, harnessing the wind to create electricity. The giant propellers seem to be trying to lift Backbone Mountain off the ground. Narrow and twisty roads await you on this ride—enjoy!

GAS

Gas is available at the start in Davis and at miles .2, 7.9, 29.3, 30.5, 31.3, 60.3, 61, 76.4, 77.7, and at the end of the ride.

GETTING TO THE START

This ride starts in the town of Davis, WV, on WV 32 at CR 29, which is the entrance road to Blackwater Falls State Park.

From the west and I-79: Take exit 119 onto US 50 East between Bridgeport and Clarksburg. Follow US 50 East into Maryland, where you'll turn south onto US 219, which will lead you back into West Virginia and to the town of Thomas. Once in Thomas, take WV 32 east into Davis. The ride begins at the intersection of WV 32 and CR 29. Zero your trip meter as you ride east through that intersection.

From the east and I-81: Follow US 250 from Staunton, VA, to Monterey, VA. In Monterey, pick up US 220 North into West Virginia. Turn left onto CR 17 (Snowy Mountain Rd.). It ends on WV 28; turn right and ride up to Judy Gap where you'll take WV 33 North to Seneca Rocks, turning left to stay on US 33 North into Harman. Once in Harman, turn right onto WV 32 and follow it up through the Canaan Valley to Davis. You'll find the beginning of the ride at the intersection of WV 32 and CR 29. Zero your trip meter as you turn back south on WV 32 at its intersection with CR 29.

OVERVIEW

Blackwater Falls State Park sits on 1,688 acres and has lodge rooms, 26 cabins, a restaurant, and lots of amenities—none of which compares to the breathtaking views deep into the Blackwater River Gorge. While riding through the park, watch your speed and *watch for deer*. Avoiding deer is pretty simple if you're going slow enough. Leaving the park, start this ride by turning right onto WV 32 South and ride through Davis.

This small town was built on the north bank of the Blackwater River out of necessity for the timber industry. It was incorporated in 1889, and electric power came to the town shortly thereafter. It's said that the town of Davis had electricity before most of New York City—something to consider when you hear the stereotypical comments about "backwards" West Virginia. In 1902, Davis was home to an opera house that seated 1,200. Today, Davis draws outdoor enthusiasts of all stripes and booms in the winter months due to the excellent skiing (alpine *and* nordic) in the Canaan Valley. To feed all those hungry skiers, several great restaurants have sprung up in the area. Lucky for motorcyclists, the restaurants remain open year-round, regardless of the snow conditions or lack thereof. While Davis is a very small town, its restaurant choices are vast. In Davis you'll find Tex-Mex, Southern style, Italian, and vegetarian food.

Leaving Davis with a full fuel tank and belly, you'll cross the Blackwater River on an old bridge with a skeleton-like steel superstructure. WV 32 now begins to roll south, offering a few sweeping curves before reaching one of the straightest sections of road in West Virginia. About six miles from the start of the ride, the road goes straight as an arrow, but still rolls lazily over the hills along the boggy wetlands flanking the roadside as you ride through the heart of ski country. On the right you'll pass the Canaan Valley Resort State Park with a lodge offering accommodations in 250 rooms, 24 cottages, and several

TOTAL DISTANCE
79.5 miles

TIME FRAME
3 hours from start to finish.
Add time to eat or visit
Cathedral State Park.

campsites. It also has a great restaurant overlooking Chimney Rock at 4,081 ft. and Pointy Knob at 4,145 ft. Its labyrinth of cross-country ski trails doubles as hiking trails in the snowless months.

You'll turn off of WV 32 onto CR 45/3, Back Hollow Rd. CR 45/3 is a "share road"—just a single lane of pavement with gravel on either side to make the road as wide as a normal one, but the paved section is only about 10 feet across. As the name implies, you'll have to share the road with oncoming traffic. Generally, the drivers in the area are aware that motorcyclists don't want to careen off into the gravel, so they'll usually give you plenty of clearance. Watch for the other guy in curves and on hillcrests. Oh, yeah, curves and hillcrests—you'll

Out of Davis, a rare straight West Virginia road.

Back Hollow Road is a "share" road.

ride through plenty of those as you navigate the backcountry of West Virginia. Back Hollow Rd. passes part of the Canaan Valley Resort State Park and several cattle farms. Cattle along this road have the ability to graze on the steep slopes of Pointy Knob Mountain, seeming more like mountain goats than bovines.

CR 45/3 ends at WV 72, where you'll turn right. Although WV 72 is state-maintained, it is still a share road for the first several miles. Passing more cattle farms before reaching the views of the Dry Fork River on the left side of the road, you're sure to enjoy the scenery along this stretch of remote roadway. You'll enter a woodsy section of the ride before crossing the Blackwater River, which empties into the Dry Fork River about 80 ft. on the left side of the bridge over the Blackwater River. At this confluence, the two rivers become the Black Fork River. Just before turning off of WV 72, you'll see a large gravel pullout on the right side of the road with a nice waterfall to enjoy. The water from this falls empties into the Black Fork River and flows through the town of Parsons.

Turn left onto US 219 and ride through Parsons. Parsons is the largest town in Tucker County, with a population of over 2,000. For dining, there's fast food and C.J. Pizzeria & Ristorante. After crossing the Black Fork River, watch carefully for the signs for US 219, because it makes a sharp left turn here. If you miss the left turn, you'll end up in a shopping center and lumberyard. Nearing the heart of downtown, you'll see the Tucker County Courthouse on the right side of the road. This impressive four-story red brick structure was built in 1898, finally ending the feud between the towns of St. George and Parsons. You see, under the cover of darkness on August 1, 1892, Ward Parsons led a peaceable if sneaky band of thieves into the town of St. George and seized the county records, moving them to the town of Parsons, thereby moving the county seat from St. George to the town of Parsons. As you probably have guessed, Ward Parsons named the town of Parsons for himself and was therefore greatly interested in its success. The two towns struggled for years over which one would serve as the official county seat. Neither recognized the other as legitimate until the construction of the Tucker County Courthouse in Parsons in 1898. Once the courthouse was built, the leaders of St. George conceded that the county seat had left St. George forever. You'll see later that Parsons has prospered, while St. George has withered away.

US 219 Ts off in Parsons, where this ride makes a right onto WV 72. No sooner do you have a full head of steam on your motorcycle than the ride makes another turn, actually a fork to the right onto CR 1, Holly Meadows Rd. Within the first mile of CR 1, you'll cross the Cheat River, which is formed in Parsons by the confluence of the Black Fork River and the Shavers Fork River. After crossing the river, look to the mountains ahead to get a glimpse of the wind turbine generators atop Backbone Mountain. CR 1 is a share road, paved on the shoulder of the Cheat River flood plain, which serves as grazing land for cattle. You'll be guided in and out of the forest along the edge of the pasture as you near St. George.

St. George is small and offers no amenities at all, and there are few clues about the town's interesting past. Not only did the county records get stolen in the middle of the night, the town was nearly ripped apart by internal strife during the Civil War when St. George's people voted (actually, back then, it was only the white males who voted) whether or not to secede from the Union. The vote to secede won by a very narrow margin. The Confederate flag was raised over the town, only to be replaced by the Union Jack after the defeat of the Confederate States of America. CR 1 makes a left at the T intersection in town, then makes an immediate right to get back onto CR 1.

Leaving St. George behind, you'll ride a series of tight twists and turns as you begin to climb Limestone Ridge. Don't turn off of the road as you head up Limestone Ridge; CR 1 makes a left turn, but CR 3 continues straight ahead, making a seamless transition between the two roads. As you near the top of Limestone Ridge and White Ridge, you'll see a distant view on the right side of the road that overlooks a quaint and silent farm along this scenic, tree-lined roadway.

On a clear day, you can also see all 44 wind turbines atop Backbone Mountain. These generators use triple blades to harness the energy of the wind, the whole propeller spanning about 150 ft. The movement of the propeller is then converted into electric energy, enough clean power for about 20,000 homes everyday. Each of the 44 generators in this array produces 1.5 megawatts of electric energy. While the initial cost was high, these generators won't need maintenance for their entire expected 25-year life-span. Why only 25 years? Well, it's believed that significant improvements in wind turbine generators will occur during that time, making these obsolete. If the weather prevents you from seeing the generators from Limestone Ridge or White Ridge, take heart, this ride will

Built in 1898, the Tucker County Courthouse now marks Parsons as the county seat.

take you to the base of one of these mammoth structures atop Backbone Mountain.

The ride makes a left off CR 3 onto CR 112, which leads you to US 50 in Aurora, WV. After turning right onto US 50, you'll see the entrance to Cathedral State Park on the left. This scenic, 132-acre West Virginia State Park offers hiking trails and picnic areas in the shadow of its towering hemlocks. These trees stand over 100 ft. tall, and some have a circumference of 26 ft. Just beyond the entrance to the state park is an old stone tavern. Now a private home, this former tavern once housed guests much like a modern motel does today. After passing the stone tavern, turn right onto WV 24 and ride its smooth surface to US 219. US 219 is freshly paved and well-banked and has plenty of signage, but watch for gravel in the curves. This section of US 219 climbs Backbone Mountain, which, as you know already, has the wind turbine generators on top. It also has a gravel pit. Watch for dump trucks pulling out onto the road and gravel dust near the apex of US 219 on Backbone Mountain.

At the apex of the mountain, pull off to the left side of the road. The gravel pit is on the right side, and the heavy commercial traffic there will certainly make your bike dirty with gravel dust. From the left side of the road, you can see one of the towers on which the three blades of the wind turbine generator are mounted. As you stand atop Backbone Mountain you might remark that it doesn't seem too windy there. But it's mighty windy just above the tree line, where the wind comes up the mountainside and spills over the ridge into the waiting propellers. The whooshing of the propellers is a uniquely haunting sound.

Windmills atop Backbone Mountain.

Descending from Backbone Mountain, continue to watch for gravel and gravel dust in the roadway. You'll follow US 219 into the town of Thomas, where you'll fork to the left onto WV 32. Thomas was built literally over the coal mining industry. The town stands on a hillside that today is like a honeycomb underneath, the part of the worker bee having been played by the coal miners who removed the coal to heat homes and generate electricity in steam plants. The mines closed years ago, but the town has continued to grow, thanks in part to the area's unique beauty and outdoor activities. WV 32 becomes a one-way road for a few blocks as you ride toward Davis. If shopping for Christmas items falls on your "to do in West Virginia" list, stop in at the Christmas Shop in downtown Thomas. If that's not on your agenda, try some culture at the playhouse in town that offers well-produced plays for residents and visitors alike.

All too soon, this adventure ends where it began, at the access road to the Blackwater Falls State Park. For more riding in the area, flip to the *Seneca Rocks!* ride (p. 180) and take in its scenic and wild roadways.

RIDE ALTERNATIVES

There are no alternatives on this ride. Pay close attention to the directions to ensure you don't get lost on a remote stretch of roadway.

ROAD CONDITIONS

In West Virginia, some roads are known as "share roads," because that's what you'll have to do to use them. You have to share the road with oncoming traffic because these types of roads are paved only a single lane wide, with gravel shoulders extending about four feet on either side of the 10-ft. paved width. Most of the County Roads on this loop fall into this category. Oncoming motorists generally understand about motorcycles and will usually yield so you won't have to careen off into the gravel. However, stay on the right side of the paved section, particularly around blind corners and hillcrests. The share roads are what some might refer to as "lumpy," while other riders might describe their bumps as "sprightly." Either way, don't expect a smooth road surface on the county roads. All of the roads on this loop are paved, with the state routes being in better shape than their county road counterparts. Signage is nonexistent on county roads, so you'll have to adjust your speed around curves as the curve exits come into view.

POINTS OF INTEREST

Blackwater Falls State Park, Canaan Valley Resort State Park, Dry Fork, a waterfall, wind-powered turbines, Cathedral State Park, and the towns of Davis, Parsons, St. George, and Thomas.

RESTAURANTS

There are several great restaurants along this ride, many of them in the small town of Davis and one in Parsons. Don't let Davis's size fool you, the restaurants here have a good following and offer meals to satisfy any taste. You can dine on Italian cooking at **Sirianni's Pizza Café**, have a home-cooked meal at the **Bright Morning Inn and Restaurant**, down a handcrafted microbrew and burger at the Blackwater Brewing Company, or get your day revving with a buckwheat pancake from the Saw Mill Restaurant. To read more about Sirianni's Pizza Café and the Bright Morning Inn and Restaurant flip to p. 185 in the *Seneca Rocks!* chapter.

The **Blackwater Brewing Company** (304-259-4221) offers six fresh-brewed, handcrafted beers that rival their Bavarian counterparts. The food at the Brewing Company is equally Bavarian. With German dishes like bratwurst and wiener schnitzel, you'll be glad to see that the menu is translated! There're also some delicious Italian dishes on the entree list. For dinner you'll spend about $9 for a German sausage and $9 for a huge plate of lasagna; the menu has items as expensive as $19. The Blackwater Brewing Company is open Monday through Thursday from 4 to 9 pm and on Friday and Saturday noon to 10 pm. Check them out on the web at www.blackwater-brewing.com.

The **Saw Mill Restaurant** (304-259-5245 ext. 125) is part of the Davis Alpine Lodge, the hotel in town. Open from 6 am to 9 pm, it serves up a delicious breakfast of buckwheat pancakes for less than $4. You can also get eggs cooked to order. Lunch is a bit more costly at $6 for a good burger with fries. Dinner will set you back as much as $14 for the 14-oz. T-bone steak, or as little as $7 for the salad bar.

DETAILED DIRECTIONS

Mile 0—Turn right from the road to Blackwater Falls State Park and head south on WV 32. *You'll see the Blackwater Brewing Company and the Saw Mill Restaurant on the left less than a block from the start of the ride. Ride through downtown Davis, WV.*

Mile 0.6—Fork to the right to stay on WV 32 South, crossing the Blackwater River on an old bridge with an iron superstructure. *Starting at mile 6, the road gets mighty straight as you ride through the Canaan Valley. The entrance to Canaan Valley Resort State Park is on the left at mile 10.4.*

Mile 11.2—Turn right onto CR 45/3 (Back Hollow Rd.). *If this is your first experience with "share roads," remember to stay to the right, because this narrow ribbon of asphalt is actually a two-way road.*

Mile 13.5—Turn right at the fork in the road onto WV 72. There are no signs to indicate that it is actually WV 72, so you gotta trust me on this one. *You'll see the Dry Fork River through the trees on the left side of the road, and you'll cross the Blackwater River again. There's a small waterfall on the right side of the road at mile 28.3 with a large gravel parking area for you to use to get a closer look at the falls.*

Mile 28.4—Turn left onto US 219 and ride toward Parsons. You'll cross the Black Fork (that's what the Blackwater River and the Dry Fork become after they converge). *The mouthwatering aromas of fresh pizza and pasta fill the air around mile 28.9 as you pass C.J.'s Pizzeria on the right side of the road. The road makes a left bend at mile 30. Just before the T intersection, the*

Tucker County Courthouse, built in 1898, is on the right.

Mile 30.5—Turn right onto WV 72 at the T intersection in Parsons.

Mile 32—Fork to the right onto CR 1 (Holly Meadows Rd.). *From the "share road" that is CR 1, you'll get your first glimpse of the wind turbines at mile 34.5.*

Mile 37.5—Turn left to stay on CR 1 and ride into St. George. *Near mile 41, you'll be in what is now the heart of St. George.*

Mile 41.1—Turn left and then make an immediate right to remain on CR 1 (now known as Limestone Gap Rd.). *The narrow and twisty section of CR 1 seamlessly becomes CR 3 as it winds you through some tight twists and turns to mile 50, where you'll have a clear view of all 44 wind turbines atop Backbone Mountain.*

Mile 52.9—Turn left onto CR 112.

Mile 59.5—Turn right onto US 50. *The entrance to Cathedral State Park is on the left at mile 61.2 (hiking trails and picnicking) and the Stone Tavern is also on the left at mile 62.*

Mile 62.1—Fork to the right onto WV 24 South.

Mile 67.9—Fork to the right onto US 219 South. *At mile 72 you'll get an impressive view of a couple of wind turbines through the trees. Take a closer look at the turbines atop Backbone Mountain at the gravel parking area on the left at mile 72.8.*

Mile 76.9—Fork to the left onto WV 32 South, and ride through the heart of Thomas to end the ride at the entrance to Blackwater Falls State Park—mile 79.5.

County Feud Loop

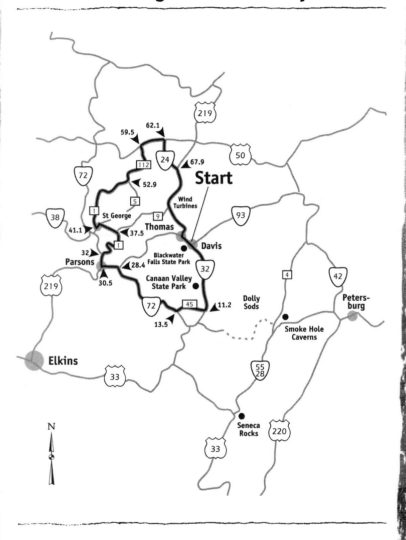

Appendix

Places to Stay, Play, Eat, and Shop

VIRGINIA MOTORCYCLE-ONLY CAMPING

Willville Motorcycle Campground
1510 JEB Stuart Hwy.
Meadows of Dan, VA 24120
www.willvillebikecamp.com

Rustling Leaves Resort
130 Rustling Leaves Ln.
Buena Vista, VA 24416
540-264-0042
www.rustlingleaves.com

VIRGINIA MOTORCYCLE-FRIENDLY CAMPING

Tye River Gap Campground
1932 Tye River Tpk. (VA 56)
Vesuvius, VA 24483
540-377-6168
www.tyerivergap.com

VIRGINIA LODGING

Highland Inn
P.O. Box 40
Main St.
Monterey, VA 24465
888-466-4682
www.highland-inn.com

The Inn at Gristmill Square
P.O. Box 359
Warm Springs, VA 24484
540-839-2231
www.gristmillsquare.com

The Homestead Resort
1 US 220
Hot Springs, VA 24445
800-838-1766
www.thehomestead.com

Damascus Old Mill Restaurant, Inn, and Conference Center
215 Imboden St.
Damascus, VA 24236
540-475-5121
www.damascusmill.com

Tuggles Gap Restaurant and Motel
3351 Parkway Ln. S.
Floyd, VA 24091
540-745-3402

Blue Ridge Motel
2295 JEB Stuart Hwy.
Meadows of Dan, VA 24120
540-952-2244

Pine Tavern Lodge
Rt. 4 Box 13 B
(US 221 North from downtown Floyd)
Floyd, VA 24091
540-745-4428

Hotel Roanoke & Conference Center
110 Shenandoah Ave.
Roanoke, VA 24016
800-222-TREE
www.hotelroanoke.com

Peaks of Otter Lodge
Blue Ridge Parkway/VA 43
Bedford, VA 24523
800-542-5927
www.peaksofotter.com

Quality Inn
179 Sheraton Dr.
Salem, VA 24153
800-459-4949

Econo Lodge
65 Econo Ln.
(US 11/I-64)
Lexington, VA 24450
540-463-7371

Buena Vista Motel
447 E 29th St.
Buena Vista, VA 24416
800-286-6965

Natural Bridge Hotel
Natural Bridge of Virginia
US 11/VA 130
P.O. Box 57
Natural Bridge VA 24578
800-533-1410
www.naturalbridgeva.com

Days Inn Of Luray
138 Whispering Hill Rd.
Luray, VA 22835
540-743-4521
www.daysinn-Luray.com

Luray Caverns
(Caverns, Motel)
790 US 211 W
Luray, VA 22835
888-941-4531
www.luraycaverns.com

Blue Ridge Motel
1370 N. Shenandoah Ave.
Front Royal, VA 22630
540-636-7200

Quality Inn of Front Royal
10 Commerce Ave.
Front Royal, VA 22630
540-635-3161
www.qualityinnfrontroyal.com

Hotel Strasburg
213 South Holliday St.
Strasburg, VA 22657
540-465-1882
www.hotelstrasburg.com

VIRGINIA MOTORCYCLE SHOPS

Predator One Cycles
9896 US 340
Shenandoah, VA 28849
540-652-8831

Bud's Motorcycle R & R
3815 Williamson Rd.
Roanoke, VA 24012
540-265-2986

Roanoke Valley Harley-Davidson
1925 Peters Creek Rd.
Roanoke, VA 24019
540-562-5424
www.rvhd.com

Motorcycles and More
525 E. Washington Ave.
Vinton, VA 24179
540-857-0707

Cycle Shack
1407 Williamson Rd. NE
Roanoke, VA 24012
540-242-1800

Custom Cycle and Restoration
1036 Goodview Rd.
Goodview, VA 24095
540-890-3224
www.cyclerestoration.com

Competition Cycles
5005 Williamson Rd. NW
Roanoke, VA 24012
540-366-0403

Mike's Custom Motorcycles
1918 Morgans Mill Rd.
Goodview, VA 24095
540-890-3230

Kent's Hog Pen
4549 Shenandoah Ave. NW
Roanoke, VA 24012
540-342-7400

Cycle Center
5120 Peters Creek Rd.
Roanoke, VA 24019
540-366-8500
www.cyclecenter.net

Allsport Cycles
3664 Colonial Ave.
Roanoke, VA 24018
540-772-2500
www.allsportcycles.com

KRI Choppers
King's Restoration, Inc.
36 Cloverdale Pl.
Cloverdale, VA 24077
540-966-3911

Berglund Outdoors
2590 Lee Hwy.
Cloverdale, VA 24077
540-992-5777

Jimmy's Cycles Sales
5784 Virginia Ave.
Bassett, VA 24055
540-629-3999

Duncan Honda Motorsport
Rte. 430
Christiansburg, VA 24073
540-552-1949

Motorcycle Parts and Accessories by Gio's
2109 Williamson Rd. NE
Roanoke, VA 24012
540-563-0401

Bedford Kawasaki
1489 Boxwood Ter.
Bedford, VA 24523
540-586-8541

Sumrell Motorcycle and ATV Works
1366 Madcap Rd.
Rocky Mount, VA 24151
540-483-7524

Black Wolf Creek Harley-Davidson
18100 Hubbard Ln.
Abingdon, VA 24211
276-628-5822
www.blackwolfcreekharley.com

Shenandoah Harley-Davidson
2800C West Main St.
Waynesboro, VA 22980
540-942-1340
www.shenandoahhd.com

Harley-Davidson of Lynchburg
20452 Timberlake Rd.
Lynchburg, VA 24502
434-237-2381
www.hdoflynchburg.com

Iron Sports Custom Cycles
3520 Williamson Rd.
Roanoke, VA 24012
540-366-0042

W & W Cycle
3764 Lithia Rd.
Buchanan, VA 24066
540-254-2120

Harley-Davidson of Wytheville
430 Lithia Rd.
Wytheville, VA 24382
276-228-9000
866-HARLEYS
www.hdwytheville.com

Mark IV Suzuki/Kawasaki/Honda/ Yamaha
2073 Chapman Rd.
Wytheville, VA 24382
276-228-3118

VIRGINIA RESTAURANTS

Bedford

Peaks of Otter Lodge
Blue Ridge Parkway/VA 43
Bedford, VA 24523
540-586-1081
www.peaksofotter.com

Buchanan

Sunflower Grill
19834 Main St.
Buchanan, VA 24066
540-254-1515

Fanzarelli's Pizzeria Ristorante
19857 Main St.
Buchanan, VA 24066
540-254-3070

Damascus

Damascus Old Mill Restaurant, Inn, and Conference Center
215 Imboden St.
Damascus, VA 24256
540-475-5121
www.damascusmill.com

Eagle Rock

Ma & Pa's Diner
14683 Church St.
Eagle Rock, VA 24085
540-884-3240

Front Royal

Daily Grind
215 E. Main St.
Front Royal, VA 22630
540-635-3556

Grapes and Grains
401 E. Main St.
Front Royal, VA 22360
540-636-8379

Floyd

Tuggles Gap Restaurant and Motel
3351 Parkway Ln. S.
Floyd, VA 24091
540-745-3402

The Pine Tavern
611 Floyd Hwy. North (US 221)
Floyd, VA 24091
540-745-4482
www.thepinetavern.com

Odd Fellas Cantina
110 N. Locust St.
Floyd, VA 24091
540-745-3463
www.oddfellascantina.com

Goshen

Mill Creek Café
VA 39/VA 42
Goshen, VA 24439
540-997-5228

Hot Springs

The Homestead
US 220
Hot Springs, VA 24445
800-828-1766

Meadows of Dan

**Poor Farmers Market
Sandwich Shoppe**
2126 JEB Stuart Hwy.
Meadows of Dan, VA 24120
276-952-2670

Mabry Mill
Blue Ridge Parkway
milepost 176
Meadows of Dan, VA 24120
276-952-2947

Chateau Morrisette
Blue Ridge Parkway/CR 777
Meadows of Dan, VA 24120
540-593-2865
www.chateaumorrisette.com

Monterey

High's Restaurant
Main St.
Monterey, VA 24465
540-648-1600

Mouth of Wilson

Ona's Country Kitchen
US 58/VA 16
Mouth of Wilson, VA 24363
540-579-4440

Roanoke

Corned Beef and Co.
107 S. Jefferson St.
540-342-3354

Texas Tavern
114 W. Church Ave.
540-342-4825
www.texastavern-inc.com

Kara O'Caen's Irish Pub
303 Jefferson St.
540-344-5509

Roanoke continued

Satori's Café and Spirits
202 Market Square
540-343-6644

Metro!
14 E. Campbell Ave.
540-345-6645

Roanoke Wiener Stand
25 Campbell Ave.
540-342-6932

Awful Arthur's Seafood
208 Campbell Ave.
540-344-2997

Mill Mountain Coffee & Tea
112 Campbell Ave.
540-342-9404

Coffee Pot
2902 Brambleton Ave.
540-774-8256

Edgar's Restaurant
4608 Williamson Rd.
540-362-5002

Sandy's Place
2404 Orange Ave.
540-345-6900

Stuart

Honduras Coffee Co.
121 N. Mail St.
Stuart, VA 24171
877-466-3872
www.hondurascoffeecompany.com

VIRGINIA CHAMBERS OF COMMERCE

Abingdon Convention & Visitors Bureau
335 Cummings St.
Abingdon, VA 24210
800-435-3440
www.abingdon.com/tourism

Floyd County
115 W. Main St.
Floyd, VA 24091
540-745-6340
www.floydvirginia.com

Patrick County
101 Stonewall Ct.
Stuart, VA 24171
276-694-6012
www.patrickchamber.com

Bath County
P.O. Box 718
Hot Springs, VA 24445
800-628-8092
www.bathcountyva.org

Roanoke Valley Convention & Visitors Bureau
114 Market St.
Roanoke, VA 24011-1402
800-635-5535
www.visitroanokeva.com

Lexington & Rockbridge Area Visitor Center
106 E. Washington St.
Lexington, VA 24450
877-4-LEXVA2
877-453-9822
www.lexingtonvirginia.com

Shenandoah County Tourism Office
600 N. Main St., Ste. 101
Woodstock, VA 22664
888-367-3959
www.shenandoahtravel.org

Luray-Page Chamber of Commerce Visitor Information Center
46 E. Main St.
Luray, VA 22835
888-743-3915
www.luraypage.com

Greene County Economic Development Authority
P.O. Box 852
Stanardsville, VA 22973
434-985-6663
www.GreeneVA.com

**Harrisonburg-Rockingham County
Convention & Visitors Bureau**
10 Gay St.
Harrisonburg, VA 22801
540-434-2319
www.hrcvb.org

**Front Royal/Warren County
Chamber of Commerce**
305 E. Main St.
Front Royal, VA 22630
540-635-3185
www.frontroyalchamber.com

**Shenandoah Valley Travel
Association**
P.O. Box 1040
New Market, VA 22844
877-VisitSV
www.svta.org

VIRGINIA PARKS

Blue Ridge Parkway
199 Hemphill Knob Rd.
Asheville, NC 28803
828-298-0398
www.nps.gov/blri

**Shenandoah National Park/
Skyline Drive**
3655 US Hwy. 211E
Luray, VA 22835
540-999-3500
www.nps.gov/shen

Luray Caverns
790 US 211 W
Luray, VA 22835
540-743-6551
www.luraycaverns.com

Natural Bridge of Virginia
US 11/VA 130
P.O. Box 57
Natural Bridge, VA 24578
800-533-1410
www.naturalbridgeva.com

National D-Day Memorial
202 East Main St.
Bedford, VA 24523
800-351-Dday
www.dday.org

Grayson Highlands State Park
829 Grayson Highlands Ln.
Mouth of Wilson, VA 24363
276-579-7092
www.dcr.state.va.us/parks/
graysonh.htm

VIRGINIA POLICE
LOCAL: 911
STATE: 804-674-2000

**National Park Service
Blue Ridge Parkway**
1-800-PARKWATCH
1-800-727-5928

Skyline Drive
1-800-732-0911

WEST VIRGINIA MOTORCYCLE-
FRIENDLY CAMPING

The Rivers Whitewater Rafting Resort
P.O. Box 39
Lansing, WV 25862
800-879-4783
www.riversresort.com

Yokum's Vacationland
(camping, motel, cabins)
HC 59 Box 3
Seneca Rocks, WV 26884
800-772-8342
www.yokum.com

WEST VIRGINIA LODGING

Opossum Creek Retreat
P.O. Box 221
Lansing, WV 25862
888-488-4836
www.opossumcreek.com

Comfort Inn
Laurel Creek Rd.
Fayetteville, WV 25840
800-789-9741
www.comfortinnnewriver.com

Snowshoe Mountain Resort
P.O. Box 10
Snowshoe, WV 26209
887-441-4FUN
www.snowshoemtn.com

Marlinton Motor Inn
Rt 219 S.
Marlinton, WV 24954
800-354-0821
www.marlintonmotorinn.com

The River Place
814 First Ave.
Marlinton, WV 24954
304-799-7233
www.riverplacewv.com

BrazenHead Pub & Inn
Rt 219 S
Mingo, WV 26294
866-339-6917
www.brazenheadinn.com

Smoke Hole Motel & Cabins
HC 59 Box 39
Seneca Rocks, WV 26884
800-828-8478
www.smokehole.com

Brandywine Motel
(Fox's Pizza Den)
Brandywine, WV 26802
304-249-51346

Franklin Inn
(Fox's Pizza Den)
Franklin, WV 26807
304-358-2118

Hermitage Motel and Restaurant
Rt. 250
Bartow, WV 24920
304-456-4808

Bright Morning Inn & Restaurant
P.O. Box 576 (Rt. 32)
Davis, WV 26260
866-537-5731
www.brightmorninginn.com

Best Western Alpine Lodge
(Sawmill Restaurant)
Rt. 32
Davis, WV 26260
304-259-5245

WEST VIRGINIA MOTORCYCLE SHOPS

B & Bs Harley-Davidson
100 Alexander Ave.
Clarksburg, WV 26301-4361
304-623-0484

Boss Cycles
Rt. 38
Philippi, WV 26416
304-457-1110

C & L Cycles
602 Nicholas St.
Rupert, WV 25984
304-392-2480

Craig's Cycle Repair
US 220 S
Petersburg, WV 26847
304-257-4371

Demotto Honda
Rt. 33W
Elkins, WV 26241
304-636-5489

Elkins Suzuki
Beverly Pike
Elkins, WV 26241
304-636-7732

Hoggies Cycle3 Shop
132 W. Main St.
Petersburg, WV 26847
304-257-2460

Lost Hawg
Main St.
Lost Creek, WV 26835
304-745-5305

Ricks Cycles
318 Frankford Rd.
Reconceverte, WV 24970
304-647-3742

Romney Cycle Center
Rt. 50 E
Romney, WV 26757
304-822-3933

Skips Honda Center
US 220 S
Keyser, WV 26726
304-788-1615

Smitty Suzuki Kawasaki
Island Ave (Rt. 151)
Buckhannon, WV 26201
304-472-4824

Summersville Cycles
1137 Broad St.
Summersville, WV 26641
304-872-6626

Waynes World Motorcycle Shop
2101 Dry Run Rd.
Martinsburg, WV 25401
304-267-1059

Young's 2 Wheel
Poor House Rd.
Martinsburg, WV 25401
304-267-9679

WEST VIRGINIA RESTAURANTS

Cathedral Café and Bookstore
304 S. Court St.
Fayetteville, WV 25840
304-574-0202

Sedona Grill
106 E. Maple Ave.
Fayetteville, WV 25840
304-574-3411

The Roadhouse Bar & Steakhouse
823 First Ave.
Marlinton, WV 24954
304-799-4383

The River Place
814 First Ave.
Marlinton, WV 24954
304-799-7233
www.riverplacewv.com

French's Diner
Main St.
Marlinton, WV 24954
304-799-9910

Blackwater Brewing Company
Rt. 32
Davis, WV
304-259-4221
www.blackwater-brewing.com

Bright Morning Inn & Restaurant
P.O. Box 576 (Rt. 32)
Davis, WV 26260
866-537-5731
www.brightmorninginn.com

Sirianni's Café
Box 626 Rt. 32
Davis, WV 26260
304-259-5454

The Sawmill Restaurant
Rt. 32
Davis, WV 26260
304-259-5245

WEST VIRGINIA CHAMBERS OF COMMERCE

Greenbrier County
111 N. Jefferson St.
Lewisburg, WV 24901
800-883-2068
www.greenbrierwv.com

New River Convention and Visitors Center
310 Oyler Ave.
Oak Hill, WV 25901
800-927-0263
www.newrivercvb.com

Pendleton Tourism Committee
P.O. Box 124
Franklin, WV 26807
www.visitpendleton.com

Pocahontas County
P.O. Box 275
Marlinton, WV 24954
800-336-7009
www.pocahontascountywv.com

Randolph County Convention and Visitors Bureau
315 Railroad Blvd. Suite 1
Elkins, WV 26241
800-422-3304
www.randolphcountywv.com

Tucker County Convention and Visitors Bureau
P.O. Box 565
Davis, WV 26260
800-782-2775
www.canaanvalley.org

WEST VIRGINIA STATE PARKS

Babcock State Park
HC 35 Box 150
Clifftop, WV 25831-9801
304-438-3004
www.babcocksp.com

Blackwater Falls State Park
Drawer 490
Davis, WV 26260
304-259-5216
www.blackwaterfalls.com

Canaan Valley Resort State Park
Rt. 1 Box 320
Davis, WV 26260
304-866-4121
www.canaanresort.com

Cass Scenic Railroad State Park
Rt. 66 Box 107
Cass, WV 24927
304-456-4300
www.cassrailroad.com

Hawks Nest State Park
177 W. Main St
P.O. Box 857
Ansted, WV 25812
304-658-5212
www.hawksnestsp.com

Watoga State Park
HC 82, Box 252
Marlinton, WV 24954-9550
304-799-4087
www.watoga.com

WEST VIRGINIA POLICE
LOCAL: 911
STATE: 1-866-989-2824
         (866-WVWATCH)

Notes

Notes

Notes

Notes

Notes

Milestone Press
Outdoor Adventure Guides

MOTORCYCLE ADVENTURE SERIES
by Hawk Hagebak

- Motorcycle Adventures in the
  Southern Appalachians—
  North GA, East TN, Western NC
- Motorcycle Adventures in the
  Southern Appalachians—
  Asheville NC, Blue Ridge Parkway,
  NC High Country
- Motorcycle Adventures in the
  Central Appalachians—
  Virginia's Blue Ridge, Shenandoah
  Valley, West Virginia Highlands

FAMILY ADVENTURE SERIES
by Mary Ellen Hammond
& Jim Parham

- Natural Adventures in the
  Mountains of Western NC
- Natural Adventures in the
  Mountains of North Georgia

Can't find the Milestone Press book you want at a bookseller near you?
Don't despair—you can order it directly from us.
Call us at 828-488-6601
or shop online at
www.milestonepress.com.

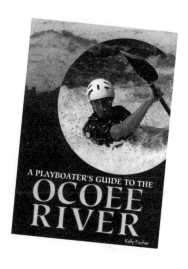

**OFF THE BEATEN TRACK
MOUNTAIN BIKE GUIDE SERIES**
by Jim Parham

- Vol. I: Western NC—The Smokies
- Vol. II: Western NC—Pisgah
- Vol. III: North Georgia
- Vol. IV: East Tennessee
- Vol. V: Northern Virginia

- Tsali Mountain Bike Trails Map
- Bull Mountain Bike Trails Map

PLAYBOATING
by Kelly Fischer

- A Playboater's Guide to the
  Ocoee River
- Playboating the Nantahala River—
  An Entry Level Guide

Can't find the Milestone Press book you want at a bookseller near you?
Don't despair—you can order it directly from us.
Call us at 828-488-6601
or shop online at
www.milestonepress.com.

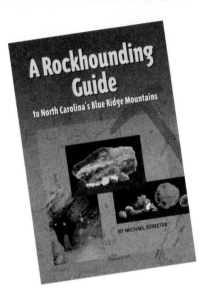